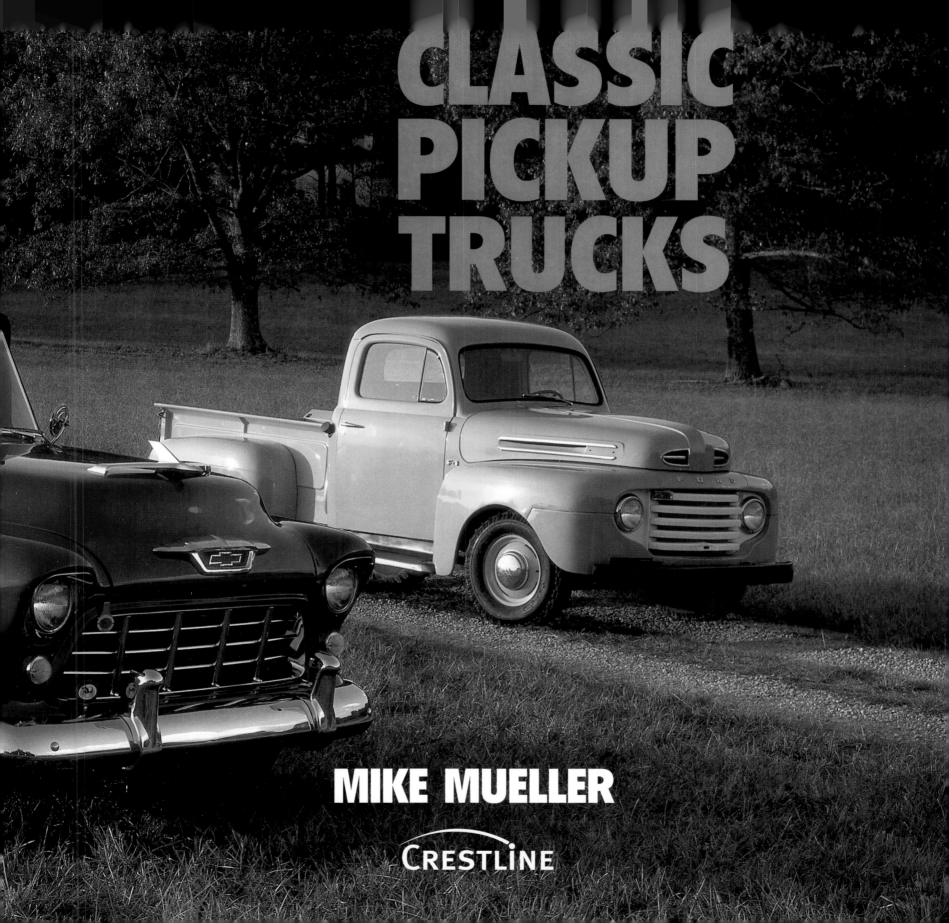

CLASSIC PICKUP TRUCKS

MIKE MUELLER

CRESTLINE

This edition published in 2011 by
CRESTLINE
a division of BOOK SALES, INC.
276 Fifth Avenue Suite 206
New York, New York 10001
USA

This edition published by arrangement with Motorbooks
International, an imprint of MBI Publishing Company.

First published in 2003 by Motorbooks International, an imprint
of MBI Publishing Company, 400 First Avenue North, Suite 300,
Minneapolis, Minnesota, 55401

© Mike Mueller, 1999, 2003

First published in 1999 as *The American Pickup Truck* by
MBI Publishing Company. First published in 2003 as
Pickup Trucks by MBI Publishing Company

ISBN-13: 978-0-7858-2777-1

Reprinted in 2013

On the front cover:
What a difference 50 years make. Even today's monstrous Super
Duty 4x4s from Ford offer more comfort, convenience, and
class than the company's light-duty half-ton F-series trucks did
when first introduced. And when the 1951 F-1 shown here was
built, the biggest engine available was a little flathead V-8. The
pictured 1999 F250 Super Duty is powered by a V-10.

On the frontispiece:
Though his 1927 Ford Model T Runabout is equipped with a
factory-installed electric starter, Bill Braughton demonstrates the
lost art of "swinging the crank." Hand cranking an antique car
is tricky. If the trottle and spark levers aren't set just right, an
engine backfire can injure the operator.

On the title page:
Ford and Chevrolet both have had milestone years in their
histories. For Ford, the year 1948 is the birthday for its legendary
line of trucks—the F-series. Over at Chevrolet, 1955 is
remembered as the year of new V-8 power and great new styling.
Here a 1948 Ford F-1 (right), owned by Sam Smith, and a 1955
Chevrolet 3100 owned by Rich New, proudly represent those
historic years.

On the back cover, left: Financial limitations forced Studebaker
to build the 2R-series in essentially identical fashion well into
the 1950s. This 1953 Studebaker closed the book on Robert
Bourke's original look. A new grille represented the only major
change for 1954—sheet metal remained unchanged up until
1950. **Right:** A lot can happen over three decades. The 1954
Chevrolet 3100 pickup at left was cutting edge for its day.
By 1970 Chevy trucks were sporting damn near as much style
as many of their car-line counterparts.

Edited by Keith Mathiowetz
Designed by Katie Sonmor

Printed in China

CONTENTS

ACKNOWLEDGMENTS

A major project like this one obviously doesn't just fall together. In this case it crumbled. But missed deadlines and disgruntled editors aside, the final product did somehow manage to make its way out of my fumbling hands into yours by way of all the wonderfully forgiving folks at MBI Publishing Company in Osceola, Wisconsin. Keith Mathiowetz, Mike Haenggi, Zack Miller, and the rest for some reason continued to put up with me for the two years it took to build *The American Pickup Truck*. Of friends like these I am certainly not worthy.

The list of other not-so-little people who made this moment possible is a long one. It's also deserving of far more mention than space constraints allow here. So if I appear unappreciative, it's not really my fault—blame it on Mathiowetz, Haenggi, Miller, and the rest.

But if there's one name above all that truly deserves ample ink, it belongs to my brother, and sometimes best friend, Dave Mueller, of Thomasboro, Illinois. Dave has been with me through thick and thin from the beginning. His hard work and enthusiastic inspiration has helped transform nearly all of my book projects from jobs into adventures. He never let me down once. I only wish the same could be said for the reciprocal. Maybe that's why I dedicate this book to you, Dave. I'd like to think this is my best work yet. I dare say that only because you truly helped make it possible in ways you're not even aware of.

Kudos to other family members who also supplied cheap labor and free room and board can be claimed by Jim and Nancy Mueller (parents), Jim Mueller Jr. (another brother), and Frank Young (brother-in-law), all of Champaign, Illinois. Frank's wife Kathy (otherwise known as my sister) and their kids, Michelle and Jason, deserve credit, too, for the incredibly tolerant natures they continually displayed during my extended stays.

Another Champaign friend, Ray Quinlan, might as well be family, what with all the fatherly guidance he continually contributes to my efforts. And I can't possibly forget my ace right-hand person, Joyce Tucker, in Marietta, Georgia. Joyce just may qualify as the hardest working woman in show business. That and she can cook, too.

So many others are also well deserving of hardy thanks. Vintage photography came from many sources: Lynn Maday at General Motors Media Archives in Detroit; Julia Brunni at Navistar International in Chicago; Mark Patrick of The National Automotive History Collection at the Detroit Public Library; Barbara Fronczak and Lou De Simone at the Chrysler Historical Collection in Detroit; Don Schumaker and Snowy Doe at the Mack Trucks Historical Museum in Allentown, Pennsylvania; automotive historian Robert Ackerson in Schenevus, New York; Richard "Mr. Studebaker" Quinn in Mokena, Illinois; Penny Chandler, marketing coordinator for Bob Chandler's Bigfoot 4x4, Inc. in St. Louis; and Paula Lewis and Dan Erickson at Ford's Graphic Arts & Photomedia Services in Dearborn.

Good friends Tom Glatch of Brookfield, Wisconsin, and Steve Statham of Austin, Texas, also lent a few photos to this book, as well as a written word or two. And various pieces of fabulous pickup truck artwork were supplied by literature collector/dealer Walter Miller in Syracuse, New York.

Research support came from Kim Miller at the Antique Automobile Club of America Library and Research Center in Hershey, Pennsylvania; Larry Scheef, managing director of the American Truck Historical Society in Birmingham, Alabama; Dodge truck men Don Bunn in Bloomington, Minnesota, and Roy Brister in Sacramento, California; and Don Hays and Bud Hennesey at the Hays Antique Truck Museum in Woodland, California.

Additional help was supplied by Barbara Kinnamon and Anne Booker at the Ford Regional Public Affairs Office in Atlanta. Also assisting in mass quantities were the great men and women of two particular American Truck Historical Society groups, the Black Swamp Chapter based in Fremont, Ohio, and the North Georgia Chapter headquartered in Cleveland, Georgia. Many, many other people also played a part in this production either by helping locate various photo subjects or by allowing their homes and property to be used as photo sites. I can't possibly list them here, but you know who you are.

Last, but certainly not least, I must thank all the people who truly did make this book possible—the men and women who own the fabulous trucks featured on these pages. In general order of appearance, they are: 1950 GMC three-quarter-ton, Roger and Eileen Bridges, Windsor, Illinois; 1950 Studebaker,

Ken Burton, Rockford, Illinois; 1940 Studebaker Coupe-Pickup, Glen and Vera Reints, Lyndenwood, Illinois; 1950 Ford F-1, Jim Miller, Millbrook, Alabama; 1940 Plymouth, Marvin Stringer, Coosada, Alabama; 1946 Chevrolet and 1990 Chevrolet SS 454, Jim and Bonnie Semon, Westlake, Ohio; 1949 Diamond T Model 201 and 1938 Federal one-ton, Bob Dean, Baton Rouge, Louisiana; 1947 Ford street rod roadster pickup (with 1938 Ford passenger car nose), Jim Richards, Reading, Pennsylvania; 1903 Knox three-quarter-ton, 1908 Galloway half-ton, and 1909 Sears Model K runabout, Hays Antique Truck Museum, Woodland, California; 1907 Autocar, W. F. Markey Jr., Dallastown, Pennsylvania; 1908 Reo and 1909 Maxwell delivery car, Bill Kirby, Asheboro, North Carolina; 1912 International Harvester Auto Wagon, John Lamb, Camargo, Illinois; 1928 International Six-Speed Special, Jerry Lomax, Dahlonega, Georgia; 1927 Ford Model T, Bill Broughton, Willington, Alabama; 1926 Ford Model T "Huckster," Jane Cress, Bismarck, Illinois; 1934 Ford V-8 roadster, Larry Bailey, Cleveland, Georgia; 1918 Chevy Model 490, Tom Snivley, Waterville, Ohio; 1940 Chevrolet, Richard Walters, Fremont, Ohio; 1918 Dodge Screenside, Roy Brister, Sacramento, California; 1946 Hudson, Paul Minor, Franklin, Tennessee; 1948 Diamond T Model 201, Bob and Alice Bageant, Bluefield, Virginia; 1950 Federal one-ton, Richard Walters, Fremont, Ohio; 1942 Crosley fire truck, Preston and Angie Kizer, Maryville, Tennessee; 1964 Chevrolet Corvair 95 Rampside, Billy Bruce, Tyrone, Georgia; 1966 Ford Bronco, Cleve McAffe, Cleveland, Georgia; 1961 Ford Econoline, Kenneth Hustvet, Trego, Wisconsin; 1959 Datsun 1200 and 1998 Nissan Frontier, courtesy Kevin Gwin, Nissan Motor Manufacturing Corporation U.S.A., Smyrna, Tennessee; 1960 Volkswagen Model 261, Brian and Dawn Holcomb, Johnson Creek, Wisconsin; 1954 Chevrolet 3100, Frank Senkbeil, Cleveland, Georgia; 1951 Ford F-1, J. R. Morton, Lilburn, Georgia; 1953 Studebaker, John and Matilda McGhee, King, North Carolina; 1952 Dodge, Dwight Tew, Franklin, Tennessee; 1948 Nash prototype, Jim Dworshack, Richfield, Wisconsin; 1947 Studebaker M-5, Buzz and Fran Beckman, Manitowoc, Wisconsin; 1955 Chevrolets, 1st and 2nd series, Rich New, Adairsville, Georgia; 1957 Chevrolet 3200, Terry Adreon, Bloomington, Illinois; 1956 Ford F-100, Mark Harrison, Hartselle, Alabama; 1960 Ford F-100, Billy Thrash, Albertville, Alabama; 1960 Dodge, Sam Webster, Fremont, Ohio;

1958 Chevrolet Apache Fleetside, Ralph Westcott, Largo, Florida; 1953 Dodge Spring Special, Val Weakley, Greenwood, Indiana; 1955 Chevrolet Cameo Carrier, Olin Hoover, Lexington, South Carolina; 1957 Chevrolet Cameo Carrier, Troy Robertson, Huntersville, North Carolina; 1957 Dodge Sweptside, Jim Elser, Marietta, Georgia; 1957 Ford Ranchero, Dick Stern, Rancho Palos Verdes, California; 1979 Ford Ranchero Limited Production, Gene Mackrancy, Port Vue, Pennsylvania; 1970 Chevrolet El Camino SS 396, Carl Beck, Clearwater, Florida; 1973 GMC Sprint Sport, Cleve McAffe, Cleveland, Georgia; 1981 Chevrolet El Camino Royal Knight, Daryl Miller, Normal, Illinois; 1985 GMC Caballero, Jody Rhodes, Marietta, Georgia; 1961 Studebaker Champ, Jerry Carpenter, Cleveland, Georgia; 1966 Ford F-100 short-bed (red/white), L. Q. Harrison, Hartselle, Alabama; 1973 Ford Explorer, Kerry Haggard, Commerce, Georgia; 1963 Chevrolet C-10 Stepside, Tim Simmons, Gadsden, Alabama; 1965 Chevrolet C-10 Fleetside, Jerry Williams, Altoona, Alabama; 1970 Chevrolet, Larry Bailey, Cleveland, Georgia; 1973 Dodge Adventurer, Dan Topping, Tifton, Georgia; 1979 Dodge Li'l Red Truck and 1996 Dodge Ram Indianapolis 500 Official Truck, Jim Elser, Marietta, Georgia; 1968 International and 1976 International Scout Terra, Scott Weeks, Hamilton, Alabama; and 1935 Chevrolet Suburban, Walter and Penny Deck, Ridge Farm, Illinois.

—*Mike Mueller*

The author's brother, Dave Mueller, puts the finishing touches on Roger Bridges' 1950 GMC during a September 1997 photo shoot outside Windsor, Illinois. Dave's help was invaluable during the production of this book, as well as many others.

INTRODUCTION

You see them everywhere these days—on the road, off the road, on the job, off the beaten path. American light-duty trucks—pickups to you and me—are showing up in greater numbers each year, and they're taking up space in places never thought possible not long ago. Relegated to the construction site, loading dock, or lower 40 in Dad's heyday, pickups have undergone a complete image makeover as performance, style, and even luxury have become part of the practical transportation equation in recent decades.

Today's pickups drive to the office, go to the show, and hang out at the club. They play as hard as they work. In conventional two-wheel drive form or fitted with 4x4 muscle, our thoroughly modern trucks are just as much at home towing boats as they are hauling sheets of plywood. As it is, fewer than 15 percent of pickup owners polled in the 1990s reported use in business or work as their trucks' primary occupation. When not occasionally punching a time clock, their trucks are out hunting, fishing, or just frolicking in the mud. A quick blast of the garden hose, and it's back to the boulevard for a night out on the town.

All this newfound versatility, coupled with the practical virtues present in a pickup's makeup since the beginning, has transformed trucks into the main attraction in today's market. The top-selling vehicles in North America for the past 21 years are Ford's F-series pickups, followed in second place during most of those years by Chevrolet's full-sized C/K trucks. Americans in 1997 bought more than 1.8 million full-sized pickups and nearly 1 million more compacts. Add to this all the other utility-minded machines drawing major attention—minivans and the wildly popular sport utility vehicles—and you now have a truck industry topping 7 million a year in sales.

Car sales peaked at an all-time high of 11.4 million units in 1986. Since then, the truck market has established seven subsequent sales records, including one each for the five consecutive years up through 1997. Those 7.2 million trucks sold in 1997 accounted for 47 percent of the new vehicle market, up from 30 percent in 1986 and 20 percent in 1972. At this rate we definitely will be seeing trucks outselling cars a few years into the next century. Already in January 1998 light-duty trucks were making up 60 percent of total Big Three sales. How far the pendulum swings will be up to buyers.

"An end to the upward trend in the importance of the U.S. truck market is not imminent," claimed a 1998 Ford Motor Company strategic market analysis report. "While demographic shifts seem to have capped the minivan segment, it is apparent that more and more families have decided that at least one of the vehicles in their household should be an SUV or pickup truck. These products can and do perform the normal functions of a car (commuting, errands, etc.), but they also provide the added dimension of versatility that traditional passenger cars cannot match. Barring an unexpected market shock, such as a disruption of fuel availability or the imposition of more restrictive regulations,

OVER THE LONG HAUL

Studebaker's pickups were always stylish, if not successful. The 1950 model on the left was among the first light trucks out of Detroit to be designed from nose to tail with aesthetics fully in mind. The 1940 Coupe Pick-Up (or Coupe Delivery) on the right represents an idea tried by many automakers before the war—stuff a small cargo box in the trunk and convert a car into a truck.

Dearborn officials in 1998 not only celebrated yet another year atop the sales heap but also marked the 50th anniversary for their F-series pickup. F-series trucks have been America's best-selling vehicle for two decades now.

In terms of design, nothing was overlooked on the 1950 Studebaker truck line, as this stylish steering wheel and horn button attest.

the fundamental sociological forces underlying the market's long-term shift toward a higher mix of trucks likely will continue. That doesn't mean that the market eventually will reach 100 percent trucks. And it certainly doesn't assure success for all new truck entries (nor survival for all old ones). It does suggest, however, substantial ongoing profit opportunities for those manufacturers who best understand and respond to the needs and wants of prospects considering the purchase or lease of a truck."

Profit opportunities in the pickup market, particularly in full-sized models, continue to dwarf those of the auto world as the 1990s wind down, although at a predictable cost. As *USA Today*'s James Healey explained in May 1997, "General Motors, Ford Motor, Chrysler and Toyota have committed hundreds of millions of dollars to increase big-pickup production, often at the expense of car production." According to Healey, most sources claimed manufacturers "can earn twice as much on a big pickup as on a small one." While they're taking advantage of the huge profit margins inherent in today's trucks sales, automakers are losing ground on the car side to the point where many once-popular models are teetering on the brink of extinction, and many still running are doing so because both manufacturers and dealers are offering incentives to customers in the way of large, profit-reducing discounts. Robbing Peter to pay Paul? To some degree, certainly. But as long as trucks remain the biggest game in town and customers continue to ante up, Detroit will keep throwing the dice with abandon.

Ford, the industry leader by leaps and bounds in the late 1990s, presently can't build its pickups fast enough. "We're very appreciative of the trust that truck buyers continue to place in the Ford brand," said Ford Division General Manager Jim O'Connor in June 1997. "The entire Ford team is totally focused on exceeding the expectations of today's and tomorrow's truck buyer. Employees at our

assembly plants have been working maximum overtime to meet the demand for Ford trucks. It's been 20 years since F-series sales have exceeded 70,000 three months in a row, and it's certain to happen again in June." At that point, Ford was on pace to surpass two million in annual truck sales for the third straight year.

It only seems right that Ford today rides high atop the pickup pack, since it was Henry himself who probably deserves the lion's share of the credit for originating the breed. While trying to pin the label of "America's first pickup" on the tailgate of one model is not exactly a cut-and-dried proposition, it is Ford's "Model T Runabout with Pick-Up Body" that is commonly identified as this country's first true light-duty pickup truck. Introduced in 1925, this polite little truck was not much more than a Model T roadster with a small cargo box mounted in place of the rear deck. It earned "first pickup" honors thanks to its factory-built status.

Similar light trucks had existed before 1925, but essentially all were sold by their makers as bare-chassis or cab-only vehicles. It was then left to the buyer to contract an aftermarket firm to add on whatever cargo-carrying bed, box, or body desired or a cab if needed. Ford's first Model T roadster truck almost overnight helped curb this practice, just as Henry had planned. He had grown tired of seeing outside companies raking in what should've been his revenues for a final product that Dearborn's high-output assembly lines could be rolling out just as easily.

Complete-from-the-factory light-duty trucks also were known before Ford began transforming Model T roadsters into pickups. Some of the earliest commercial vehicles produced in this country around the turn of the century were obviously light in nature, a result of the natural ramp-up process inherent to an entirely new technology. Just as America's first automobiles were small, simple machines, so too were the very first trucks. Horseless carriages were joined by horseless wagons, some as large as their buckboard forerunners, others as diminutive as the horse-drawn surreys they mimicked. Once proven on city cobblestones and rutted rural roads, however, early trucks quickly grew into monsters: slow, brooding beasts built to extremes to handle extreme loads.

Long known for its brawny, burly big-rigs, semi-truck giant Autocar's first commercial vehicle, arriving in 1907, was basically a petite motorized carriage with a small cargo box on back. The original big Autocar, a much more purposeful one-ton machine, debuted immediately in 1908, followed soon afterward by a popular two-ton brute.

International Harvester's first vehicles also debuted in 1907. IHC's Auto Buggy "high-wheelers" (rolling on wooden wagon wheels as tall as 44 inches) reflected the company's heritage in the farm equipment business, a legacy that could be traced back to 1831. The appropriately named Auto Wagon was introduced in 1909. As the moniker implied, this machine looked very much like a buckboard powered by an engine instead of being drawn by a horse. By 1916, International was building five different truck models ranging in size from three-quarter ton to three-and-a-half tons.

Before Ford took over the lead in the 1970s, Chevrolet had dominated truck sales back to 1930. Chevy's new six-cylinder engine, introduced in 1929, instantly transformed its commercial and utility vehicles into highly popular machines. This 1931 Chevrolet ad depicts one of the pickup truck's close cousins, the sedan delivery.

Any pickup fan will recognize the truck on the right—Ford's popular F-1, this being a 1950 model. The 1940 Plymouth at left, however, represents the family of short-lived, rarely seen pickups that came and went before World War II.

The hub of the vintage truck universe may well be found in Alabama—Birmingham to be exact. This southern steel city is home to the American Truck Historical Society, recognized officially "as the duly authorized organization founded to record and develop trucking industry historical data." While the Society is dedicated to the collection and preservation of the dynamic history of trucks, the trucking industry, and its pioneers, all sizes of trucks and their enthusiasts are welcome from the big-rigs and big-time trucking firms to the small and light trucks, including pickups. Consider that the vast majority of trucks featured within these pages are owned by ATHS members. And ATHS-sanctioned truck shows feature everything from Peterbilt to Plymouth, from Brockway to Buick, from Kenworth to Crosley.

The roots of the group can be traced back almost 30 years. Articles of incorporation for a general not-for-profit corporation were signed in Illinois on March 24, 1971. ATHS members met for the first time in Chicago on May 6, 1971, when Howard Willett and A. H. Nielsen were elected president and first vice president, respectively.

A similar group, the United States Truck Historical Society, had already been incorporated in Illinois in September 1970 by Robert Gerstacker, Wilbur Dean, and Harry Wood. Wood would also become ATHS historian the following summer. USTHS meetings began in March 1971. The two groups then existed in parallel for more than a year before a merger brought the pair together to form the "new" American Truck Historical Society. Newly elected ATHS President Jim Godfrey established headquarters for the reorganized group in Dearborn, Michigan.

Godfrey started a regular newsletter and also came up with the idea for the ATHS's official logo, which was designed by Whiteco Associates in Shelby, Indiana. Framed in a red-and-blue shield, that logo features an upward-traveling wheel trailing twin centerline stripes. The stripes represent the open road, the wheel signifies the "momentum of a great industry," and the shield is meant to remind us of federal highway marker signs.

Bart Rawson became managing director in 1974. Having just then retired as *Commercial Car Journal* editor, Rawson soon was in charge of the ATHS newsletter, which he later helped transform into the organization's fine magazine, *Wheels of Time*. *Wheels of Time* debuted in October 1980 with 20 pages. Today the bimonthly publication is 48 pages long.

Initial growth for the organization itself was slow, with ATHS membership totaling only 350 by 1977. Then Harris Saunders, Sr., became president. His first move was to relocate the group's headquarters to Birmingham. There, he put his daughter, Zoe James, in charge of the archives and membership affairs. Within three years the organization's roll call had swelled to 1,000 thanks to the dedication and hard work of Saunders and James. Membership hit 12,000 in 1991; in 1998 it stands at more than 20,400, including this book's author. In

AMERICAN TRUCK HISTORICAL SOCIETY

Wheels of Time

VOL. 1, NO. 1   OCTOBER, 1980

IRVING F. JENSEN CO

- **Forty-seven Years of Truck Progress, page 2**
- **Highway Post Offices, page 16**
- **Firestone "Ship By Truck" Parade, page 10**

The American Truck Historical Society's fine magazine, *Wheels of Time*, originated with this issue in late 1980. *Wheels of Time* goes out bimonthly to more than 20,000 ATHS members today. *American Truck Historical Society*

1991, the group was more than proud of its 44 regional chapters in the United States and Canada. Seven years later, there are 75 chapters.

American Truck Historical Society membership represents probably one of the better bargains you'll find. Annual dues are $25 for an individual, $35 for a family membership. Life and company memberships are also available. Canadian rates are $35 single, $45 family. The rates for overseas members are slightly higher.

A national vintage truck show has been an ATHS tradition since 1980. Vehicles ranging from pickups to big-rigs show up for these popular events. The 17th annual show, held in May 1996 in Ottawa Lake, Michigan, attracted more than 600 trucks of all types, making it the largest happening to date for the ATHS. Shown here is the 1997 Greensboro, North Carolina, event, which honored Autocar trucks, built from 1907 to 1995. *American Truck Historical Society*

Joining the ATHS means you receive *Wheels of Time* every other month. If you like reading about trucks, or just looking at pictures, this publication is for you. If you're shopping for a vintage truck or parts, all that's in there, too.

Truck historians can also take advantage of the ATHS library and archives in Birmingham. You don't have to be a member to visit the ATHS library. "But we'd sure like to see them sign up while they're here," explains present ATHS Managing Director Larry Scheef with a chuckle. Serious researchers and the casually interested alike are more than welcome to stop in. Available for perusal are 1,500 books, 2,000 manuals, 20,000 magazines, and 30,000 pieces of rare and beautiful sales literature. More than 100,000 archival photos are also on hand, some available for purchase at modest prices. Research services are also offered on special request.

Annual national conventions have been held since 1972. In 1980 a vintage truck show was added to the event. Moving to a different location each summer, the ATHS convention and antique truck show has grown rapidly right along with the organization. As many as 5,000 onlookers have turned out for these events,

with show entries ranging anywhere from 300 trucks to the 622 that rolled out for the 1996 convention held in Ottawa Lake, Michigan. Upcoming ATHS national shows will be held in Minneapolis, Minnesota, (1999); Valley Forge, Pennsylvania, (2000); and Reno, Nevada, (2001).

Those curious about what these events are all about can order one of the "ATHS Show Time" collector's special issues, priced at $20. Available for each yearly show dating back to 1994, this full-color publication depicts many of the finest vintage pickups, heavy haulers, and tractor-trailer rigs in the country. Looking through it is almost as much fun as being there. But seeing an ATHS national in person is still the only way to go. Those in attendance in Phoenix, Arizona, for the 1998 show will attest to that.

Potential members can contact the American Truck Historical Society at P.O. Box 531168, Birmingham, Alabama 35253. The street address is 300 Office Park Drive. Call (205) 870-0566 for directions. If you're an open-road trucker, a company owner, a collector, or whatever, you can't lose by joining the American Truck Historical Society. Some 20,000 truck lovers can't be wrong.

Ford still has a long way to go to match Chevrolet's longevity record as America's top-selling truck maker. None did it better for nearly all years during the 1930s, 1940s, 1950s, and 1960s. The half-ton Chevy on the right is a 1946 model. The black-and-bad boy on the left is an SS 454, introduced in 1990.

Various big-truck builders also tried their hands at pickup production in the 1930s and 1940s. Among these were Mack, Federal, and Diamond T. Easily the most successful was Diamond T—a 1949 Model 201 is shown here on the left. To the right is a one-of-a-kind 1938 Federal one-ton pickup.

size until Reo too was a member of the big-rig fraternity.

Most commercial vehicle companies (and there were many) doing business during the years leading up to World War I concentrated on large, sometimes huge, trucks, some as big as five tons. Lighter-duty trucks were fewer and much further between, although some manufacturers, like White, did offer a wide range of load ratings, the lowest on the scale appearing as light-duty machines from a relative perspective. White offered three-quarter-ton trucks for many years before World War II then began concentrating on the big boys. As late as the 1920s, heavy-capacity trucks were outselling primitive pickups by a 10-to-1 margin.

White's earliest trucks, introduced in 1900, were extra-light-duty delivery cars powered by steam. Countless other firms known more for their larger, harder-working products also broke into the business by taking smaller steps. Dart's first trucks in 1903 were half-ton models, as were Ranier's around 1910 and Stewart's in 1912. Like Stewart, both Brockway and Republic also got things rolling in 1912, each with a three-quarter-ton offering.

Later, some of these big-truck makers returned to the light-duty market with pickup models. Most notable was the stylish Mack Jr, built for Mack by Reo in 1936 and 1937. The "Buddy Stewart" half-ton pickup debuted earlier

Ransom E. Olds' Reo Motor Car Company got into the commercial car market in 1909 (some sources indicate production began in 1908) with a light truck, the so-called "Flare Board Express." Three-quarter-ton developments then led up to the debut of Reo's fabled Speed Wagon in 1915. Reo trucks continued growing progressively in in the 1930s. Federal began building light commercial vehicles in the 1920s, then unveiled a beautiful three-quarter-ton pickup in 1939. Diamond T's "light heavyweight," the one-ton Model 201 pickup, debuted the previous year and was produced up through 1949.

On the flip side, the 1930s also showcased America's first compact pickups, built by American Bantam and Crosley. More car than truck, these tiny machines nonetheless did have a bed in back, and that was enough to allow them entry into the fraternity.

Other companies known more for their automobiles also built commercial vehicles, from light to heavy, in small numbers from 1910 through the 1930s—Buick, Oldsmobile, Cadillac, Pierce-Arrow, Packard, Pontiac, Plymouth, and Hudson were the major players here. Additional manufacturers proved themselves equally capable on both sides of the fence. Studebaker, Willys-Overland, and of course Ford, Chevrolet (along with its corporate twin GMC), and Dodge all built trucks as well as they built cars from their earliest days.

As for the name "pickup," the term itself evolved somewhat ambiguously, just as the truck family it eventually defined developed slowly through a similarly murky history. No one really knows when the word originated or who first spoke it, although the reasoning behind its choice is fairly obvious. When Reo's image-makers initially tried type casting their trucks, known during the 1910s for their swiftness, they chose "Hurry-Up Wagon." The less-clunky, easier-off-the-tongue "Speed Wagon" almost immediately took over. Apparently no one streetside ever could top the

FOR US,1963 BEGAN IN 1917!

The first Dodge truck ever built quickly earned a reputation for toughness and dependability. We have jealously guarded this reputation for 45 years, constantly striving to make each succeeding Dodge truck tougher, more economical to operate.

During the past 15 months alone, we have made more than 50 improvements in our trucks. (A few are described below.) These engineering advance-

ments were not held back for a so-called "new model" announcement, but were added as soon as we had thoroughly proved them and knew they would benefit Dodge truck owners.

Whatever time of year you buy a Dodge truck, you can always be sure of getting the latest in design and engineering features. It's always "Happy New Year" at your Dodge Dealer's. See him.

Dodge's truck heritage dates back to 1917, although its earliest "screenside" commercial cars are commonly identified as 1918 models. True Dodge Brothers' pickups didn't come along until the 1920s.

Ford gets credit for offering the first factory-built pickup in 1925. The Model T Runabout was a light-duty half-ton with a steel cargo box. Dodge technically beat Ford to the punch with a "factory-built" pickup in 1924, but this rarely seen truck was a three-quarter-ton with a wooden box. Notice the rear tires compressed under the load. *Ford Motor Company*

Pickups have long been able to play as hard as they work. One of the more radical examples of this reality was Bill Golden's "Little Red Wagon," a Dodge A-100 pickup powered by a Hemi V-8 engine. Golden first began doing this high-flying trick in 1964 and is credited with originating drag racing's wheelstanding exhibition performances.

first commonly accepted generic description for any vehicle that could easily pick up light loads and haul them away.

Some manufacturers originally used the label "express" or "express delivery" for their lightest trucks, those with a cab in front and a bed in back. Studebaker was among the first to officially use "pickup," this reference coming in its sales brochures for 1913. Actually, the hyphenated "pick-up" was the common construction then, and that's how International spelled it in 1921 when describing its new S-series trucks—the "S" standing for "speed." The popularity of the term (with hyphen) really took off in the 1930s when the breed truly took root.

The half-ton pickup as we know it today started shaping up once Henry Ford introduced his Model T rendition. Chevrolet followed suit with its own roadster pickup in 1926, then introduced its "Cast Iron Wonder"—the division's overhead-valve six-cylinder engine—three years later. The popularity of these powerful "Stovebolt" trucks quickly soared. Ford temporarily regained the light-duty truck lead early

in the 1930s. But Chevrolet quickly grabbed it back in 1933 and continued to dominate the industry's top spot up into the 1970s.

Detroit's modern Big Three pickup line-up—Ford, Chevy/GMC, and Dodge—first formed in the 1930s, after Dodge was purchased by Walter Chrysler in 1928. Few witnesses noticed when a Dodge Brothers pickup bowed in 1924. Even fewer bought them, helping explain how Henry Ford hogged all the credit the following year—his first pickup model in 1925 sold more than 30,000 copies. But once Dodge became a Chrysler Corporation division, there was no stopping these ramrods. Nor their Chevy and Ford rivals. The die was then cast and the newly formed triumvirate was off and running, leaving the independents to struggle on down their long roads toward eventual obscurity. More than half of the 600,000 trucks built in this country in 1937 came from Chevrolet, Ford, and Dodge. While this figure includes all trucks, big-rigs and the rest, the half carved out by Detroit's three trucksters was made up mostly of pickups. And mostly of Chevys and Fords.

Light-duty trucks then picked up in the 1940s, right where they had left off when World War II temporarily interrupted their rise into the American mainstream. Pickups actually got the jump on automobiles in the reforming postwar market due to the fact that auto production had been shut off in 1942 while truck manufacturing, by necessity, simply shifted gears and continued on as a major contributor to the war effort.

When peace came in 1945, almost all truck builders were ready to face a new world. Ford, Chevrolet, Studebaker, and International, in rapid-fire fashion, all rolled out new pickups in the late 1940s. More power, more room, and countless new engineering advancements were among the carrots dangled in front of new model-hungry buyers. All-new attractions also popped up. Dodge and Willys took what they learned building bulletproof military machines by the boatload during the war and were immediately off and running in 1946 in the burgeoning off-road, four-wheel-drive field.

With the 1950s came even more new developments as rampant competition created a "keep up with the Joneses" atmosphere. Ford's first F-100 in 1953 drew raves for its newfound user-friendliness. Chevrolet then one-upped its long-standing rival with its stunning Task Force trucks in 1955. Chevy that year also brought out its Cameo Carrier, a truly elegant pickup that for the first time proved that class and cargo capacity could indeed peacefully coexist. Ford in 1957 then showed how car and truck could work together within the same sheet metal. Dearborn labelmakers called this split-personality pickup "Ranchero." Two years later Chevy people were calling their copycat creation "El Camino."

High style became a major selling point in the 1950s. First came eye-catching two-tone paint schemes from Dodge, Studebaker, International, and even Willys' Jeep pickups. Chevrolet then established a new design trend with its smooth-sided Cameo. Ford followed in 1957 with its first fenderless pickup, the Styleside. Chevy's Fleetside and Dodge's Sweptline debuted in 1958 and 1959.

By 1960, truck sales in America was hovering around the one million mark and made up 12.5 percent of the total vehicle market. Sales surpassed two million in 1971, and the market share hit 20 percent the following year. Contributing to this rise was a corresponding increase in pickup promotion. Ford promo people in 1965 couldn't brag enough about how

A Hays man has always known trucks. Hauling the goods was the family business from 1929 until A.W. Hays Trucking, Inc., finally sold out in 1978. The gauntlet was then passed on to A.W.'s son, Don, who had been manager since 1951. Don ran his own company, Hays Transportation, for about a dozen years beginning in 1980.

Trucks remained in A.W. Hays' blood even after his retirement. He began restoring vintage examples in 1977. First came a 1929 Chevrolet similar to the one he had purchased new almost a half century before. Many other vehicles soon followed until the elder Hays decided to share his fabulous collection with the public. In 1982, he opened his first antique truck museum, in Woodland, California, outside Sacramento.

Meanwhile, an acquaintance of Hays, Fred Heidrick, was hard at work trying to keep the lid on an expansive collection of his own. Heidrick had spent about 40 years packing various barns full of vintage tractors and farm equipment. There they sat, hidden from view, until A.W. Hays passed away in November 1992. "After dad died," explained Don, "Fred and I kept talking about putting our collections together side by side."

Talk quickly turned into action. The doors to the Heidrick Ag History Center opened on September 20, 1997. Located at 1962 Hays Lane in Woodland, the Heidrick Ag History Center is actually two separate museum facilities joined by two enclosed walkways around a pleasant courtyard. Each display area encompasses about 45,000 square feet, while the entire complex totals 130,000 square feet.

On the Fred C. Heidrick Antique Ag Collection side are about 170 restored examples of farm machinery history, all in working order. All the popular names—John Deere, Caterpillar, Allis-Chalmers, International Harvester, Case—are represented. Museum brochures claim this is "the world's largest and most unique collection of antique agricultural equipment." No arguments here.

Don Hays is the full-time director of the adjoining Hays Antique Truck Museum, which is "also recognized as the largest of its kind in the world," according to the same brochures. Once again, it ain't braggin' if it's true. About 130 trucks of all sizes and power sources representing nearly 100 years of trucking will attest to that claim, if you have the time to listen to each one's story. Mack, Nash, Autocar, Fageol, Reo, Diamond T, Pierce-Arrow, Peterbilt, Powell, Republic, Oldsmobile—the list goes on. And on. And on.

The Hays display hauls you through the entire history of the trucking industry from the beginning, when cargo-carrying vehicles, like the museum's 1909 Sears, were nothing more than motorized buggies with shoebox-sized cargo areas in back. The first unique truck you'll meet on your tour is a Knox, an air-cooled two-cylinder motor wagon built in 1903 that emerged from a New York City road test that year as the first recognized leader of the cargo-hauling pack. Gasoline, diesel, electric, steam—all these types of motivation are represented among the significant moments in trucking's time line.

Each museum on its own would be worth the trip to the West Coast. Together, they represent a truly memorable destination for anyone in the world interested in how this country used to work. Even the most experienced truck or tractor hounds will probably learn something.

"Our primary mission, like any museum, is educational," explained Joanne Milberger, director of the Heidrick Antique Ag Collection. "We want to make people aware of our agricultural roots, the roots of the trucking industry. We think the two collections are compatible, in that agriculture and the commercial trucking business are dovetailed historically. We want to remind people of these roots, to keep them alive for future generations." Future generations are already starting to learn, to the director's delight. "We're getting more and more kids in here," she continued. "We're very excited about that."

According to Milberger, about 100 visitors a day now file through the doors. Once inside, they are commonly greeted by one of the center's 80 or so volunteers. Bud Hennessy is president of a volunteer council made up of many members of local American Truck Historical Society chapters, devoted truck enthusiasts like Bev Davis, Al Garcia, and Roy Brister, who, when not handling everything from groundskeeping to polishing the brass, are more than willing to answer any questions and tell any story—with expertise as well as energy. "There's a lot of enthusiasm among our volunteers, a lot of knowledge," said Milberger.

Even Hays himself admits to having found a nugget or two. "With the short time the Hays and Heidrick museums have been side by side, the tie between trucking and agriculture becomes more evident," he wrote in the Hays Antique Truck Museum's fine quarterly newsletter, *Old Truck Town News*. "Listening to visitor comments about how they used a truck on the farm and how each industry was important to them has enlightened me. We learn so much from the visitors and are able to pass the information on." Subscriptions to *Old Truck Town News* are available to anyone who loves trucks—old, new, or otherwise.

Visitors can find the Hays Antique Truck Museum open seven days a week during the summer. The center is closed on Mondays and Tuesdays in the winter. Regular admission is $6. The fee is $4 for seniors (62 and older) and youngsters age 6 to 14. Kids 5 and under are free. For more information on the world's greatest truck museum, call (530) 666-1044.

Chevrolet's modern pickup legacy dates back to this stylish roadster. Earlier roadster pickups from Chevy were cars with cargo boxes fitted into their trunks. In 1930 Chevrolet introduced a true droptop pickup, featuring automotive sheet metal up front, followed by a true truck bed in back.

The Hays collection features a little bit of everything, including this unrestored Powell pickup. Powells were built on Plymouth chassis in 1955 and 1956 in California.

Trucks in all types, shapes, sizes, and power sources—electric, steam, gasoline, diesel—can be found in the Hays collection. This 1922 MacDonald was built in San Francisco specifically for dockside cargo carrying. A low bed floor was incorporated to help handle heavy goods in the days before forklifts. This design demanded the use of front-wheel drive. And to make this seven-and-a-half-ton beast easier to handle, innovative power steering and hydraulic brakes were also added.

International Harvester probably ranks as American truck history's most diverse manufacturer over the long haul. I-H gained the early lead in the business before the Depression by offering a wide range of trucks, and this practice continued after World War II, when the company commonly ranked third behind Chevrolet and Ford.

A new conventional line with GVW from 4,200 to 23,500 lb.

The leading line of multi-stop delivery trucks with Metro bodies.

Other forward-control units — Metro-Mite, Metro-Lite, Metro Van.

Medium and heavy-duty four and six-wheelers of compact design.

Famous R-line 4 and 6-wheel chassis with 6-cylinder engine power.

Off-highway giants with up to 60,000 lb. GVW, choice of engines.

INTERNATIONAL TRUCKS—The World's Most Complete Line

This catalog introduces only a minor fraction of the total number of International Truck models offered for your selection. Each of the basic types illustrated on this page is representative of a great many other models differing widely in power and capacity. Whatever your transportation needs, you will find superbly engineered International Trucks with the desired design, weight rating, power and equipment offered by your International Truck Dealer or Branch.

Sightliner models with bumper-to-back-of-cab slashed to 48 inches.

Another hydraulic tilt-cab COE line, diesel-powered, GCW to 76,800 lb.

A big line of conventional V-8 four and six-wheel trucks and tractors.

Fire trucks in all sizes with engines to meet pumping needs.

A third line of COE's equipped with 6 or V-8 gasoline or LPG engines.

School bus chassis, conventional and forward-control, in all sizes.

their supposedly innovative Twin I-Beam front suspension would revolutionize the way a pickup traveled over rough roads.

Suddenly, comfort and convenience were deemed important to truck owners. Power options and air conditioning began making their way into pickup cabs. And more V-8s began showing up under the hoods. Real performance also showed up. Dodge's Custom Sports Special, when fitted in 1964 or 1965 with the 426 wedge V-8, was a certified hot rod, complete with bucket seats and racing stripes.

Sporty appearance packages and plush interior appointments came into vogue in the 1970s. Ford Explorer, Chevy Cheyenne, Dodge Adventurer—these were everyday drivers that could compare closely with many cars of the day in the way they both pampered their drivers and impressed the neighbors. And when muscle cars began to wane in the early 1970s, pickup power rose to the forefront. Featuring better power-to-weight ratios and not hindered by nearly as many government regulations as their emissions-controls-choked, low-compression car-line counterparts, pickups in the 1970s could still get up and go. By 1978, America's quickest performance machine wasn't a car; it was Dodge's Li'l Red Truck.

More power may have represented the main reason more buyers were choosing trucks in the 1970s. Sales of standard pickups went from 1,163,535 in 1970 to an all-time high of 2,234,389 in 1978, a record that still stands. The total truck market that year breached the four million barrier for the first time, and it was to be another eight years before that record (4,307,901 units) would be broken.

Contributing to this standard, however humbly then, was a new breed: the compact pickup. Inspired primarily by Japanese imports, Detroit-built compacts first showed up in 1961 from Chevrolet and Ford. A third from Dodge appeared three years later. All three of these forward-control vehicles, however, were history by 1970, a year in which compact pickup sales in America totaled only 62,099 units, a mere 3.2 percent of the total truck market.

Demand for little trucks then began to rise along with gas prices in the 1970s. The compact's market share hit 8.2 percent in 1978, with 353,756 units. Just four years later, the figure was 773,537 and the share was 29.8 percent, the latter a high that remains unsurpassed. Compacts peaked at 1,436,581 vehicles sold in 1986. Although production has since receded, small truck sales remain healthy at about one million a year.

An explanation for this decline involves the rise of minivans and compact sport utility vehicles in the 1980s. Combined, the two segments claimed only 2 percent of the truck pie in 1982. Ten years later, their wedge was 40 percent; it was 43 percent in 1997. Larger SUVs have also emerged to cut out their own distinct piece of the market. In the meantime, the total pickup share, compact and full-sized combined, has correspondingly dropped, while production numbers have been on the upswing. Pickups made up 70 percent of the market in 1982 with sales of 1,803,896. Sales soared to 2,850,204 in 1997 but the segment share shrank to 39.5 percent of the truck market.

It doesn't take a rocket scientist to determine that such stats mean little when the whole pie is expanding many times faster than the segment percentage is shrinking. SUVs may be the hottest things rolling right now, but light-duty trucks are by no means cooling off. Americans without a doubt will never become fed up with pickups, new or old.

Pickup popularity today has undoubtedly helped spur an interest in pickups of the past. Fully restored or radically modified, trucks for some time now have been rolling along right up with cars among both the hot rodding and restoration crowds.

"Trucks are undoubtedly hot right now," said Bill Moeller, cofounder of the Michigan-based International Show Car Association. According to Moeller, customized pickups in the 1990s represented probably the fastest-growing group in ISCA competition, which has featured a special truck class since the van craze hit the scene in the early 1970s.

Truck shows of all varieties have exploded on the scene over the last 10 years or so. Carlisle

THE MOTHER OF ALL MONSTER TRUCKS

Like truck enthusiasts themselves, the vehicles they love come in many shapes and sizes, from slammed minipickups to rock-climbing 4x4s. But they don't get much larger than the monster of all monster trucks, Bob and Marilyn Chandler's "Bigfoot." Based in St. Louis, the Chandlers' Bigfoot fleet of Ford trucks stand tall as the most recognized, most renowned members of the monster truck fraternity—and rightly so since they originated the breed.

Monster trucking today involves more than just crushing a bunch of old cars. Official racing circuits and promotional appearances also keep these beasts busy. Major promoters produce between 160 and 220 events annually, with lesser exhibitions at fairs and racetracks adding as many as 500 additional dates to the monster truck calendar. Rampant popularity has been a given for more than 15 years now. By 1998, between 9 and 10 million spectators were flocking to see monster trucks each year. Television coverage on Ted Turner's networks, The Nashville Network, and ESPN2 attracted millions more.

About half of those fans come to see Bigfoot vehicles. Bigfoot 4x4, Inc., tours the country year round, averaging about 700 to 800 event-days annually with its 16-vehicle fleet. Chances are, even if you somehow had never heard of Bigfoot, you would've already run into it—or it into you—somewhere by now.

In all, the Chandlers have built 14 Bigfoot trucks (three other Bigfoot exhibition vehicles were also created over the years) dating back to 1974. In those days Bob Chandler was just another guy who liked to take his pickup off-road, and the farther off the better. River racing in the wilds of Missouri had been Bob's gig since 1967. A basically stock 1967 Ford F-250 4x4 was the able competitor then. Seven years later, Bob started with a new 1974 Ford F-250 4x4. But as both the mud and his racing involvement grew deeper, his truck got taller. And taller. And taller. It wasn't long before the Ford was rolling on 18x22.5 tires driven by Dana 70 one-ton axles.

It also wasn't long before Bob discovered the need for specialized off-road parts and repairs. Even the heaviest of heavy-duty driveline and chassis parts could only stand so much abuse at those Midwestern truck pulls and mud races. No full-service source for such things was then available in the St. Louis area, so in 1974 Bob and Marilyn Chandler opened their own business, Midwest Four Wheel Drive. Word quickly spread about the fair prices and great service a four-wheeler could get "from those guys with the giant truck."

The Chandlers' "giant truck" got its name about the same time. Traveling weekends in 1974 to every hill climb, mud race, or truck pull he could find, Bob would invariably return to the shop on Monday with something broken. According to Chandler, shop general manager Ron Magruder blamed the many breakdowns on Bob's "big foot." Magruder's name stuck.

Bigfoot's first big break on the national scene came in November 1977, when the Chandlers took their tall truck to Las Vegas for the Specialty Equipment Marketing Association's annual event. This high-profile exposure led to appearances at competition events in Texas, Florida, Ohio, Kansas City, and Detroit in 1978.

Innovations that year included rear-wheel steering, even bigger 48-inch Terra tires, 2.5-ton military axles, and a supercharged 460 Ford V-8.

Bigfoot's first paid performance came in February 1979 at a Denver car show. Appearances on national television and various magazine covers followed that summer. By year's end more than 100,000 fans had seen the first Bigfoot Ford.

In 1980 Bigfoot made 30 bookings in 12 states. The truck also spent a month that summer in Dubuque, Iowa, helping film the movie *Take This Job And Shove It*, which debuted in April 1981. Forty-eight more events followed that year, as did an all-new stunt when Bob and Bigfoot first drove over a line of junk cars. Car crushing quickly grew into a supreme crowd pleaser. It also inspired many monster truck imitators. There remained, however, only one Bigfoot, which by the end of 1981 was being managed by its own company, Bigfoot 4x4, Inc.

In 1982 Bob Chandler decided there was room in this country for another Bigfoot. Built that summer, Bigfoot 2 rolled out on even taller 66-inch Goodyear Terra tires turned by five-ton Rockwell military axles, a combination later added to Bigfoot 1. Bigfoot 2 made its own movie debut in 1983, crushing a Porsche 928 in the film *Cannonball Run II*.

A dozen other Bigfoot Ford trucks were built, with the latest, Bigfoot 15 (the unlucky number 13 was skipped in the series), making its debut at the SEMA show in Las Vegas in November 1994. Three other machines also made the team, the Bigfoot Shuttle, Bigfoot Fastrax, and Ms. Bigfoot. The latter was a 1,000-horsepower Ford Ranger pickup built in 1985 for Marilyn Chandler. It was later sold. Also built in 1985, the Bigfoot Shuttle is a highly modified Aerostar van that rolls on 48-inch tires. Bigfoot Fastrax, purchased by the Chandlers in 1988, is also a Ford van—on top. Below that shell is an M84 personnel carrier powered by two blown 460 Ford big-blocks. This crawler weighs in at more than 23,000 pounds.

The biggest of the Bigfoot breed is No. 5, built in the summer of 1986. It is still the world's tallest, widest, and heaviest pickup. Dual 10-foot-tall Alaska tundra tires from Firestone push Bigfoot 5's height and width to 15 and 20 feet, respectively. It weighs 38,000 pounds. While this behemoth does occasionally venture out for an exhibition, it primarily appears on static display back at the home office in St. Louis.

Bigfoot 8 was the first monster truck built by Chandler specifically for racing. It features a tubular frame, integrated roll cage, and a computer-designed chassis incorporating a unique cantilever suspension (controlled by nitrogen shock absorbers) that allows about two feet of wheel travel. In 1990 Bigfoot 8 copped the TNT World Championship Truck Racing Circuit crown by winning 60 percent of the 40 races it entered, an achievement that also helped it garner the Monster Truck Racing Association's "Truck of the Year" honors. By 1997, Bigfoot trucks had won seven racing titles in eight years, including six straight dating back to 1992.

Race winners, movie stars, proud promotional representatives for Ford pickups—Bob and Marilyn Chandler's tall trucks have played all these roles and more over the last 20 years. If it's a really big show, Bigfoot is there.

The Bigfoot team in the late 1980s included everything from toys for the kids to Bigfoot 5 (in center facing you) with its 10-foot-tall tires. In front are Bigfoot Ranger (left) and Bigfoot Shuttle. *Bigfoot 4x4, Inc.*

It wouldn't be a Bigfoot exhibition without a few car-crushing runs. No one in the monster truck crowd does it better than Bob Chandler and his various Bigfoot Ford trucks. *Bigfoot 4x4, Inc.*

MODEL 3102, CHASSIS and FLAT-FACE COWL • MODEL 3112, CHASSIS, COWL AND WINDSHIELD
Accommodate 66" to 84" bodies. Weight of body and payload up to 2250 pounds

LIGHT-DUTY CHASSIS
116" Wheelbase, Maximum G.V.W. 4800 Lb.
FOR THE INSTALLATION OF VOCATIONAL BODIES

Available with the new Comfortmaster Cab, flat face cowl, or cowl and windshield, with full-length running boards and four fenders, these chassis accommodate standard and special-purpose bodies of many types. Power, economy and flexibility are offered in these units with the new Thriftmaster 235 Engine, new rear axle ratio of 3.9 to 1 and a choice of four transmissions, including the Synchro-Mesh Standard Three-Speed, Heavy-Duty Three-Speed,* Four-Speed* and the new Automatic.* Durability and dependability are increased by improvements in the design of many of the chassis components.

*Regular production option at extra cost.

MODEL 3103—CHASSIS AND CAB
Accommodates 66" to 78" bodies.
Weight of body and payload up to 1800 pounds

Productions, a group formed in Carlisle, Pennsylvania, in the 1970s to promote a collector car show parallel to the Antique Automobile Club of America's legendary national event held in nearby Hershey, turned to trucks in 1991. The first annual Carlisle All-Truck Nationals attracted 212 trucks and more than 12,000 truck fans that year. Nearly twice as many trucks, running from custom minipickups to 18-wheelers, showed up in 1992, along with 16,000 fans.

Such great results right out of the blocks reflect various trends, not the least of which is the growing attraction of vintage pickups. Most witnesses agree these trucks possess a certain charm all their own that appeals to a newfound sense of nostalgia, a back-to-basics, down-on-the-farm, family-value type of thing that perhaps proves someone at one time actually did listen to a Dan Quayle speech. But while changing values and refocused personal tastes have undoubtedly played a part, money is still the root of all revivals as far as rising truck popularity is concerned.

Manufacturers continued offering bare-frame trucks even after factory-built pickups became popular in the 1930s. The idea, of course, was to allow buyers to build the right truck for the job. These special applications are still available today.

Not all pickups were forced to work themselves to death, and some that did even came back to life as true fun machines. Street rodders and customizers have long included trucks as subjects for their creativity. This droptop Ford is powered by a Mustang 5.0-liter V-8.

24

Collector car values shot through the roof in the 1980s, convincing many people to begin considering vintage trucks, vehicles that are more readily available and cost less. And not only are they easier to buy initially, they also generally require less green to restore.

Preserving pickup history, of course, would be next to impossible without restoration support through vintage parts suppliers, which today rival their automotive-oriented counterparts. Golden State Pickup Parts in Buena Park, California, started as a hobby in 1975 in Seth and Meredith Doulton's garage, is among this country's largest sources for antique truck parts, used and reproduced, even though the focus is primarily postwar Chevrolets. During the 1990s Golden State reproduced more parts for the heavily popular 1967–1972 Chevy pickup than any other age group.

Even more popular than restored pickups are their modified counterparts. As *Truckin'* magazine editor Steve Stillwell saw it in 1993, these machines have become all the rage because they represent "affordable street rodding." "The days of building a nice street rod car for less than $10,000 are basically over," he said. But personalizing a pickup or even building a relatively hot half-ton are still well within the reach of the average hot rodder.

Stillwell also pointed to rampant pickup popularity growth among the younger set, primarily a result of the minitruck craze. Speaking from a Southern California perspective, Stillwell claimed minipickups in the early 1990s replaced Volkswagens as cheap, trendy transportation that offered young buyers ample opportunity for easy customization tricks.

According to Stillwell "'personalization' is the up and coming thing for truckers in the 1990s." Personalization includes such modifications as custom grilles, splashy graphics, or lowered suspensions, with the goal being to transform common transportation, whether it be compact or full sized, into an uncommon fashion statement. "Today's younger trucking hot rodders are not necessarily interested in performance or engine mods," claims Stillwell, "it's mostly body customization, paint jobs and stereos."

Tens of thousands of big Studebaker Trucks move the men and supplies of war

"Trucks that go boom," pickups (mostly minis) with ground-pounding stereos and slammed-into-the-weeds attitudes, continue to make their presence felt (with a heavy base beat) on the street scene as the new millennium nears. Whether or not they too will be short-circuited by the Y2K menace remains to be seen. We can only hope.

In the meantime, older hot rodders will continue tinkering with trucks, because these machines are able to fill an important need: the need to be different. As Gary Meadors, a founder of the Goodguys Rod and Custom Association in Alamo, California, explained, "There are only so many things that can be done to a Deuce coupe. You can show up at a show with a 1938 Ford truck with that funky art-deco front end and people'll say, 'Man is that bitchin',' and they'll walk right by a big-dollar 1932 three-window to check it out."

Such is the rich history of the American pickup—so much diversity, so many surprises, so much rock-solid continuity. This truly is a machine that means so many different things to so many different people.

What does one mean to you?

While automobile production fell victim to World War II, trucks remained in great demand, and every manufacturer seemingly was called on to fill the military's need for heavy-duty workhorses. Studebaker, Dodge, Ford, Chevrolet, and GMC were all heavily involved, and put many lessons learned in war to good use in peacetime.

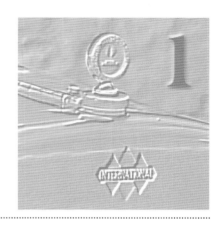

IN THE BEGINNING

A PICKUP PRE-HISTORY

It was already a steamy hot Wednesday morning in New York when a curious crowd began to gather at the corner of 58th Street and Fifth Avenue. Temperatures that day would hit triple digits—and it wasn't even June yet. Terribly hot weather at the time was a feared killer. Air conditioning was not yet discovered, nor was refrigeration. The date was May 20, 1903. That some citizens, primarily the elderly, in the crowded cities of the East and Midwest would fall victim to the heat during the months to follow was understood. For most, however, the threat wasn't nearly as critical, although keeping one's cool remained a top priority for all.

Another fact of metropolitan life, as inevitable as the changing seasons in those days, compounded a city dweller's frustration with the summer heat. As author Christopher Finch explained in his 1992 ode to the automobile, *Highways to Heaven*, "It has been estimated that there were two million horses in New York City in the 1890s, and most of these, of necessity, were stabled in proximity to human residences, an unsatisfactory situation, especially in those areas where the residences themselves were crowded upon one another. Overpopulated and under-ventilated tenements backed onto narrow alleys across which dray horses and peddlers' mules were stabled. Aromas that are reassuring in a barnyard became, in the dog days of a New York summer, intolerable stenches that rose on the night air to suffocate the residents who sought to escape the heat and humidity by sleeping on roofs and fire escapes. The horse

was indispensable, but by becoming indispensable it had made man its slave."

Horses and heat—never a good combination. Nor were horses and horsepower. That the horse and the horseless carriage stood on opposite sides of the fence was made more than obvious the very moment that Charles King, Henry Ford, and the Duryea brothers put their first internal combustion experiments in motion in the 1890s. Hay-fed transportation was immediately rendered obsolete, although it would be a decade or two before the great majority of Americans were finally convinced.

Most witnesses in the years immediately following the turn of the century remained uncertain that those confounded motorized contraptions represented the best way to ride into the future. In congested areas local ordinances inhibited the automobile's use with the horse's best interests in mind. Spooking Mr. Ed with loud bangs and pops or threatening him and his human cargo with excessive speed stood as major concerns to city fathers all over America in the early 1900s.

Illinois lawmakers in 1903 even went so far as to impose a statewide speed limit—of 12 miles per hour—with the passing of the Lyon Bill, named after the representative who pushed it through. Representative Lyon was from affluent Lake County on Chicago's posh North Shore where enraged homeowners "have for years waged energetic warfare on fast bicycle riders and automobiles," according to *The Automobile*. Lake Countians could fight all they wanted but they couldn't stop progress.

A three-quarter-ton Knox truck gained fame during America's first major public test of commercial vehicles, held in New York in May 1903. This 1903 Knox resides today at the Hays Antique Truck Museum in Woodland, California.

The 1903 Knox was powered by an air-cooled one-cylinder engine. The engines acquired the nickname "Old Porcupine" from the pins screwed into the cylinder jacket, supposedly a better aid to cooling than typical fins.

Long known for its big-rigs, Autocar's first truck was this polite motor carriage, built in 1907. Power came from a 12-horsepower horizontally opposed two-cylinder engine.

In the early 1900s, when automotive engineering was in its infancy, radiators were fully exposed for effective engine cooling. To incorporate this external component into the car's overall design, manufacturers decorated them with highly polished brass trimmings. This Autocar radiator reveals typical horseless carriage styling practices, including the delicate identification script.

It was clear even then that the horse's days were numbered, especially so within city limits. The sanitary aspect alone was enough to help hasten the departure of Mr. Ed and his friends from the crowded streets of America. Collecting the occasional dead Ed was one thing; the everyday policing of the by-products left behind by four-legged motivation was something no one relished. Deceased or dying automobiles didn't smell near as bad, nor did they present such a dangerous health risk—over the long term, maybe, but not

According to many sources, Ransom Olds didn't begin building trucks until 1909. But this express model, recognized as a 1908, reportedly was originally sold in 1907. Hidden beneath the seat is a 10–12 horsepower one-cylinder engine.

Like Autocar, Reo used a beautiful brass identification script to decorate its truck radiators. The Reo name, incidentally, came from the initials of the company's founder, Ransom Eli Olds.

in the 1900s. Sure, internal combustion's by-products have never been good for us. But at least we can't step in them.

Above it all was the plain fact that a four-legged animal would never compete with its four-wheeled rival. Early autowriter David Wells took a shot at explaining this reality in 1907:

"The horse, in spite of the romance that clings around 'Black Beauty' and 'Billy, the Fire Hero,' is too slow and too expensive a means of locomotion to do the business of the world when one machine can do the work of 'Billy,' 'Black Beauty,' and several others, better and quicker. 'Black Beauty' very prettily noses into his master's pockets for sugar, but the sugar costs, so do the oats, and the groom, and the veterinarian, and the horseshoer. A hard cold

will reduce 'Billy' to a simple figure in the profit and loss column. It is cheaper if less romantic to put in his place a car, which does not eat, costs little for a physician and does 10 times the work."

Winning over followers in New York, Chicago, and the rest represented only a slightly taxing proposition for the horseless carriage. City slickers could read the balance sheet every day, and they knew the score. Country folk, on the other hand, were typically not so progressive. They proved nowhere near as willing to trade in their whip for a Whippet. And their answer was loud and clear.

"The automobile is not putting the horse out of use," wrote rural Illinois newspaper editor C. L. Livingston in August 1910. "It is estimated that

The William Galloway Company of Waterloo, Iowa, was a popular mail-order farm implement supplier early in this century. From 1908 to 1911, the company also took orders for trucks, which were built by Waterloo's Dart Manufacturing Company. This 1908 Galloway half-ton is also part of the Hays collection in California.

More than one early automaker turned out a few utility vehicles, including Maxwell. This 1909 delivery car is nothing but a Maxwell automobile wearing a covered cargo-carrying body.

235,000 automobiles will not more than cover the manufacture of that vehicle this year and that the value is about $235,000,000. But there are 2,000,000 horses in Illinois alone and they are worth $256,000,000. Horses never commanded such good prices as now and horse-breeding is, in fact, the most important and profitable branch of the livestock industry in the country today. The horse is still man's greatest and most serviceable friend and he is likely to remain. No man now living will see 'the horseless age.'"

Mr. Livingston, we presume, must've been blind.

The horseless age, of course, wasted little time emerging. Conflicts between car and horse

declined considerably after World War I as the former took control and the latter finally let go of the reins. Records show the commercial vehicle population in New York City was 12,148 in 1915; five years later that figure had ballooned to 83,746. International in 1915 for the first time sold more trucks targeted for urban use (delivery, hauling, etc.) than those headed for the farm.

The boys who would never be kept down on those farms again after seeing Gay Paree had demonstrated the truck's abilities the hard way while fighting over there. A demand for similar demonstrations here at home grew by leaps and bounds once the war ended in 1918. The public demanded better roads, leading to the introduction of more than 20 highway bills in the 66th Congress, including measures to establish a federal highway commission and create a national highway network.

On the backroads, however, horses continued to hang on to their jobs, some well into the 1930s.

The horse still owned the streets in New York City in 1903, although at least one group then was out to prove that a new landlord was stepping up. Automobiles had barely made a dent in the technological timeline in the early 1900s, yet there was already a well-recognized organization present to investigate their merits, test their mettle, and hopefully promote their further development. That organization was the Automobile Club of America, and it was A.C.A. actions that had brought New Yorkers running to 58th and Fifth Avenue on that morning in May.

Summer's early arrival that day may have made hotheads out of most citizens, but it represented just the ticket for the event at hand— the A.C.A.'s first-ever Commercial Vehicle Contest. Various A.C.A.-sanctioned hillclimbs, road races, and endurance runs had already put the automobile to the test. Now it was the truck's turn. And the heat would only make this trial even more worthwhile, for it would force the entrants to prove just how hard they could work in tough conditions.

Contestants were assembled by 8 A.M. that day. The competition consisted of three stages

run over two courses. Stage One began at the A.C.A. clubhouse on 58th and ran up Fifth Avenue and other byways across the Harlem River to 230th Street. Then it was back south on Broadway, Amsterdam, and Central Park West to return to the clubhouse. Stage One was 20 miles long. Stages Two and Three covered identical 10-mile routes from the clubhouse to the Battery and back. Each stage would be run against the clock, once a day on both Wednesday and Thursday, May 20 and 21.

All three competing power sources, gasoline, steam, and electricity, were represented at the starting point that morning. The test certainly looked promising from a variety perspective. But looks were deceiving. As *The Horseless Age* reported on May 27, 1903, the contest was "a disappointment as far as the interest evinced by the majority of the manufacturers was concerned, for out of the hundreds of concerns in the automobile industry today less than a score took the trouble to enter machines, and the makes of concerns who have done most in this particular branch of the business were highly conspicuous by their absence."

Of the few that did sign up, not even all of these could answer the bell first thing Wednesday. Continued *The Horseless Age*'s long-winded report, "Never before was the trend of the automobile manufacturers' efforts more clearly shown than when 12 business vehicles out of the 14 entered lined up on 58th Street, near the A.C.A. club room and started on their run from the same point where over 60 vehicles of the strictly pleasure class left for Boston last fall, and an almost equally large number started on a 100-mile run to Bridgeport, Connecticut, and returned last Decoration Day."

Trucks obviously drew the short end of the stick during the motorized market's earliest days. "The field of automobiles for commercial purposes has hardly been scratched," explained David Wells later in 1907. "While many firms are manufacturing delivery wagons and trucks to the capacity of their plants, the possibilities for commercial vehicles have hardly begun to be exploited."

Patience, David, patience. The automotive concept as a whole then was still a long way from finding its place in mainstream America. That the technology would also require an extra moment or two to evolve from a novelty into a fully functioning tool was only logical. Equally understandable was the extra time needed to reshape that tool from a hand auger into a three-speed, reversible, power-driven hammer-drill.

With so little attention given to the commercial aspects of this young technology early on, is it any wonder then that the utility breed's pioneers have also been overlooked by history? America's first automobiles have been honored many times over. Who built the very first truck? Good question.

From a worldwide perspective, most reports claim this planet's first gas-powered commercial vehicle was built in France by Panhard et Levassor in 1893. Precursors to a similar accomplishment on this side of the Atlantic include an

This cargo-carrying motor carriage was delivered to its owner in 1909 in boxes, by way of the Sears, Roebuck and Co. catalogue. About 3,500 Sears Model K runabouts were sold this way. An air-cooled two-cylinder engine was included in the deal.

International Harvester's first trucks were "high-wheelers"—no explanation for the name is needed. This is a 1912 IHC Auto Wagon. The two rear seats could be removed to open up space in the bed for cargo.

electric surrey built by William Morrison in Chicago in 1891. Morrison's machine, along with being the first four-wheeled electric vehicle in America, was also the first motorized carriage to carry passengers. Two other Bills from Chicago, one named Harris, the other Hollingsworth, constructed an experimental gas-powered sight-seeing bus in 1892. Henry Morris and Pedro Salom built their "Electrobat"—a wagon converted from horse-drawn motivation to electric power—in Philadelphia two years later. In 1895 two gas-powered tricycles were used to deliver mail on a rural route in California.

A third motive force entered the fray in 1896 when the Baldwin Steam Company in Providence, Rhode Island, built a steam-powered delivery van for a local department store. That same year the American Electric Company in Chicago completed two electric-powered delivery wagons. Another steam vehicle, the Boss Steam delivery van, was introduced by the Boss Knitting Machine Works in Reading, Pennsylvania, in 1897. Andrew Riker began rolling out electric delivery vans in Brooklyn about the same time.

In 1898, the Winton Motor Carriage Company in Cleveland, Ohio became the first American firm to offer a gas-powered truck. This was a light delivery van based on the Winton automobile chassis. The Dr. Pierce Medicine Company ordered 100 of these vans, but reportedly only 8 were built that first year. Total Winton sales of all vehicles in 1898 was 22. The figure soared to 100 in 1899, and Alexander Winton soon found himself ranking as this country's leading automaker. Whether or not he also qualified as America's pioneer truck builder is your call.

Not long after Winton's delivery van appeared, the S. Messerer Motor Wagon Company in Newark, New Jersey, debuted its line of half-ton delivery wagons powered by four-cylinder gas engines. In 1899 Charles and Frank Duryea began manufacturing gas-powered three-wheeled delivery vans at their Reading, Pennsylvania, works. In stark contrast to the Duryeas' trike was an eight-ton behemoth built that year by the Patton Motor Vehicle Company in Chicago. Fitted with a three-cylinder, two-cycle engine that drove

electric motors at each rear wheel, this monster was perhaps the earliest heavy truck manufactured in America.

Other trucks of all sizes and power sources quickly followed as the century turned. Among the more prominent were the steam-powered delivery vans introduced by Thomas White and his sons in 1900. The Cleveland-based White Company followed these up with various hard-nosed trucks ranging in size from three-quarter-ton to a brutish five-tonner. Gasoline engines appeared in 1909. By the time the firm was reorganized in 1916 as the White Motor Company, it was well recognized as the builder of some of this country's hardest-working big trucks—the so-called "mules of the motorway."

White's long, legendary history involved many other bright names. In 1932, the company bought Indiana Truck from Brockway. A brief, futile merger with Studebaker also came and went

Studebaker's hardworking legacy dated back to 1852, when the Indiana firm built its first horse-drawn wagon. When the horseless carriage began appearing in greater numbers around the turn of the century, the Studebaker brothers decided it was better to switch than fight. Studebaker light-duty pickups, however, wouldn't start showing up until the 1930s.

The "waterless Knox" impressed many with its steadfast durability in this century's first decade. Pneumatic tires were a Knox innovation, and later the company originated the fifth wheel design, but this early mover-and-shaker failed to survive the 1920s. *Antique Automobile Club of America Library and Research Center*

INTERNATIONAL AUTO BUGGY WITH ONE SEAT.

were gasoline vehicles, one from Blaisdell and a pair from both Union and Knox. One other entry apparently didn't make the start.

When the dust had finally cleared after two days of bouncing over rutted, unpaved streets, plodding through muddied roads, huffing and puffing up hills, and fighting all the traffic (the snorting, clip-clopping kind) on Broadway, it was a Knox gasoline-powered three-quarter-ton delivery wagon that rolled away with the A.C.A. laurels, after speeding through each test with ease. "The first stage on the first day's run was covered in 1 hour and 25 minutes, the driver taking advantage of the 'Bailey' law, which allows 15 miles an hour where the houses are 100 feet apart," wrote Joseph Tracy of *The Horseless Age*.

The truck's driver was Harry Knox, who had founded the Knox Automobile Company in Springfield, Massachusetts, in 1900. According to ads, his company offered "the car that never drinks," this a reference to its air-cooled one-cylinder engine. Knox vehicles also were nicknamed "Old Porcupines," because the 2-inch-long pins screwed into the cylinder barrel to aid cooling by increasing surface area resembled the quills of a porcupine. Though odd-looking, the setup worked exceptionally well, a fact Joseph Tracy couldn't say enough about.

"The performance of the two waterless Knox delivery wagons was probably the most interesting feature of the test," he wrote. "A good many people have been skeptical in regard to the efficiency of the Knox system of air cooling, especially during extremely hot weather and under a heavy load. The record of these two vehicles in making their full two days' run without a single stop finally sets these fears at rest. Both vehicles completed the test without a hitch of any sort in the mechanism." Remember, the temperature surpassed 100 degrees on both days of the test. As for the heavy load, the winning Knox delivery wagon carried 1,224 pounds during the contest, as called for in the A.C.A rules.

The waterless Knox's performance in May 1903 may have wowed the press, but apparently Harry Knox himself wasn't impressed. In 1904 he resigned to pursue other automaking ventures.

that year. In 1951 White purchased Sterling, then merged with Freightliner. Autocar was absorbed two years later, as were Reo in 1957 and Diamond T in 1958. White itself was bought out by Volvo in 1981, and Volvo merged with General Motors in 1986. GMC-Volvo finally dropped the vaunted White nameplate after 1995.

White's earliest contemporaries consisted of countless long-forgotten names, including the eight companies that showed up for the A.C.A. Commercial Vehicle Contest in 1903. These trucks were as varied as the day is long, ranging in size from the 14,500- and 10,225-pound Herschmann steam wagons to the 1,500-pound Mobile, also powered by steam. A Waverly electric, weighing in at 2,420 pounds, was also present, as were two other big steam-powered machines from Coulthard and Morgan. The rest

Four years later, the Knox company began using water-cooled engines for its trucks and cars. The firm continued on rather successfully until a recession after World War I helped bring about its ultimate demise in 1924.

Knox made more than one major contribution to truck history. Its first four-wheeled commercial vehicles, introduced in 1902 (three-wheelers were the company's original products), were among the earliest light trucks to roll on pneumatic tires. Knox was also a pioneer in the fire truck field, delivering its first fire-fighting vehicle to the Springfield Fire Department in September 1906. Three years later, Knox man Charles Hay Martin effectively invented the tractor-trailer rig layout by designing the "Martin Rocking Fifth Wheel."

For every innovator like Knox, dozens of other early truck makers did little more than fill out history's roll call. Still others did make history, but—like Knox—they are forgotten today. Auglaize, Dorris, Jeffery, Randolph, Sears, Vim, Zimmerman. Some came and went overnight, others lasted 20 years or more. Catercar, Galloway, Marmon, Kelly-Springfield, Selden. Some you probably recall, while others have not a chance. Chase, Garford, Franklin, Maxwell, Republic, Tiffin. The complete list could fill a book, and has, but not this one.

With due respect to so many long-lost great truck makers, two names simply can't be dusted off—International Harvester and Reo. Both were among trucking's pioneers and each over its long career blanketed the truck market from top to bottom, light to heavy. While Reo is long gone, International still exists today as Navistar. Pickups, however, were dropped from the I-H line-up two decades ago. Reo's heyday in the light truck field came before World War II.

International Harvester's history dates back to before the Civil War. In 1831 Cyrus Hall McCormick invented the grain reaper, then went into business manufacturing farm equipment in Chicago. In 1902 the McCormick Harvesting Machine Company merged with four other similar firms—the Deering Harvester Company; Warder, Bushnell and Glessner Company; the

Milwaukee Harvester Company; and the Plano Manufacturing Company—to form the International Harvester Company. IHC also acquired the Weber Wagon Company in 1904.

One of the goals of this grand merger was to branch out into the automotive world. As early as 1889, Deering had begun experiments with gasoline engines. In 1892 Deering engineer George Ellis built a self-propelled wagon. About the same time, McCormick man Edward Johnston was toying with his own gas-powered vehicle. He eventually designed IHC's Auto Buggy, which went into production on the fifth floor of the McCormick works in Chicago in February 1907.

The Auto Buggy was a "high-wheeler," a motorized carriage complete with large, wooden-spoked, carriage-styled wheels. A 20-horsepower air-cooled two-cylinder engine promised speeds as high as 20 miles per hour. Reportedly 100 Auto Buggy high-wheelers were built in Chicago before production was transferred in October 1907 to a newly built assembly plant in Akron, Ohio.

IHC's Auto Buggy was joined by the Auto Wagon in 1909. The Auto Wagon featured a cargo-carrying bed in back, but it also came with removable seats stretched across that box, so this might be considered the first multirole utility vehicle. Whatever they were, customers loved them. Although official productions figures vary, common estimates claim more than 9,000 high-wheelers were built between 1907 and 1912. By the time the last of these quaint throwbacks was built in 1916, the production total stood at somewhere in excess of 19,000.

The Auto Buggy was dropped after 1911 as International Harvester began concentrating solely on the building of what in 1912 became known as "Motor Trucks." New that year was a choice between engines. Model AW high-wheelers continued to carry the 196-cid air-cooled two-cylinder. A water-cooled two-cylinder was

In the beginning, trucks were sold in bare-chassis or cab-chassis form, with bodies and beds being supplied by countless outside contractors. This tradition continues today, although not nearly as strongly as before 1930.

introduced for the Model MW line. MW displacement was the same as the waterless two-cylinder. Output was quoted at 15 horsepower.

Other changes included a switch to left-hand steering in 1913. In 1914 the familiar "IHC" badge was traded for "International" script. A new model line-up appeared the following year with the Model M showing up as a true half-ton—the capacity rating for earlier high-wheelers was actually 800 pounds. The tougher Model E in 1915 was rated at 1,500 pounds.

A third model, the F, also debuted in 1915 just in time to phase out the old, trusted high-wheelers. This three-quarter-ton was truly a modern machine. Gone were the wagon wheels, wooden construction, chain drive, and two-cylinder engine. The F got a rugged steel frame, shaft drive, smaller wheels, a sliding-gear transmission, and a water-cooled four-cylinder engine. The radiator was mounted behind that four-cylinder in Renault-like fashion, a trick also tried by other truck builders of the day. Stronger and more durable, this new International truck left the high-wheeler days to the history books and quickly made a little history of its own. On June 14, 1916, a Model F became the first truck to climb Colorado's Pikes Peak.

By 1920 International Harvester had 981 truck distributorships across the country. And as if the products they sold weren't attractive enough already, International did itself one better in 1921. The fabled Model S debuted that year with flashier, updated styling, this time crowned by a radiator in the typical location up front. The one-ton Model 21 retained the Renault-style sloping hood and rear-mounted radiator.

Putting the speed in the Model S was a 19-horsepower 192-cid Lycoming four-cylinder. This big inline four, when planted in the lightened Model S, made for a top end as high as 30 miles per hour, faster than most rivals at the time. Along with all that new styling and power, the Model S also came right out of the box with

pneumatic tires, a battery ignition system, an electric starter, and electric horn and lights—all firsts as far as International truck standard equipment was concerned.

Like the first Auto Buggy before it, the Model S immediately got its own exclusive assembly plant. This time, an old farm implement factory in Springfield, Ohio, was converted over to Model S production in 1921. More than 33,000 speed trucks were sold through 1926, after which a revamped S-series was rolled out. International sold its last S-truck in 1930.

Another new plant was opened in Fort Wayne, Indiana, in 1923 to replace the antiquated Akron facility, which then closed in 1925. International yet again opened a new plant, this one dedicated to engine manufacturing, in Indianapolis in March 1938. Three years later, the company sold its one millionth truck. In International Harvester's heyday, only Ford and Chevrolet did it better.

Reo tried. Like their I-H rivals, Reo trucks came in all shapes and sizes over the company's 60-year run. Reo truck registrations in the 1920s ranked as high as fifth in the industry's yearly pecking order—16,300 went on the books in 1928. Medium-sized machines were the firm's bread and butter then, but light-duty pickups did make the line-up in the late 1920s and 1930s. Reo also originated the speed truck genre with its legendary Speed Wagon, introduced one world war earlier.

Although Reo's heritage wasn't anywhere near as old as International's, the two rivals' truck legacies did begin about the same time with similar products. Company history dated back to January 1904, when Ransom Olds left the firm—"for certain reasons," claimed press releases—that he had founded in 1897. Olds was, of course, thoroughly angered about the new direction his partners had planned for the company that wore his name. He then jumped ship and named another company after himself, using his initials this time as the Olds Motor Works claimed rights to his surname. Ransom E. Olds' new automobile was already in the works in October 1904. By 1907, Reo Motor Car Company, in Lansing, Michigan,

One of the more memorable work trucks of the pre-Depression era was Reo's Speed Wagon, a truck that debuted in three-quarter-ton form just before World War I. Heavier versions of the Speed Wagon were later offered in the 1920s. *The National Automotive History Collection, Detroit Public Library*

International introduced its own "speed truck," appropriately labeled Model S, in 1921. This three-quarter-ton pickup looked fast even while standing still. This is a 1924 Model S. *Navistar International* was this country's third-ranking automaker, behind Ford and Buick.

Ransom Olds' first truck appeared in 1909, perhaps even as early as late 1907. Either way, it was quite "wagon-like" in appearance, with its wooden "flareboard" express body and 36-inch-tall wooden-spoked wheels. A water-cooled 10–12 horsepower engine was beneath the seat, and drive was by double side chains. The maximum load was 1,500 pounds. The price was $750.

Additional merits were explained by the promotional guys. "The Reo Delivery Wagon and one man does the work of three horses and wagons and three men, and its daily cost, including operator, is about the same as one horse and wagon and man," claimed advertisements. "It enables you to extend your business to a wider radius; it advertises your business; it works 24 hours a day if necessary; it does not slip, get lame, sick or die; it requires less attention than a horse; and it doesn't eat unless it works." If this prose wasn't enough to convince Americans to give up the bridle, what was?

More trucks from Ransom Olds probably helped. In October 1910, Olds announced the founding of the Reo Motor Truck Company to further this effort. Earliest advertisements featured a three-quarter-ton Model H and quarter-ton Model J. Model H sales from 1911 to 1913 numbered about 2,300 units.

Advertisements in 1915 were bragging about Reo's new "Hurry Up Wagon," soon renamed "Speed Wagon." A 45-horsepower four-cylinder engine inspired this three-quarter-ton truck's name, as well as at least one doubtful claim. While factory specifications listed the early Speed Wagon's top end at 22 miles per hour, some reports had a loaded model hitting 40 miles per hour. Believe it or not. All bloated boasting aside, the first Speed Wagons did feature pneumatic tires, electric starters, and electric lights, meaning Reo's trucks were right on the industry's cutting edge at the time.

Reo would use the Speed Wagon name—later spelled with a hyphen, then as one word—for various-sized trucks over the years, but the original was still the original. About 140,000 three-quarter-ton Speed Wagons were sold between 1915 and 1926.

By 1925 International Harvester had grown into this country's largest full-line truck builder. In 1927, the company introduced its Six-Speed Special, a one-ton truck able to both hunker down under heavy loads and haul butt on the open road, thanks to an innovative two-speed rear axle. This is a 1928 I-H Six-Speed Special.

The Six-Speed Special carried the company's triple-diamond logo on the radiator shell and rear axle, presumably to let everyone know you were driving an International.

Reo trucks grew progressively larger through the 1930s. Although some relatively light trucks were built later on, the company's main fare after World War II consisted of heavy-duty commercial rigs.

In 1954 Detroit's Bohn Aluminum and Brass Corporation bought Reo. Three years later, White purchased the company from Bohn, then followed that with the acquisition of Diamond T in 1958. Diamond T production was transferred to the Reo plant in Lansing, where both old veterans were operated as separate divisions of the White Company for nearly 10 years. The two were finally consolidated into Diamond Reo in 1967.

By that time it had been long since established that no man then living would ever see the horseless age . . . would ever see the horseless age end.

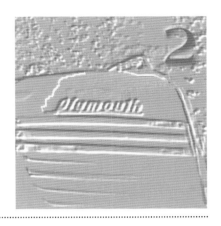

HENRY GETS EVEN

BIRTH OF THE AMERICAN PICKUP

Henry Ford was no stranger to beating a dead horse. For all his historic achievements, the father of the mass-production assembly line more than once rode a bet well past a point of diminishing returns, if not into the ground. Even his crowning glory, the Model T, probably rolled on for a few years too long. More than 15 million Model T buyers couldn't have been wrong, but by the time the last of those customers showed up at a dealership the competition was already stealing the attentions of the next guy in line, as well as a few thousand after him.

Henry often refused to let progress guide his hand. In his mind, simplicity was always among his company's strongest selling points. Simple yet obsolete buggy springs suspended Fords at both ends through the 1940s—because the old man demanded so. He remained adamant even after Chevrolet introduced its new knee-action independent front suspension in 1934. "We use transverse springs for the same reason that we use round wheels," he once admonished listeners, "because we have found nothing better for the purpose."

Apparently hydraulic brakes and modern Hotchkiss drive were also no better than the age-old mechanical stoppers and antiquated torque tubes used by his cars in the 1930s. Mechanically operated brakes continued offering Ford drivers "the safety of steel from toe to wheel" until 1939, once again because the boss said so. A Hotchkiss-type drive shaft didn't replace the torque tube until 1949, two years after Henry Ford's death. Those antique buggy springs also were buried in 1949.

Henry was equally stubborn about what went beneath his cars' hoods. Like the Model T it powered for nearly 20 years, Ford's old reliable four-cylinder just kept going. And going. And going. From the 1910s into the 1920s. From the 1920s into the 1930s. Chevrolet stole the industry sales lead in 1927, then introduced a six-cylinder engine in 1929, and Henry Ford apparently still refused to budge. As he once explained during the Model T's heyday, "I've got no use for a motor that has more spark plugs than a cow has teats."

The head man finally did give in, however. Ultrasecret experimental work on new, larger engines was under way as early as 1921. Henry *was* actually looking to the future, on this occasion with an eye toward doing the competition more than one better. As he told engineer Fred Thoms in the late 1920s, "We're going from a four to an eight, because Chevrolet is going to a six." Ford's famed "flathead" V-8 debuted in 1932. Of course, it then soldiered on well past its prime into the 1950s, as if to make one final lasting salute to Henry Ford's steadfast stubbornness.

Old Henry always had his way, right up to the end.

What he didn't have was the honor of being the first to drive a horseless carriage on the streets of Detroit, despite common beliefs to the contrary. Young Henry was riding a bicycle along behind Charles Brady King's first automobile as

Ford helped make the term "pickup" a household name in 1925 by offering the first complete-from-the-factory version of the light-duty half-ton truck. This is a 1927 Model T Runabout. The pickup box included with this model could also be ordered separately for any Model T—and when it was, it came painted black.

King made the city's premiere showing of internal combustion power on March 6, 1896. Ford's more famous Quadricycle set off on its maiden voyage around Detroit on June 4. King never had a chance from there as Ford raced off with automotive history in tow.

Ford built his second car in 1898, then helped organize the Detroit Automobile Company in August 1899. Detroit Automobile completed its first vehicle, an enclosed delivery wagon designed by Henry, on January 12, 1900. Ford's initial business venture failed to survive the year, however. He tried again in November 1901, incorporating the Henry Ford Company to pick up where Detroit Automobile left off. No such luck; he resigned from the first company to wear his name in March 1902. This firm then evolved into the Cadillac Automobile Company.

The Ford Motor Company we all know and some love today was finally established on June 16, 1903. Two years later, the firm rolled out its first commercial vehicle, a delivery car that Ford paperwork called the "Model C fitted with our Delivery Top." It was designed to use as many Model C passenger car parts as possible. Reportedly only 10 were built, with a price tag of $950 each.

Henry Ford's first "truck" was a delivery wagon he designed for the Detroit Automobile Company in January 1900. Other similar panel delivery designs appeared later as Ford products. *Ford Motor Company*

Apparently Henry had paid no attention to the Automobile Club of America's Commercial Vehicle Contest in 1903. Trucks mattered little to him, if at all; so much so that another delivery car model wouldn't be offered again until 1912. This time considerable effort was made to build a better beast of burden. This wasn't just a modified passenger car; it featured a unique delivery body and was "tougher than an army of mules and cheaper than a team of horses," according to ads. Nonetheless, "The Car That Delivers The Goods," as Ford called it, didn't

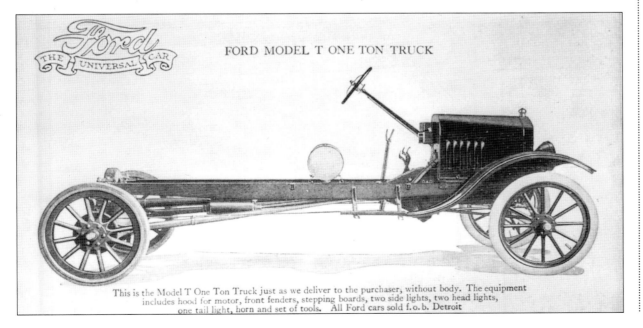

FORD MODEL T ONE TON TRUCK

THE FORD UNIVERSAL CAR

This is the Model T One Ton Truck just as we deliver to the purchaser, without body. The equipment includes hood for motor, front fenders, stepping boards, two side lights, two head lights, one tail light, horn and set of tools.   All Ford cars sold f. o. b. Detroit

Dearborn's truck legacy officially began July 27, 1917, with the introduction of the one-ton Model TT chassis. Ford trucks seen before this date were all aftermarket conversions. Adding a bed and cab was left up to the buyer. *Ford Motor Company*

OPPOSITE: Model T Fords were converted into a variety of special models targeted for commercial use. This 1926 T was fitted with a "huckster" body, an open shell used to show off a dealer's wares.

Was this actually the first factory-built pickup? Dodge Brothers offered this truck as a complete package in 1924, one year before Ford's Model T Runabout. In Dodge's case, production was low, the truck was a three-quarter-ton, construction was wood, and the body was supplied by Dodge Brothers' Graham Brothers affiliate. You make the call.

Reo began offering its half-ton Junior Speed Wagon in bare-chassis form in 1928. At $895, the Junior Speed Wagon was touted by Reo brochures as the "lowest priced six-cylinder truck of its size in America."

OPPOSITE: Chevrolet's first trucks arrived in 1918. The half-ton Model 490, shown here, was priced at $595. The larger one-ton Model T cost $1,325. Beneath that beautiful blue hood is a 26-horsepower 170-cid overhead-valve four-cylinder engine. These trucks were typically sold as bare-chassis models—again, adding cab and bed was the customer's prerogative.

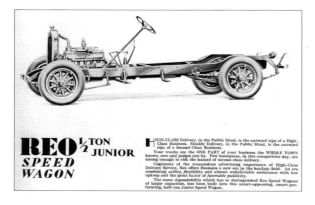

REO ½ TON JUNIOR SPEED WAGON

HIGH-CLASS Delivery, in the Public Mind, is the outward sign of a High-Class Business. Shoddy Delivery, in the Public Mind, is the outward sign of a Second-Class Business.

Your trucks are the ONE PART of your business the WHOLE TOWN knows, sees and judges you by. Few businesses, in this competitive day, are strong enough to risk the hazard of second-class delivery.

Cognizant of the tremendous advertising importance of High-Class Delivery Service, Reo offers Business a new era in the haulage field. An era combining *utility, flexibility and almost unbelievable endurance with low upkeep and the great factor of favorable publicity.*

The same dependability which has so distinguished Reo Speed Wagons of larger capacities, has been built into this smart-appearing, smart-performing, half-ton Junior Speed Wagon.

exactly deliver the customers. It was discontinued in December 1912.

Along with that $700 delivery car, Ford in 1912 introduced a commercial roadster model that featured a removable rumble seat to make additional space for hauling things back there. Creating the commercial roadster opened the door for creative customers who quickly learned how to convert their Model Ts into light-duty pickups. Out went the rumble seat, in went a cargo box, however crude. These homebuilt haulers were not alone on the streets. Quick-thinking entrepreneurs also made conversions on request.

Various businesses had emerged by 1913 to offer buyers the chance to transform their Model T into a truck. At the top of the list was the A. D. Smith company, which sold The Smith Form-a-Truck conversion. The parts included here turned a polite Model T into a lengthened one-ton, chain-driven workhorse. The Convertible Equipment Company offered a

similar kit that also extended the frame and beefed the suspension and driveline.

With Ford again out of the commercial vehicle business after December 1912, it was left to the aftermarket to supply utility bodies for the Model T chassis. Panel delivery conversions were sold by, among others, the Columbia Body Company in Detroit, the Highland Body Manufacturing Company in Cincinnati, the Brown Auto Carriage Company in Cleveland, and William G. Hess & Son in Leavenworth, Kansas. The Union Truck Manufacturing Company in New York built screenside express bodies. The Miffinburg Body Company fashioned stylish "Suburban" models—station wagons with added seating. The Gustav Schaefer Wagon Company in Cleveland even transformed Model Ts into tractor-trailer rigs, as did Union. Slip-in pickup boxes were also sold through various firms.

The aftermarket business was flourishing during the second decade of the century, and Henry Ford apparently couldn't care less. Independent companies could make a buck converting his products into trucks if they wanted; he was too busy building cars as fast as customers could snap them up. But Henry wasn't alone. Many early manufacturers concentrated on automobile production and treated utility models like stepchildren.

There were major exceptions. Reo, Autocar, and White did quite well building both cars and trucks in this century's early years. International even traded cars for trucks completely in 1911. Other major carmakers "dabbled" in the truck business. The company Henry inadvertently helped create, Cadillac, and Oldsmobile were both building commercial vehicles right out of the blocks in 1904. Packard began offering trucks in 1905, Buick in 1910. But as far as primitive pickups—true light-duty trucks with an open cargo box behind a cab—were concerned, most seen on American roads before the 1920s were owner-converted cars, either rough-and-tough homebuilts or simple kit creations.

Henry Ford's company finally fully acknowledged the truck market in 1917. On July 27,

longer wheelbase), beefed-up suspension in back, tougher worm-drive rear axle, and artillery-type rear wheels wearing solid rubber tires. The Model TT was both wonderfully rugged and warmly welcomed—by 1919, Ford had built 100,000 one-ton chassis.

Henry Ford, however, continued to let others get into his pockets. Bare-chassis Model T and Model TT trucks remained the only factory-delivered choices for Ford buyers into the 1920s. Henry reportedly feared a bad-press backlash should he ever start taking business away from all those aftermarket firms—picture for a moment the image of a big bully national corporation from decadent Detroit beating up on a defenseless mom-and-pop outfit operating in friendly Anytown, U.S.A.

Then apparently the boss finally got wise. Perhaps the TT's appearance had proven to him that neither mom nor pop would mind his expansion onto their turf. Or maybe he got fed up with watching all that cash flow into Anytown when it could be emptying into Dearborn. Either way, he became fearless and decided he could no longer overlook such a highly profitable opportunity. Henry chose not to get mad. He got even.

In October 1923, Dearborn announced it finally would be offering truck bodies for the TT chassis. The first, a pickup-style express body, was actually the product of a collaborative effort between Ford's Highland Park Plant, the Budd body company in Philadelphia, and Simplex Manufacturing in Kansas City, Missouri. Ford's first true factory-designed truck compartment, an open C-cab, was introduced in January 1924. Later in December, an eight-foot stake bed debuted. Then a Ford-issue enclosed TT cab appeared in the spring of 1925.

Buyers desiring a light-duty pickup, meanwhile, were still left with a Model T chassis conversion as the only choice. But that all changed on April 15, 1925, when Ford announced the arrival of its "Model T Runabout with Pick-Up Body."

Temporarily overlooking the fact that the Dodge Brothers firm apparently introduced a

Ford's last open-cab pickup was built in 1934. Production that year was only 347. This 1934 roadster Ford is powered by a flathead V-8.

Dearborn officials announced the production of its one-ton chassis, the Model TT. Though still a modified passenger car platform, the Model TT exhibited true truck-like qualities, thanks to its lengthened, reinforced frame (with a 2-foot-

Old Henry never did care much for keeping up with the Joneses. But when Chevrolet went from a four to a six in 1929, Ford upped the ante by two more cylinders in 1932. Here, Henry Ford ponders the merits of his famed "flathead" V-8, which powered Ford pickups and autos up until 1953.

complete three-quarter-ton pickup in 1924 (with a lot of help from the brothers Graham), it is Ford's 1925 Model T roadster that is commonly honored as this country's first factory-delivered light-duty truck. A few points can be made in support of Dearborn's accomplishment. Henry Ford needed no assistance whatsoever to create his first pickup. Dodge's body and box were Graham Brothers' pieces, and that flareboard box was made of wood. Ford's pickup box was all steel. Finally, the Model T light truck was a certified sales success—33,795 hit the streets the first year alone. Dodge/Graham's slightly heavier pickups were almost unheard of in the 1920s.

The 1925 Ford pickup's cargo box simply attached to the Model T chassis in place of the car-line's rear deck. The box was 56 inches long, 13 inches deep, and 40.75 inches wide. In typical pickup fashion, it also featured four stake holes and an adjustable tailgate. Additional equipment included a heavier nine-leaf buggy spring in back. The price for the whole deal was $281. The box itself could be purchased as a separate option for $25.

Model T roadster pickup sales soared to 75,406 in 1926. The Model A pickup debuted two years later, first in roadster-only form. An enclosed cab model appeared later in August 1928. As mentioned, Ford's first V-8, the 221-cid flathead, joined Henry's tried-and-true four-cylinder in 1932. All Ford pickups beginning in 1935 were V-8-powered. A four-cylinder returned in 1941, joined by a new six-cylinder.

Pickup styling in the 1930s remained mostly car-based until 1937, when a distinctive grille was added. Much more radical was the "barrel-nosed" look introduced the following year. Also new for 1938 was a front-opening hood. Styling reverted back to car-line features in 1940 and 1941. Though these pickups looked like their passenger-car cousins, few parts actually interchanged. Car-line impressions disappeared in 1942, just in time for World War II to interrupt production. Three years later, the truck line picked up where it had left off, and never again would a Ford pickup wear a car-like facade.

Like Ford, Chevrolet's earliest pickups were also nothing more than cars with cargo boxes bolted in back. Chevy's first truck, introduced in 1918, even shared its model number with its car-line counterpart. The company's 490-series automobile, itself introduced two years before, was named for its base price—$490. The Model 490 half-ton truck, with its lengthened 102-inch wheelbase and 26-horsepower 170-cid overhead-valve four-cylinder engine, was priced at $595. Its one-ton big brother, the 125-inch-wheelbase Model T, wore a $1,325 price tag and never once apologized to Henry Ford for borrowing its name from his cars. Both 1918 trucks were sold only as bare chassis, the assumption being that a Chevy customer would also turn to one of the many aftermarket cab and body suppliers.

Chevrolet's first venture into the utility vehicle market, which came seven years after the company was established by Billy Durant, was barely noticed in 1918. Total output of both models that year was only 879 units. Once word got around, though, there was no stopping the Chevy truck, especially the Model 490 half-ton, a nicely affordable, wonderfully functional machine. "The Chevrolet Light Delivery Wagon was designed to meet the requirements of those who have need of a commercial car with slightly less capacity and of considerably lighter weight than is afforded by a one-ton truck," explained a company sales catalogue later in 1920. Led by the 490, Chevrolet truck production in 1919 exploded almost tenfold to 8,179. Ten more years were all that were needed for all-time Chevy truck production to hit the half-million mark.

General Motors' low-priced division almost overnight went from a small fry to a heavyweight challenger in the utility vehicle market. Ford, the reigning champ, began feeling the heat in the mid-1920s. A shocking knock-down blow then came in 1927, as the Bow-Tie bested the Blue Oval with 104,832 calendar-year registrations against Ford's 99,451. The factory downtime needed in 1927 to prepare for the Model A's introduction greatly inhibited dealers' stock in 1928, resulting in a drop to 65,247 for Ford. Chevy, meanwhile, was soaring to 133,682—better than twice the 1928 sales of its new/old rival. A revitalized Ford regained its crown in 1929, holding it until 1932. Chevrolet then

grabbed it back in 1933 and almost never looked back again for nearly four decades.

Chevrolet's early technical progression differed slightly from Ford's. Aftermarket sheet metal continued as the norm atop a light-duty Chevy truck chassis for about 10 years. But around 1920, Chevrolet began installing those subcontracted bodies on its own assembly lines. Most of these bodies were manufactured by the Martin-Parry Company in Indianapolis, Indiana. Other popular suppliers included Superior and Hercules.

An all-steel enclosed cab was introduced in 1925. The following year, Chevrolet rolled out a roadster pickup by simply shoving a supplier-built cargo box into the trunk of a drop-top Chevy car. A "true" roadster pickup, one with a conventional box mounted behind a truck cab, debuted in 1930. Late that year, Chevrolet bought Martin-Parry, which at the time was among the world's largest truck body manufacturers. From then on it was official: A Chevy pickup was an all-Chevy pickup, it now qualified fully as "factory built." As for the box-in-the-trunk idea, it would return in 1936—on a coupe body this time—and survive up through 1942.

Even bigger news in 1929 was the installation of Chevrolet's new overhead-valve six-cylinder engine in place of the aging four-holer. Advertised as "A Six for the price of four," this incredibly durable 194-cid powerplant produced 46 horsepower. More important, it gave Chevy pickups the added prestige of having two more cylinders than comparable rivals from Ford and Dodge, something company ads were more than willing to point out to prospective buyers. Even after it went down two cylinders to the competition, the revered "Stovebolt" six still managed on its own to propel Chevy pickups above their eight-cylinder rivals to the top of the sales ladder year in, year out until 1955, when the division's modern OHV V-8 emerged to help carry some of the weight.

Chevrolet pickup popularity continued to climb in the 1930s. The division sold its one millionth truck in 1933, and needed only six

Dodge's first truck was typically a car with heavier springs and a purpose-built body. Dodge Brothers' screenside delivery model debuted in 1917 as a 1918 model. A true pickup was a few years down the road, as was an eventual merger with Walter P. Chrysler's young conglomerate.

more years to deal out its second million. In 1934, Chevy pickups received their own individual sheet metal for the first time—almost no more car components were used. Standard hydraulic brakes were added in 1936, the same year annual sales surpassed 200,000.

Chevrolet's corporate cousin, GMC, collected its fair share of truck industry milestones. The first four-wheel brakes. The first two-speed rear axle. The first recirculating ball-bearing steering. The first dual-range transmission. The first full-pressure lubrication and hydraulic lifters for its engines. The first air suspension. GMC over its long history has built everything from pickups to big-rigs, from taxis to buses, and it's done all this in the shadows of all those Chevrolet trucks rolling out each year.

The complex GMC legacy began in 1909 when Billy Durant bought up two Detroit truck builders, the Rapid Motor Vehicle Company and the Reliance Motor Company, as part of his early push to assemble his General Motors empire. The General Motors Truck Company was formed to oversee sales of the Rapid and Reliance trucks. The GMC label first appeared in 1911 and the two truck lines were renamed GMC models in 1912. In 1913 all GMC truck production was centralized in Pontiac, Michigan. Medium- and heavy-duty models represented the main priorities early on.

GMC entered the light truck field in 1927 or 1928, depending on how you look at it. General Motors' Pontiac Division introduced a half-ton panel delivery vehicle in 1927. This very same machine was marketed as GMC's T-11 model in 1928. Half-ton pickups appeared as well and later, in the 1930s, began sharing sheet metal with Chevrolet's trucks. Unique drivetrains, some from Pontiac, others based on Buick designs, always set the GMC pickup apart from its Chevy running mate. The plan was to market GMC pickups as an upscale step above the lower-priced, less-prestigious Chevrolet trucks. This differentiation has been all but lost in recent years, as all trucks now are loaded down with as much prestige as they can carry.

In the 1930s GMC typically hung around the fifth slot in the annual sales rankings. Always

just above it in those rankings was the company founded by John and Horace Dodge in 1914.

Talented engineers with ties to both Ransom Olds and Henry Ford, the Dodge brothers began planning to manufacture their own automobiles in 1910. They had made small fortunes supplying Ford with engines, transmissions, and axles for eight years; now it was time to put their own name on the automaking map.

The automotive press began to buzz immediately after the word went out in 1914 that John and Horace would be building automobiles by the end of the year. "When the new car comes out, no question it will be the best thing on the market for the money," claimed the *Michigan Manufacturer and Financial Record.* "The Dodge brothers are the two best mechanics in Michigan."

About 22,000 dealership applications landed in Hamtramck, Michigan, even before the plant there rolled out its first car on November 14, 1914. Some 45,000 more Dodge Brothers cars left the line in 1915, vaulting the newborn firm to third place in industry sales rankings.

Dodge Brothers began building civilian commercial vehicles (military models were built in 1916 for use in World War I) in 1917. A screenside commercial car went into production on October 18 wearing a 1918 model-year

By 1929, Dodge was selling complete, all-steel half-ton pickups. This 1929 Model BE could have been powered by either a 45-horsepower four-cylinder or a 63-horsepower six. *Chrysler Historical Collection*

By 1940, Chevrolet light-duty trucks had evolved into streamlined, all-steel leaders of the pickup pack. Sealed-beam headlights were new that year. Behind that attractive grille is an 85-horsepower six-cylinder.

commercial car. These two vehicles remained Dodge Brothers' primary utility offerings through 1928. Custom variations did exist during that time as once again buyers added their own bodies to bare chassis. Other models also emerged by way of an agreement with an independent truck builder from the Hoosier state, this deal coming about after tragedy struck in 1920.

Both Dodge brothers died that year, John in January, Horace in December. Neither had been particularly fond of commercial vehicles during their short tenures atop the company that bore their name; building the two delivery vehicles was sufficient in their minds. Overwhelming automobile orders kept them busy enough as it was. But with the brothers gone, new company president Frederick Haynes almost immediately went to work expanding the firm's horizons by widening the scope of its truck line.

Early in 1921, Haynes signed a contract with Graham Brothers of Evansville, Indiana. Graham Brothers first began doing truck conversions on others' chassis in 1919, then quickly started manufacturing its own models. The deal Ray, Robert, and Joseph Graham made with Haynes two years later essentially transformed the Indiana firm into an unofficial division of Dodge Brothers. Graham Brothers would concentrate solely on building one- and one-and-a-half-ton trucks at its Evansville plant, based on Graham-designed chassis that featured parts manufactured by Dodge in Michigan. Graham-built cabs and bodies went atop those frames, which included a Dodge-built driveline. The finished products were then sold and serviced through Dodge dealerships alongside those existing commercial and business cars. Graham Brothers built its first truck under this agreement in April 1921.

Graham Brothers offered customers a wide range of body choices, including an express version. This pickup-styled package included a cargo box with wooden sides topped by wooden flareboards, all held together by iron straps. In 1924 a smaller three-quarter-ton truck was introduced and sold as a Dodge product. It was marketed with either a stake or pickup

designation. The screenside moniker meant just that—the open compartment in back was walled-off on each side by a wire screen. That screen could help keep wandering hands away from the goods while still allowing a huckster to show off his wares. Roll-down canvas side covers could also discourage prying eyes come closing time.

Advertisements for that first screenside truck claimed it was "precisely the kind of car you would expect Dodge Brothers to build." Except for heavier springs, larger tires, and the screenside body, the company's commercial car was indeed a Dodge Brothers automobile—an automobile with a 1,000-pound payload. It featured a big 35-horsepower, 212-cid four-cylinder backed by a cone-type clutch and three-speed transmission. The price for the complete package was $885.

In March 1918, an enclosed panel delivery, called a business car, joined the screenside (express) body behind an open or closed cab. As before, the driveline and chassis were Dodge-built, the cabs and bodies were Graham products. Like the express box, the enclosed cab was also made of wood.

As discussed earlier, these three-quarter-ton express trucks may or may not represent this country's first factory-built pickups, allegedly beating Ford's Model T by a year. The issue primarily hinges on whether or not you believe the Graham Brothers plant was officially a Dodge Brothers factory. It's more or less a matter of semantics. It also may have been a classic case of which dog barked the loudest. Only 347 open-cab Dodge pickups were built in 1924, joined by 152 of the wooden-bodied closed-cab models.

Things didn't become truly official until late 1924. In October, Dodge Brothers finally consummated the relationship that dated back to 1921—Graham became a fully recognized division of Dodge. But almost nothing changed, as Graham Brothers remained an autonomous entity with its own officers and identity. The division continued rolling out its own Graham Brothers trucks, and in fact had its best year ever, building 10,743 vehicles.

Graham more than doubled that record in 1925, the year John and Horace's widows finally sold out. In May, Dillon, Read and Company in New York purchased Dodge Brothers for $146 million—at the time a record figure for a business buyout in America. Haynes, who remained president, announced in June that Robert Graham was the new director of the Commercial Car and Truck Division.

The plot thickened even further later that year. In November 1925, Dillon, Read and Company obtained a 51 percent majority interest in Graham Brothers. Personnel shuffling then began, with Haynes moving up to chairman of the executive committee and Ray Graham taking over as general manager of Dodge Brothers, Inc. Graham Brothers President Joseph Graham and Vice President Robert Graham joined Dodge Brothers' board of directors. Brother Joseph was also named Dodge Brothers' Vice President of manufacturing two

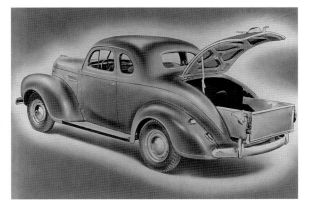

The trendy cargo box conversion for cars seemed to be all the rage in the 1930s. Hudson, Studebaker, Chevrolet, and Ford all tried this trick. Chrysler did too—shown here is a 1939 Plymouth coupe transformed into a truly light light-duty pickup. *Chrysler Historical Collection*

months later. The Graham Brothers division meanwhile continued operating independently. Graham built 37,463 trucks in 1926.

But just as there were no Dodge brothers in Dodge Brothers, by 1926 there were no longer any Graham siblings left at the company named after them. All three Grahams resigned their posts in the Dodge/Graham executive arrangement after Dillon, Read and Company acquired the remaining 49 percent of Graham Brothers in April 1926.

In yet another twist, the Dodge Brothers badge was dropped completely in 1927. All trucks sold that year were named Graham Brothers, even though Graham was the division and Dodge was the parent company. All production also was transferred to the Graham Brothers plants in Evansville, Detroit, and Stockton, California. The last Dodge-built, Dodge-named truck rolled off the line on October 4, 1926. This practice continued into 1928, the year Graham Brothers introduced an attractive half-ton panel truck.

Of course 1928 was also the year that Walter Chrysler acquired the company he had coveted since he had founded Chrysler Corporation four years before. The deal that shook Detroit was completed on July 30. This wasn't a case of a big company buying up a much weaker competitor. This was Detroit's wet-behind-the-ears No. 3 player joining forces with the former third-place runner to radically increase the sum of the parts. In collecting Dodge's vast dealer network, massive manufacturing facilities, and successful reputation, Walter Chrysler now had the weapons to do battle in a big way with

International expanded downward into the growing pickup truck ranks late in 1932 with its D-1 half-ton. A rebadged version of Willys-Overland's stylish C-113 pickup, the D-1 International, was officially introduced in January 1933. *Navistar International*

would remain Dodge's base light truck engine up into 1933. Technical innovations in 1929 included four-wheel hydraulic brakes.

A fresh, modern restyle helped mark the appearance in 1933 of the first pickup designed and built from tire tread to top as a Chrysler product. Crowning things off was one of Detroit's best-known, longest-running corporate symbols—the Dodge ram's head ornament. Dodge officials a year or two before actually paid for a study to determine if the ram would be a suitable mascot for their products. Once they learned how swift, strong, and sure this proud animal was, the Dodge boys knew it was the only choice to represent their trucks—their powerful, rugged, impressive-looking trucks. Impressions were further enhanced in 1933 by a 190-cid six-cylinder L-head engine, as four-cylinder power became a thing of the past.

Another major restyle arrived in 1936 for the "Fore-Point" Dodge trucks, so named because the engine and cab were relocated farther forward for better weight distribution and to allow a longer bed in back.

Further updates included new grilles in 1937 and 1938, followed in 1939 by yet another full-fledged reskin, a look that would carry over into the postwar years. Also surviving beyond World War II was Dodge's famed "Job-Rated" ad slogan, first used in 1940.

Dodge's truck division spent the 1930s battling tooth and nail with International for Ford and Chevrolet's leftovers. I-H ranked third in industry sales from 1930 to 1932 and again from 1937 to 1939. In between, Dodge copped the third position from 1933 to 1936. When one firm was in third place, the other landed in fourth. Dodge sales jumped up considerably for each of its four years on top of International, reaching a record high of 85,295 in 1936. Numbers then lagged a bit, beginning in 1937.

Chrysler's other truck division, Plymouth, experienced a meteoric rise that year, perhaps helping explain why Dodge dropped about 20,000 units. Peter robbing Paul? Maybe a bit, but this was how Walter Chrysler wanted to play the game—just like GM.

Detroit's two mega-manufacturers, GM and Ford. A truck division as part of the deal only sweetened the pot.

With the papers signed, Chrysler people immediately invaded Hamtramck, sacking everyone, including president E. G. Wilmer. K. T. Keller then became head of Chrysler's new Dodge Division. All trucks sold by Chrysler in 1929 were Dodge Brothers models again, as the Graham Brothers badge was finally deleted—even though early 1929 editions were Graham carryovers from 1928. A new Dodge truck, partially redesigned and built by Chrysler people, rolled out in May 1929 to help usher in the age of the "Big Three" pickup builders. The Dodge Brothers moniker lingered into the 1930s before the second word faded away.

Leading the charge was Dodge's first half-ton pickup, an attractive little hauler powered by a four-cylinder engine supplied by Plymouth, Chrysler's newly founded low-priced division. Larger trucks in 1929 used Dodge's passenger-car six-cylinder. The Plymouth four, which displaced 175 cubic inches and produced 45 horsepower,

GM's pricing pecking order was reproduced by Chrysler just before Dodge Brothers came into the fold. Dodge immediately settled in between higher-priced DeSoto and lower-priced Plymouth. Both of these divisions originated in 1928. Yet another division, Fargo, was also born that year to allow Walter Chrysler a slice of the truck market pie. This founding, of course, came before he bought out Dodge Brothers.

Fargo products included half- and three-quarter-ton commercial vehicle chassis, 7,680 of which were sold before the Depression came along and helped kill off Chrysler's first truck company. Although the young division's untimely death came in 1930, some leftovers apparently were sold as 1931 models. The legacy didn't end there, however. The name would carry on atop the corporation's national fleet sales organization. Fargo trucks emerged again in 1933 as rebadged big Dodges heading for overseas export markets. A Fargo pickup appeared in 1936, but only in Canada, as Chrysler's counterpart north of the border began marketing light trucks that were again rebadged Dodge models. Chrysler of Canada would offer Fargo trucks and vans up through 1972.

When the Depression struck in 1929, Walter Chrysler hardly needed two truck divisions. Dodge was the established winner, so it was Fargo that had to go. And to think Chrysler also had early plans for Plymouth to enter the truck market, too. Three semisuperfluous utility vehicle divisions in tough times might've been too much to bear.

As it was, Plymouth did offer a small number of commercial sedans in 1930 and 1931. Sedan deliveries appeared in 1935 and remained on the scene until 1942. And once Dodge settled into its niche and the cash began to flow again, Chrysler's price leader also began marketing pickups in 1937. These were basically Dodge truck clones wearing a slightly smaller price tag. Pricing was undoubtedly the key to Plymouth's immediate jump up into the industry's sixth slot in the sales rankings. Registrations for 1937 totaled 13,709. But that was as good as it got. Although responses remained

Willys-Overland began offering commercial vehicles based on its compact Whippet car line in 1927. These trucks probably should be included in chapter 4 of this book, as the Whippet, when introduced in the fall of 1926, was America's smallest car. Pickup versions were built alongside the delivery model shown here. *Chrysler Historical Collection*

Willys-Overland's half-ton pickups of the 1930s and 1940s were rather compact themselves. They were also quite attractive, thanks to the car-line sheet metal used up front. *Chrysler Historical Collection*

healthy for the attractive Plymouth pickup, Chrysler officials grew tired of competing against themselves. When Plymouth truck production was shut down by the war in 1941, it was shut down for good.

By then the Big Three were thoroughly in control of the pickup market, with Ford and Chevrolet miles ahead of everyone and Dodge a distant third. Or fourth. As mentioned, International Harvester was often in third place, but its numbers were always well padded with its larger trucks. Dodge, on the other hand, did it mostly with light-duty machines, as did Chevy and Ford.

The lightest International trucks before 1933 were three-quarter-tonners. While these hard-working haulers had always done the company proud, they still proved unable to fend off the Depression. Sagging sales after 1930 convinced I-H officials that something more was needed to keep the company competitive. Or

Studebaker entered the pickup race in 1937 with its first Coupe Express, a model that was not much more than a Dictator passenger car with a softly contoured cargo box molded on in back. The Coupe Express was built for three years only. It was canceled in July 1939.

some extra cash, while International execs at the time were almost willing to trade their kingdom for a pickup. Presto. Late in 1932, I-H contracted W-O to build International-badged Willys pickups at its plant in Toledo, Ohio. International then sold these trucks as its D-1 series. The only major difference in the two was a larger six-cylinder beneath the D-1's hood. I-H's D-1 truck was introduced in January 1933, just in time to help push International sales up by 70 percent.

International continued marketing the Willys-built D-1 up into 1934, when it was replaced by I-H's own pickup, the stylish C-1. A new, restyled D-series debuted in 1937, followed by the more-modern K-series midway in 1940.

Willys trucks almost faded from the scene after the International deal was made in 1932. Only panel delivery versions of its attractive, restyled series 77 four-cylinder trucks were offered in 1933 and 1934. With its slightly truncated 100-inch wheelbase, Willys' series 77 half-ton trucks came off looking smaller than they actually were. They also looked just like Willys-Overland automobiles.

A pickup joined the team in 1935. And another restyle in 1937 put the series 77 Willys right up with the most distinctive-looking light trucks of the prewar era with its unmistakable "ship's prow" nose and sculpted-in, fender-mounted headlights. Although the ship's prow hood was retained, overall looks were refined in 1939 as the headlights went into the fenders, Ford-style, and an understated chrome grille replaced the garish louvers used previously. Willys pickups from 1939 to 1941 may well rank among the most attractive of all time.

Pickups that looked like cars were commonplace before the war, since so many light trucks were conveniently based on their car-line counterparts, as were Willys-Overland's products. Some even were cars. More than one automaker played the "stuff the cargo box in the trunk" game: Chevrolet with its roadster pickups from 1926 to 1929, Durant with the same over the same span. Chevrolet returned with a coupe version in 1936.

perhaps something less. The low-priced, light-duty pickup had already carved out a niche in the truck market. Why not extend the model line down into this rapidly growing arena? The problem was that International wasn't capable of simply pulling a pickup out of a hat on short notice.

A solution presented itself in the form of Willys-Overland, the firm created after John North Willys took over the four-year-old Overland company in 1907. Willys-Overland first began offering commercial vehicles in 1911. Definitely light Overland "half-ton" (capacity was more like 800 pounds) express models were being marketed by World War I. In 1927 a truly compact pickup, based on the new Whippet car platform, was introduced. Diminutive Whippet pickups were superseded by W-O's new C-113 model half-ton trucks in January 1931.

By then Willys-Overland was also feeling the financial crunch. Willys was in dire need of

Hudson and Ford copied this idea in 1937, Plymouth in 1938.

When Studebaker entered the light-duty truck field in 1937, its first half-ton pickup was not much more than a Dictator passenger car with a bed bolted on back. The so-called Coupe Express shared so many automobile parts, it even had vent windows in the doors, a feature found on few light trucks before modern times. Studebaker built this stylish pickup up through 1939 before disappointing sales forced its cancellation. Yet another box-in-the-trunk model, the Champion coupe delivery, was the company's only light utility vehicle offered in 1940. A true modern pickup, the M5, was introduced in 1941 and carried over into the postwar years.

Hudson's pickups closely resembled the Studebaker Coupe Express ideal, with shorter bedwalls. Hudson was 20 years old when it first offered a light-duty commercial vehicle line, named Dover, in 1929. In 1930 the Dover commercial cars became Essex models, Essex being Hudson's smaller, lower-priced running mate. The company unveiled its attractive Terraplane series for the Essex line in 1932, and a Terraplane-based Essex pickup was introduced the following year. A major restyle in 1934 emphasized the car-line connection for the Terraplane—no longer just a series, Terraplane became an individual marque of its own that year. The Terraplane half-ton pickup wore a rakish grille, flowing fenders, and overall low lines that worked in concert to make impressions like no other truck. These beautiful pickups remained Terraplane models until 1938 when they were repackaged as Hudson-Terraplanes. The Terraplane moniker was dropped in 1939.

A restyle in 1940 resulted in the same Hudson pickup shell that returned to the market after the war in 1946 to look definitely out of place in a field full of competing light trucks that no longer shared images with their car-line cousins. Hudson then built its still-fashionable pickup one more time before leaving the past behind in 1947.

Another carmaker who gave the crossover trick a valiant try was William Crapo Durant,

Billy to his friends and creditors alike. Durant, the tragic figure who founded General Motors then lost it—twice—organized Durant Motors, Inc., in January 1921, almost immediately after leaving the GM presidency for good. Durant built cars until 1932. The company also began marketing commercial vehicles beginning in 1923. These were based on Durant Motors' Star automobiles and were basically assembled models. They used Continental four-cylinder engines and Martin-Parry bodies. A Continental six-cylinder made big news for the Star truck line in 1926. Two years later, the Star name was traded for Rugby, a moniker previously used by Durant for export models. Rugby trucks continued rolling on, however feebly, up through 1932. The Durant company went out of business that year. Billy Durant was reportedly penniless by 1936. He died in New York in 1947.

Reo gave up building cars the same year that Durant declared bankruptcy. Officials in Lansing announced in the summer of 1936 that their company would end its 31-year-old automotive legacy immediately to concentrate on commercial vehicle production. Reo then was America's eighth-biggest truck builder after standing as high as sixth earlier in the decade. It had managed to survive reasonably well through the Depression years by offering a wide range of working machines. Reo entered the

Walter Chrysler's desire to run with Detroit's two big dogs led to the production of a second light-duty truck line, this one dressed up in Plymouth garb. Plymouth pickups were first offered in 1937. Their short-lived lineage ended with the coming of war in 1941. This is a 1940 model.

Plymouth pickups were basically Dodge trucks with a Plymouth engine, grille, and hubcaps. Like all early Plymouth vehicles, this 1940 Plymouth truck carries the company's famous "sailing ship" hood ornament.

light-duty field in 1927 with its half-ton Speed-wagon Junior, an $895 truck labeled by company ads as "the lowest priced six-cylinder truck of its size in America." Hydraulic brakes were included in the deal.

Half-ton pickups from Reo continued into the 1930s, with the most notable being the classy Speed Delivery models built from 1937 to 1939. Reo also supplied Mack Trucks with its Mack Jr pickups in 1936 and 1937. Its own Speed Delivery trucks were marketed in two

LEFT: General Motors founder William Durant also gave truck building a try in the 1920s under the Star and Rugby names. Shown here is a 1928 display of Durant's Rugby trucks. *The National Automotive History Collection, Detroit Public Library*

Hudson's earliest trucks were Essex-based models named Dover. A 1929 Dover is shown here. *The National Automotive History Collection, Detroit Public Library*

forms: the 450 model with a four-cylinder engine and the 650 with a six. Both engines were Continental "Silver Crown" L-head units. Output was 45 horsepower for the 140-cid four, and 70 horses for the 209-cid six. Hydraulic brakes and a synchromesh three-speed transmission put the Speed Delivery pickup in a class with the most modern light trucks then offered. But few apparently noticed. Estimates put production for the three years at about 2,000. Reo

gave up on the light-duty market in 1940 and never built another half-ton truck.

As was becoming more and more the case, Reo's departure from the light truck business left more of the pie for the Big Three to wolf down. Once lousy with names, the utility vehicle roster had shrunk considerably by the time peacetime production resumed in 1945 and 1946.

And it was destined to get even smaller.

Hudson, too, offered both the box-in-the-trunk design and a car-based pickup line in the 1930s and 1940s, and was the last truck maker to carry on with a "half-car, half-truck" model into the postwar market. Hudson's last pickup was built in 1947. Shown here is a 1946 model. The bright running boards and tonneau tie-downs are owner-added customizations, as is the typical pickup "theft-deterrent" system hanging in the rear window.

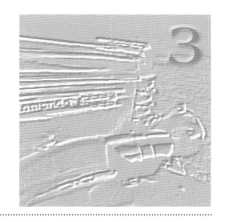

THE BIG BOYS' TOYS

ONE SIZE DIDN'T FIT ALL

The truck market has always been a diverse place from a size perspective, although more often than not with a bias toward the heavy-duty end. Manly, even monstrous, commercial machines dominated truck production before the Depression. The more personal pickup began flourishing in the 1930s, but it was a few decades before the light-duty family began outselling its big brothers.

The market players themselves have also represented a diverse lot over the last 90 years or so. So many different jobs to do, so many different truck buyers, so many different trucks. Compact and full-sized 4x4 pickups from Willys-Overland and Kaiser-Jeep. Truly minute minitrucks from Crosley and American-Bantam. Cars disguised as pickups from Studebaker, Hudson-Terraplane and, later, Ford and Chevrolet. Pickups disguised as cars from Willys and Ford. Big-bully Power Wagons from Dodge. Classy Cameo Carriers from Chevy. Canadian-marketed M-100s from Mercury and Fargo pickups from Chrysler-Plymouth. South-American-sold commercial rigs from DeSoto. And so on.

The long list of these players also includes various cross-dressers. Predominant car builder Plymouth built a few pickups. Predominant truck builder International Harvester built a few early automobiles. Another major truck builder, Reo, built many cars. General Motors founder Billy Durant tried building cars and trucks after leaving GM in the 1920s.

Detroit's Big Three, of course, manufactured both cars and trucks by the boatload. Studebaker, the aged outsider from Indiana, also built both, but in much smaller quantities—and at an ever-decreasing rate after World War II. When the going was good, Studebaker was successfully selling utility vehicles of all sizes from the car-based Coupe Express, to true pickups, to tractor-trailer rigs. One size never fit all in South Bend.

Studebaker obviously wasn't alone in its diversity. While smaller independent firms like Willys kept busy focusing sharply on their own tight niche (in this case, postwar four-wheel drives), other larger, better-equipped truck builders with deeper pockets looked to totally saturate the playing field. Chevrolet, Ford, and Dodge truck divisions have primarily depended on pickup production almost from the get-go. But they've also rolled out their own fair share of heavy-duty haulers—cab-overs, diesels, you name it—during their long careers.

Reo blazed its own trail through the truck market's various levels. The company Ransom Olds founded gained fame up to and through the 1920s with its medium-duty line, then later evolved solely into the big-truck field. White, too, early on offered a wide range of bare-knuckled, burly machines with load capacities running from three-quarter ton to five tons, then turned its attention toward heavies only.

After starting out really small, Autocar went right to the top. Sterling also temporarily toyed with trucks as "light" as three-quarter-ton before also eventually emerging as one of this country's better-recognized big-rig builders. Dart, too, started out small, in this case with half-ton trucks

Diamond T's classic-looking machines are considered the "Cadillac of trucks." Though by no means luxurious, the Model 201 one-ton pickup easily ranks as one of the most stylish heavy-duty pickups ever built. Model 201 production ran from 1938 to 1949. Red was the common color. This is a 1948 model with optional 20-inch big-rig-style wheels.

Equipped with a specialty bed and dual rear wheels, this Model 201 fits its employer's needs to a T. Notice the bright full wheel covers. These were included with the standard 16-inch wheels as part of the optional Deluxe cab package.

Diamond T was known mostly for its heavy trucks and big-rigs. The company was also recognized for its style and flair—even its large trucks caught the eye with classic grilles and a nice dose of trim.

in the years before World War I; from there it was bigger and bigger brutes.

Perhaps the best at branching out over the long haul of truck history was International Harvester. IHC wasted little time covering all the bases in the truck game once it gave up motorcar production and began concentrating only on utility vehicles around 1910. Construction equipment, heavy haulers, open-road big-rigs, crew-cab pickups, light-duty half-tons, sport utilities—for about seven decades, if truck buyers needed it, International built it. Lighter I-H trucks were retired after 1980. In 1986 International Harvester officially became the Navistar International Corporation, which now resides at the upper reaches of the cargo-capacity pecking order.

Other big names stuck with big trucks only—Fageol, FWD, Corbitt, to name just a few. Younger readers will more readily recognize the monikers Peterbilt and Kenworth, two modern big-rig makers that never have ventured down from the truck market's heavy air.

Still other long-standing, well-known big-truck builders did try to expand their interests downward into the pickup world. Brockway, Mack, Federal, Diamond T, and Stewart over the years all attempted their own brand of market diversification. Some of these products were classic pickups; half-tons with polite personalities. A notch or so up were the "light heavyweights," three-quarter- and one-ton machines that fit in nicely with the drive-to-the-general-store crowd, yet were still able to work in ways no standard pickup could.

Of the names on this short list of "big boys' toys," it is Brockway that stands as the longest reach. Founded in 1912 by George Brockway in Cortland, New York, the Brockway Motor Truck Company at first did qualify, relatively, as a light-duty manufacturer. The company's earliest products were three-quarter-ton high-wheelers powered by air-cooled, two-cycle, three-cylinder engines.

But like Sterling and Dart, Brockway was simply starting small. By 1913 the company was also marketing two-ton trucks, followed soon afterward by three-and-a-half-ton beasts. Five-ton trucks arrived in the 1920s, as did a one-and-a-half ton Express model that looked very much like so many other early pickups of the day. These latter light Brockways, however, came and went quickly. In the 1930s, Brockway indeed meant big—the 30-ton V1200 behemoth was introduced in 1934. A long line of heavy haulers and tractor-trailer rigs followed.

Mack acquired Brockway in 1956 and continued marketing big-rigs wearing the Brockway name into the 1970s. Money then got tight and the parent company finally shut down the last major truck builder in New York in 1977.

Another New Yorker, the Stewart Motor Corporation, was founded in Buffalo in July 1912 by Thomas Lippard and R.G. Stewart. Stewart never was a big-truck builder, but it wasn't a small-timer, either. Medium-duty models represented the main line for much of the company's 30-year history.

This 1938 Federal pickup is a one-of-a-kind prototype for a one-ton model that was never put into production. During its restoration, it was discovered that its cab was simply a Federal big-rig unit cut down to smaller proportions.

The Federal's streamlined hood louvers and identification badge contain art deco styling influences.

Like Diamond T, Federal's big-rigs also began featuring trendy stylish touches in the 1930s. Federal built big trucks up until 1959. *American Truck Historical Society*

They probably don't get any bigger than the pickup shown here. This 1950 Federal M-15 one-ton truck was created specially for the Phefferkorn Awning Company in Sandusky, Ohio, to haul extension ladders and long rolls of tarps. The bed, which measures 14 feet long, was fabricated for this application by Perfection Steel Body in Galion, Ohio.

Trucks and deliveries running from one ton to three-and-a-half tons were Stewart's bread and butter. Quality and durability were prime selling points.

A modicum of diversity, supplied by various economical light-duty trucks, was also one of Stewart's attractions. A half-ton model with an express body, priced at $750 complete, was first advertised in 1916. But the really big small-truck news came 10 years later. In 1926 the Buffalo-based firm introduced its "Buddy Stewart," a three-quarter-ton pickup priced at $900 in bare-chassis form, about $1,200 with a body along for the ride. A one-ton version appeared in 1927.

Stewart's idea was to place a model in between International's Special Delivery one-ton, priced at $700, and Reo's lightest Speed Wagon, which cost more than $1,200. Apparently the Buddy Stewart's price was right, as was the power and fuel economy supplied by its 40-horsepower Continental six-cylinder engine. It was reasonably popular, in Stewart terms, for the short time it was around. The Buddy Stewart was dropped in 1930. Temporarily.

An all-new, truly stylish Buddy Stewart pickup, this one an honest half-ton, was reborn a few years later. Power this time came from a high-mileage, low-power 35-horse Waukesha four-cylinder. The four-cylinder Buddy Stewart traded

top end (40 miles per hour was about it) for fuel economy—more than 35 miles went by for every gallon of gasoline. Price, as a chassis only, was $495. Considering that a comparable Ford pickup at the time sold for about $470 with both a body and a V-8 thrown in as part of the deal, was it any wonder Stewart was out of business by 1942?

Company president Lippard jumped ship just as things really got bad for Stewart. He landed a job in 1940 at Stewart's main rival, the Federal Motor Truck Company, in Detroit. Federal even took over Stewart's ad slogan after World War II. "Federals have won by costing less to run," was the new claim to fame for Lippard's latest employer. With his previous company dissolved by then, who was going to complain?

A slogan and a company president weren't the only things the two firms had in common. Like Stewart, Federal was an "assembler," not a true manufacturer, in that it purchased many major components from outside contractors. Federal, again like Stewart, also for a time marketed pickups along with its line of medium- and heavy-duty commercial vehicles. But unlike its rival from Buffalo, Federal did offer some truly big trucks. Models as large as eight-tonners were being sold by the 1930s.

Federal was founded in 1910 as the Bailey Motor Truck Company. The founder was Martin Pulcher, who had organized the Oakland Motor Car Company in Pontiac, Michigan, in 1907. Not long after Pulcher opened his truck company he changed the name from Bailey to Federal. The Federal Motor Truck Company's first offerings were one-ton models powered by Continental four-cylinder engines.

The company's first pickup, the Model 10, was announced in December 1935 during a three-day convention held in Detroit to mark Federal's 25th birthday. According to President Pulcher, the Model 10 was created to help fill a gap perceived to exist in the 1930s truck market. Some light, bulky loads—like those encountered by launderers, dry cleaners, bakers, etc.—were too much for conventional half-ton pickups, he explained, yet were still not heavy enough to be hauled economically by a typical one-and-a-half-ton truck. Pulcher's plan was to close

While International Harvester may have represented the most diverse truck maker over the years, the Big Three players have never been strangers to bigger trucks. Pickups have long been Chevrolet's, Ford's, and Dodge's main claim to fame, but each company has also offered its fair share of heavy-duty haulers as well.

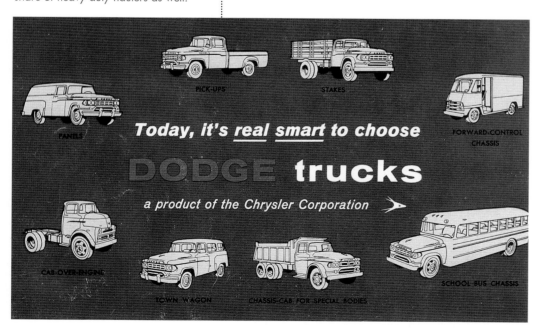

Today, it's _real_ _smart_ to choose

DODGE trucks

a product of the Chrysler Corporation ➤

PICK-UPS
STAKES
PANELS
FORWARD-CONTROL CHASSIS
CAB-OVER-ENGINE
TOWN WAGON
CHASSIS-CAB FOR SPECIAL BODIES
SCHOOL BUS CHASSIS

that gap with the Model 10, offered in three-quarter- and one-ton forms.

Three chassis lengths were initially offered, beginning with the standard 128-inch wheelbase. The two other frames stretched 143 and 152 inches between axles. Five bodies were available atop these frames. Along with the pickup, this list included a panel, a stake, a canopy, and a screen-side. Base price for the standard chassis was $545. Weight for a standard cab-chassis was a healthy 2,950 pounds.

Model 10 customers could've picked between two cabs; a standard unit with a rakish one-piece windshield or the deluxe version featuring an even more stylish split-V windshield that also sloped back in sleek fashion. High style was a Federal pickup trademark from the outset. That aggressive rake was accented up front with an impressive grille, ample trim for the hoodsides, and a chrome windshield frame. A chrome front bumper and bright hubcaps were also standard. Completing the image were big-rig-style cast-steel spoke wheels at the corners.

Federal looked to Hercules for its Model 10 engine. A 198-ci four-cylinder was chosen, its output advertised at 50 horsepower. In back of this L-head four went a 10-inch clutch and a four-speed transmission. Timken supplied the axles, with the rear units being full-floating pieces. Standard tires measured 6.00x20. Dual wheels could be added in back as an option.

As if the Model 10 wasn't good-looking enough, Federal hired famed industrial designer Henry Dreyfuss in 1938 to update its trucks. His input resulted in the restyled 1939 Models 7–8. These three-quarter-ton pickups ranked right up with the most attractive trucks ever offered before

World War II. Rakish lines, trademark Federal trim, and those eye-catching spoker wheels continued to be main attractions.

Wheelbases now numbered four: 102, 111, 119, and 128 inches. Model 7 Federals were powered by a 139-ci four-cylinder rated at 52 horsepower. A larger 205-ci six-cylinder L-head, rated at 72 horses, set the Model 8 apart from its more economical little brother. Everything else about the Models 7–8 line was the same, from the 10-inch Borg & Beck clutch, to the three-speed synchromesh transmission, to the Timken axles (again full-floating in back), to the Lockheed four-wheel hydraulic brakes, to the 6.00x16 four-ply balloon tires. These classic Federal light trucks rolled on until the end of 1940, when pickup production was interrupted by war.

Federal tried a new approach to the light-duty truck market in 1949, introducing a trimmed-down version of its big 15M-series truck. Both pickup and stake truck versions of this 15M model were announced in April that year, with a nominal load rating of three-quarter ton to two tons. These machines featured rugged, extra-heavy bodies on equally tough frames with a wheelbase measuring 135 inches. Equipment included a 93-horsepower 245-ci Hercules six-cylinder, an 11-inch clutch, a four-speed transmission, 20-inch wheels, and Timken wide-track front and rear axles. Budd wheels and a two-speed rear axle were

Stewart built its half-ton "Buddy" model off and on in the 1920s and 1930s. This 1936 Buddy Stewart was priced at $495.

The Stewart Motor Truck facility was founded in Buffalo, New York, in 1912, and operated there until 1942.

Stewart was known most for its one- to two-ton trucks. Bodystyles included everything from large panel deliveries and dump trucks, to buses. Sizes went as large as seven-tonners.

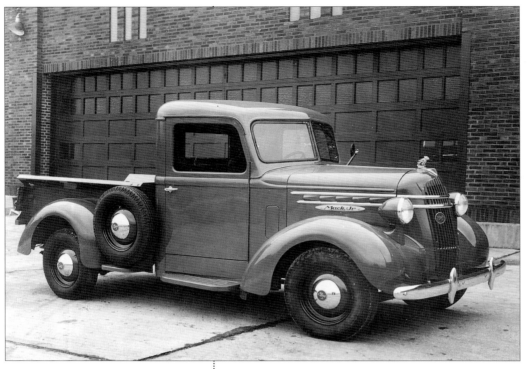

The Mack Jr half-ton pickup debuted in 1936, courtesy of Reo. When Reo restyled its Speed Delivery truck in 1937, the Mack Jr conversion took on a fresh, new, streamlined image. Notice the split-V windshield and bulldog ornament on this 1937 Mack Jr. *Mack Trucks Historical Museum*

optional. Styling for the 15M pickups remained similar to the Dreyfuss touch added in 1939. Federal's final "light truck" lasted only into early 1950, when the company introduced a new line of restyled medium and heavy trucks for 1951.

Federal's fortunes began to fade about this time. A merger with Fawick Airflex in 1952 resulted in the Federal Motor Truck Company becoming the Federal Motor Truck Division of the Federal-Fawick Corporation. Federal-Fawick was then sold to the Mast-Foos Manufacturing Company at the end of 1954. Not long afterward, Federal was purchased again, this time by Napco Industries in Minneapolis, Minnesota. Yet another merger followed as Napco, Federal and three other companies joined forces. All this paper trading and name changing finally came to end when Federal ceased production for good in March 1959.

Estimates put total Federal truck production over its 49-year history at only 160,000. From that, we can logically assume that the company's highly attractive pickups were few and far between.

Mack's humble half-ton and Diamond T's light-heavyweight pickup, both better known and

more plentiful, were introduced in the 1930s. Like Federal's light trucks, the Mack Jr and Model 201 Diamond T featured classic looks and, in the latter's case especially, a rugged, hard-working nature. What else would you expect from these two legendary names?

Mack may well represent the "T-Bird of the big-truck world." Just as anyone with eyes is familiar with Ford's little two-seaters of 1955–1957, so too are most casual witnesses able to readily recognize those big-rigs with the bulldog leading the way—and not just because he's so damned cute. That classic canine long ago came to stand for steadfast toughness and durability, qualities the company has been striving for from the beginning, with little regard to cost. "Built like a Mack truck" also long ago made its way out of the trucker's world into American lexicon. Those same casual witnesses will commonly compare anything, be it animal, vegetable, or mineral, to a Mack whenever strength and fortitude are at issue.

The company's roots run back to New York just after the turn of the century. The five Mack brothers, after gaining experience building wagons, manufactured their first motorized vehicle, a one-ton sightseeing bus, in Brooklyn in 1901. Bus building then became the Mack Brothers Motor Car Company's main business. Trucks joined buses on the production line after the company moved to Allentown, Pennsylvania, in 1905.

Further expansion led to a merger of sorts with the Saurer Motor Company in October 1911. Mack and Saurer continued separate operations under the International Motor Company banner. Two years later New York's Hewitt Motor Company also joined IMC. Soon afterward, Joe and Jack Mack gave up their IMC board of directors positions and faded into history. Luckily this wasn't the case for the line of hard-working trucks they founded.

It was IMC's purchase of Hewitt that helped vault Mack into its honored high place in trucking history. Company founder Edward Hewitt would serve as Mack's chief engineer for 30 years. He designed the AB series, which established the

Mack name firmly in the truck marketplace. The AB's lengthy career spanned from 1914 to 1936.

Hewitt engineer Alfred Masury designed the legendary AC Mack, introduced in 1916. Like many trucks of the time, the AC mounted its radiator safely behind the engine, a distinctive arrangement first popularized on France's Renault automobiles. As legend tells it, more than one early trucker found his conventional front-mounted radiator destroyed after a teamster "accidentally" allowed his wagon to roll backward into his motorized rival while awaiting a load or such. Horses and horsepower were not friends at all during the first decade of this century, especially when livelihoods were at stake.

Trucks like the Mack AC helped thwart such tactics until those wagon masters eventually lost their grip on the hauling industry. If you can't beat 'em, join 'em. Horses did remain popular in some rural areas into the 1930s. But in the hustling, bustling metropolitan marketplace, it was the truck that quickly took over as the favored way to move the goods after World War I. And teamsters eventually became Teamsters.

The AC's sloping hood also inspired the creation of the company's longstanding mascot. Reportedly British soldiers during World War I began referring to military versions of the AC as the "Bulldog Mack," this term of endearment being the product of the truck's snub-nosed frontal impressions. Alfred Masury later designed that famous bulldog hood ornament, which would eventually take its proud place atop the radiator (now mounted in its traditional location) of every Mack truck built after 1932.

The company name became firmly established in March 1922 when directors voted to trade their IMC flag for "Mack Trucks, Incorporated" colors. This was done to clear up an identity crisis; International Motor Company and International Harvester would never by confused again. Today, Mack is a division of Renault.

Mack's brief fling in the light-duty truck field—as if any Mack could ever be considered "light-duty"—came about as a result of tough economic times. Mack, like almost every other American manufacturer, was not immune to

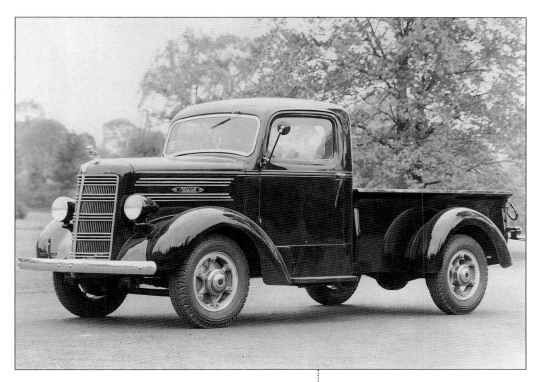

the effects of the Depression. By 1932, new truck registrations had fallen to 1,425, down from 6,823 in 1929. That same year International Harvester and Willys-Overland signed an agreement allowing I-H to market Willys' new C-series pickup as its own D-1 model. International officials found that the addition of light-duty sales was just what the doctor ordered to help ease its own depression. The lesson wasn't lost on Mack's brain trust.

In October 1934 they teamed up with their Reo counterparts in Lansing, Michigan, to draw up a similar deal using Reo's newly introduced, nicely styled light-duty truck line. Adding a different grille and badging and the bulldog mascot was all it took to roll out the first Mack Jr (Junior was never spelled out in factory literature) trucks in 1936. Load ratings went from a half-ton to three tons for the Mack Jr machines, which were

Mack replaced its Jr pickup in 1938 with the heavy-duty ED model. ED pickups were built up through 1944. *Mack Trucks Historical Museum*

Unlike the Mack Jr, which used a Reo car chassis, Mack's heavier ED pickup was based on a purpose-built frame that was ready, willing, and able to handle any job thrown at it.

Perhaps the most widely recognized Mack product was its B-series tractor-trailer rig, introduced early in 1953. B models were built for 13 years.
American Truck Historical Society

identified by an M code. Both a pickup and a panel delivery, each based on a Reo sedan chassis, were included in the half-ton 1M line. Series codes went up to 30M for the three-ton model—"30MT" for the three-ton cab-over version.

Widening the scope of its product line instantly gave Mack the boost its officials were looking for. New Mack registrations jumped up 279 percent from 1,515 in 1935 to 4,226 in 1936. Among that latter number were 2,343 Mack Jr models.

Mack's 2M models appeared in 1937, this time as rebadged versions of Reo's restyled Speed Delivery truck, an even more rakish hauler featuring a split-V windshield. As was the case with its Speed Delivery counterparts, the 2M pickup in 1937 was available with either a four- or six-cylinder engine. The four displaced 140 cubic inches and produced 45 horses. The Continental six-cylinder filled out 209 cubic inches and was rated at 72 horsepower. Standard equipment included hydraulic brakes.

Two wheelbases were also offered, 114 inches or 120. Extended model codes reflected these vari-

ations. A short-wheelbase, four-cylinder Mack Jr half-ton pickup was a 2M4A model. The same with a six instead of the four was a 2M6A. Long-wheelbase versions exchanged the "A" at the end for a "B." Short-wheelbase pickups had a six-foot-long cargo box; their long-wheelbase brothers featured a seven-foot box. Yet another letter, "S," followed the A or the B if the pickup was a three-quarter-ton model. These senior Mack Jr trucks were fitted with a larger front axle; stiffer springs; heavier, full-floating rear axles; and oversized 6.50x16 tires.

Once again, the light-duty 2M pickups were offered alongside various larger Mack Jr trucks in 1937. Pricing began at $575 for a basic four-cylinder Mack Jr 2M with cab and body; $1,200 for the biggest Juniors. This bottom line exceeded competing figures by quite a bit, but Mack salespeople hoped to offset the difference by pointing out that their price was for a "complete truck," not a bare chassis. On top of that, this wasn't just a truck, it was a Mack truck. Although that latter claim did carry considerable weight, it still couldn't quite distract a pickup buyer from reality. A 1937 Ford V-8 pickup in chassis-only form sold for $360. As mentioned earlier, Ford's whole package retailed at $470. And $470 was still a far cry from $575, explaining perhaps why Mack sold only 563 of its 2M pickups in 1937, and a mere 117 in 1938.

Sales as a whole, however, benefited greatly from the influx of new blood. While Mack Jr deliveries dropped to 2,226 in 1938, total new truck registrations for Mack Trucks rose to 5,513. Anyone with enough fingers and toes can see that this meant the company's own production was back on the healthy side of the ledger—remember, Mack Jr trucks were built by Reo. Jr numbers plummeted in 1938 to only 405, while total Mack registrations dipped to 4,406. But this still could've been considered a success since the company's in-house activities remained on the upswing. The Mack Jr was no longer needed, nor was anyone buying them, so the Reo deal was closed out in 1938. Heavyweight Mack registrations continued to rise from there:

6,670 in 1939, 7,736 in 1940, and 9,468 in 1941. Mack busted the 10,000 barrier in 1947.

Though the Mack Jr was dropped early in 1938, this didn't signal the end for the company's light truck ventures. Even as dealers were watching the last Reo-built 2M pickups roll off their lots, Mack's own ED models were showing up on the scene. These were real bulldogs: tough, big, and strong. And they were built by Mack assembly people to Mack engineers' exacting standards.

"Model ED is Mack's answer to the long-felt need for a properly balanced and coordinated truck in the light-duty range" explained Mack wordsmiths. "Here is no makeshift attempt to build up a lighter model or build down a heavier one. Model ED is the culmination of thorough study and painstaking efforts by Mack engineers to design and build a truck exactly fitted to its own particular hauling job. Uniformly rugged and perfectly proportioned throughout, Model ED is literally a small-scale, heavy-duty truck. From every standpoint—price, performance and stamina—this newest and lightest Mack challenges comparison with any truck in its class."

Mack's new E-series heavy trucks were introduced in 1936, and many historians today wonder if the Mack Jr was brought in as a quick-fix measure until a pickup version of the E model could go into full production. When it finally did two years later, the ED was everything those brochures said it was.

Beneath a wonderfully stylish skin, modeled after its big-rig brethren, was a beefy frame with huge side channels heavily braced by five rigid cross-members consisting of two channels and three boxed-girders. Brakes were big hydraulic units. Full-floating rear axles were torqued by 5.571:1 gears in standard form, while optional cogs included 5.125:1 and 6.333:1 ratios. Standard wheels were 17-inch six-spokers wearing 6.00x17 tires. A 7.50x17 tire was available at extra cost for heavier loads, as were stiffer springs. The ED's base price, as a flat chassis, was $675.

Like the Mack Jr, the Model ED was offered in two wheelbases. In this case, they were the standard 120.5-incher and the "special" 136.5-inch stretch. Power came from a 210-ci Continental six-cylinder that was also beefed to beat the band. Thirty-three studs helped keep the lid down on this L-head six, meaning head warping and gasket leaks were almost unheard of. Output was 67 horsepower. A three-speed transmission and a 10-inch clutch were standard. A four-speed was optional.

Mack manufactured the Model ED up through 1944. Production was 152 in 1938, 704 in 1939, 589 in 1940, 707 in 1941, 274 in 1942, none in 1943, and 260 in 1944. ED trucks built after 1941, all bare-chassis models, went to the U.S. military to be finished as fire trucks. Mack never again tried the light truck field after the war—understandably so considering the company was continually busy manufacturing some of the best big-rigs ever to set tread on the road or the worksite.

Mack's direct competitor in the light-duty big-truck field was Diamond T, builder of what many called the "Cadillac of trucks." Diamond Ts, no matter the size, were never short on style or class. Flowing fenderlines, aggressive grilles, rakish cabs—there was simply no way to mistake a heavy hauler from the Chicago company founded by C.A. Tilt. "A truck doesn't have to be homely," he reportedly said more than once.

According to the same reports, the company name was created when Tilt's shoe-making father fashioned a logo featuring a big "T" (for Tilt, of course) framed by a diamond, which signified high quality. The younger Tilt built his first motor vehicle, an automobile, in 1905. Regular production of three passenger-car models began two years later. In 1911 a customer requested a truck, an order that convinced Tilt that commercial vehicles represented the best way to make a buck. He immediately traded cars for trucks, and the rest is history. Diamond T's best year was 1936, when new truck registrations reached 8,750. Roughly a quarter-million Diamond T trucks were built over the company's storied 56-year history.

White Motor Company bought Diamond T in 1958. The Chicago firm remained an individual division until 1967, when it merged with another White division, Reo, to form Diamond

Reo. The Diamond T legacy came to a close as the 1966 model year ended.

In its heyday in the 1930s, Diamond T also demonstrated how diverse a big-truck maker could be. Midyear in 1936, the company joined International, Federal, Reo, and Mack as a heavy-duty player in the light-duty game with the three-quarter-ton Model 80. Two versions were offered: the Model 80S (standard) and 80-D (deluxe). The deluxe model added an electric clock and jeweled cigar lighter. Model 80 production was brief; it ended midway through 1938. Common estimates claim "a few thousand" were built during that short run.

The Model 80 was then replaced in 1938 by the classic Model 201 Diamond T one-ton. According to 1941 Diamond T paperwork, the "Model 201 is a unique vehicle in the light-duty field. Its all-truck specifications and exceptionally rugged construction set it widely apart from most trucks in this classification because they are commonly passenger car adaptations, which include the use of many units originally designed for passenger car service." Available as a pickup, panel delivery, or stake truck, the Model 201 shared nothing, save for a touch of style and grace here and there, with any automobile then rolling.

So much of the 201 Diamond T's muscular makeup will sound familiar: a supertough heavy-duty frame, Lockheed hydraulic brakes, full-floating rear axles, extra-rigid front I-beam axle, and cast-iron spoke wheels. In the latter's case, 16-inchers were standard (with dual wheels optional), or big 20-inch wheels were available at extra cost.

The 201's frame differed from its Mack counterpart in that it used a reinforced X-member design for added strength and durability. In the company's own words, "The exceptional rigidity of the X-type frame promotes longer life for cowl, cab and bodies by its freedom from weaving and distortion. In particular, the common panel body is often racked and weakened at joints and door posts when the conventional type of frame is employed."

That beefy frame meant more weight. In base chassis form, Diamond T's one-ton pickup weighed in at 2,750 pounds. "Model 201 is necessarily built heavier than the usual competition," continued the Diamond T brochure, "but this additional chassis weight is required to provide its long life and low maintenance cost. It will do its job at a lower cost per mile and per day and for a longer useful life by far than any of the lighter and less rigorously designed vehicles commonly offered in this market."

Of course, all this added mass, sprung accordingly, in turn meant heavier loads could be hauled. The maximum gross vehicle weight rating was 8,000 pounds. Helping achieve this rating were heavy-duty leaf springs in back that stacked up like a dump truck's. Each rear spring contained 13 steel leaves.

Supplying the strength to move those heavy loads was a 73-horsepower, 205-ci Hercules L-head six-cylinder (Code QXB-3) with seven main bearings. Postwar Model 201 trucks were fitted with a stronger 91-horsepower, 236-ci Hercules L-head (Code QXLD). A three-speed Warner transmission was typically standard. A granny-low T-9 four-speed was typically optional. The latter was far more plentiful than the former.

As much as all this heavy hardware would indicate, Diamond T pickups were by no means no-nonsense work trucks. By nature (or by C.A. Tilt's mandate) they offered a touch of style right off the lot. In standard form, all Diamond T pickups wore red paint on their wheels and sheet metal. Accent striping was also added to the cab. Inside, prewar deluxe models featured an attractive engine-turned dash panel. This panel was discontinued for postwar models, although the 1946–1949 cab was upgraded from the prewar standard version, and large chrome hubcaps were offered as an option.

Deluxe models were only available before the war, while varying paint schemes and options were offered for postwar Diamond Ts. Black, two-tone blue, and two-tone green were the choices. Prewar deluxe treatments included such nice baubles as chrome mirrors,

Diamond T was acquired by the White Company in 1958. It remained an autonomous division of White up through 1966. In 1967 Diamond T merged with Reo, another White acquisition, to form Diamond Reo. *American Truck Historical Society*

chrome bumpers, and bright stainless-steel windshield frames for the split-V front glass that cranked open on both sides. Along with the clock, cigar lighter, and dash panel mentioned earlier, deluxe customers also got those large chrome full wheel covers for the 16-inch rims, fender-mounted parking lights, a dome light, armrests, chrome mirrors, and a "banjo" steering wheel. The tall 20-inch wheels featured small chrome hubcaps.

Diamond T's Model 201 stayed on the scene until 1949 in almost identical fashion, save for grille variations and few mechanical modifications. After roughly 7,000 were built, it was finally replaced in 1950 by the Model 222, a big pickup that ended up being an even bigger disappointment.

Times, of course, had changed by then. A need to be so widely diversified in the truck market was no longer as great as it was in the 1930s. Add to that the fact that this country's mainstream light truck makers, led by Ford and Chevrolet, had also put a headlock on the pickup market with their own brand of limited diversity. New, modern half-tons were joined by a whole host of equally new three-quarter-ton and one-ton models, these coming at highly competitive prices and with long features lists.

In 1948, Diamond T put the model 201's price at $1,275—for the chassis only. A cab cost $215 more, a body $165. Ford's new F-1 half-ton that year wore a $1,232 price tag. And even Ford's F-3 "one-ton" (it actually was more like a one-and-a-half-ton truck) still came in a couple hundred less than a fully dressed Diamond T one-ton. The numbers said it all.

Mack logically chose not to return to the civilian light truck market after World War II ended; that Diamond T did was a testament to the company's willingness to keep a classic legacy alive for its own sake. Those who experienced and loved the model 201 pickup were thankful. The rest simply never knew what they missed.

SMALLER HAULERS

MINITRUCKS IN AMERICA ARE NOTHING NEW

Today's truck market is a busy place, with pickups and sport-utilities of all sizes, prices and nationalities seemingly stacked up as far as the eye can see. Choosing the right truck for the job—whether it be real work or home-body tasks, like transporting your six-year-old's soccer team—can be a mind-boggling experience, a task comparable to transporting your six-year-old's soccer team. Whatever happened to the days when trucks were just trucks? Whatever happened to the days when baseball was the American pastime?

The more things change, the more they don't stay the same. Forty years ago American pickups (and American cars) came almost exclusively in one general size. And we liked it that way. Now we have compact, midsized, and full-sized trucks. And a few odds and ends in between.

Pricing is equally divergent and has been so since Detroit discovered that the real money can be made in the utility vehicle business, where profit margins remain incredibly wide in apparent defiance of economic principles. Has demand really grown so rampant that truck builders can charge whatever they like without fear of competitive undercutting? Or are Americans just being led around by their collective nose?

Selling the public on the notion that trucks supply the safest way to go has certainly spurred on demand, as has the pickup's newfound ability to cater to the status-conscious. Who in 1960 would've ever guessed that truly prestigious luxury would find its way into the truck field—and bring with it a corresponding caste system similar to what car buyers have looked up to from the beginning? With the way truck stickers are stacking up today it may not be long before we start seeing an "entry-level" class, a place where the average buyer can actually put himself into a pickup at a fair price. Such a pecking order does presently exist, although it's just not labeled as such.

This order began to take real root in America in the 1960s, a time when shifting attitudes began convincing buyers to change the way they looked at their daily transportation, whether car or truck. A real need for affordable, efficient compact vehicles hadn't materialized at that point. Still-cheap gasoline didn't start turning into gold until the 1970s. Yet American compacts did begin gaining a foothold in 1960. They had to, since foreign influences, mostly from Germany, had already challenged Detroit.

Volkswagen may have led the way from overseas with compact cars in the 1950s, but it was Japan—with due respect to VW's open-box Microbus variant—that got the whole compact pickup thing rolling. Nissan landed its first truly small Datsun truck (along with an equally small, considerably homely Datsun car) in Los Angeles in December 1958 for an import auto show. The same event also showcased Toyota's initial American imports. Toyota tried cars first; its own pint-sized pickup didn't arrive until 1964.

Both Japanese automakers initially found the going slow, due primarily to the aforementioned fact that Americans were still unsure

Powel Crosley's pint-sized pickups proved to be the perfect pick in a pinch for customers like the Alcoa aluminum company. Alcoa officials equipped this 1942 Crosley to serve as a mini fire truck inside one of its factories in Tennessee. It served there up until 1950.

The revolutionary Crosley 4 cylinder Cobra is the most efficient automobile engine ever built

Powell Crosley Jr

PRESIDENT,
CROSLEY MOTORS, INC.

Crosley pickups in 1948 received fresh styling that added a flush-sided cargo box in place of the pontoon fenders used previously. Chevrolet officials would later brag of originating this style in 1955.

Powel Crosley's claim about his Cobra four being efficient may have been correct, but he said nothing about his revolutionary lightweight powerplant's durability. Its COpper-BRAzed (thus its name) sheet-steel block quickly fell victim to tiny rust holes. It was canceled after 1948.

In 1949 the Cobra four was replaced by the CIBA four, a more conventional engine with a Cast-Iron Block Assembly. The application shown is a 1950 Farm-O-Road.

about or even unaware of the merits of cost-conscious, space-saving transportation. It took an Arab oil embargo in 1973 to finally prove to red, white, and blue-blooded car buyers that less could indeed be more. So what kept the two Japanese import lines alive here before fuel economy became a major concern?

In Nissan's case, an answer was supplied by David Halberstam in his 1986 epic, The Reckoning, the definitive history of that firm's successful infiltration—and eventual reshaping—of the American automotive market. "What saved the company in the meantime, though Tokyo was loath to admit it, was Nissan's little pickup truck," wrote the Pulitzer prize-winner. "It was small, it was inexpensive, and, unaffected by the Japanese weaknesses at the time such as lack of style, it exploited the singular Japanese strength—durability."

Two other factors, timing and location, also played major roles in Nissan's success. Continued Halberstam, "Many of Datsun's best dealers signed up in the early days, not because they wanted that ugly little car or because they were so prescient that they knew that this odd Japanese company previously unknown to them would do everything right and produce an increasingly sophisticated auto, but because they knew that the pickup truck was a winner in California."

Everything seems to get its start in trend-setting, fad-conscious California. Surfing, beach music, hot rods, smog—what would the rest of America have done had SoCal pioneers not paved the way for us in these areas and many others? We probably would've survived, but Nissan might not have had its early Datsun pickups not first found such a loyal following in California. Why the West Coast?

"In western America and especially California the pickup truck had a function different from the one it had elsewhere," explained Halberstam. "Here it was both truck and passenger vehicle. Many Americans worked their small patches of farmland for an hour or two in the morning before driving off to a factory job. Some who no longer worked on the farm kept a pickup nonetheless as if to sustain their sense of self; rural they had entered this world, and though they might no longer work the land, rural they could believe they had remained, if they owned a pickup."

Halberstam also pointed to another faction responsible for the rise of compact pickup popularity. By the luck of the draw Nissan had chosen to reach into the American market through the West Coast at a time when counterculture movements were in the ground swell stage there. Just as flower children and VWs would soon be forever tied, so too would hippies and a host of other off-the-beaten-path vehicles, like compact import trucks. "Unlike most Americans, whose car conveyed their status and for whom the biggest and fanciest car signaled the greatest prestige, there were those who enjoyed the antistatus in having a little pickup truck parked in front of the house," claimed Halberstam.

The rest of the country, including Detroit, began catching on to this groovy concept about a decade after the Datsun pickup first made a home for itself in California. Both Nissan and Toyota were selling more than 100,000 compact trucks a year in America by 1979. Countering these foreign invaders were copycat responses from the Big Three. "If you can't beat 'em, join 'em," was the apparent belief. In 1972 both Ford and Chevrolet turned to the East for a little help in creating their own compact pickups. Ford's Courier was built in conjunction with Japan's Mazda firm, while Chevy's LUV—for "light utility vehicle"—began life at Isuzu Motors. Chrysler Corporation followed suit in 1979, introducing the D-50 sport minipickup, which was basically a Mitsubishi truck dressed up in Dodge clothing.

Small trucks have continued running strong ever since. Total market segment sales for 1972 (142,181) more than doubled those of just two years before. Segment sales in 1977 were 321,332; 773,537 in 1982. Compacts peaked in popularity in 1986, when total sales reached 1.4 million. American truck buyers actually bought more compacts than full-sized models that year, and they repeated this performance in 1987. In 1970, full-sized pickups made up 60.3 percent of the total truck market in this country, compared to only 3.2 percent for compacts. Sixteen years later, compacts captured 29.2 percent, full-sized models 25.3. In 1987, market share numbers read 28.1 percent for compacts, 24.2 percent for their big brothers.

Standard pickups regained their top spot in 1988 and slowly pulled ahead as compacts fell away. Compact sales dropped below one million in 1991 and did again in 1996 and 1997. By 1997 the market share for small trucks was only 13.6 percent.

Japan's slice of the pickup pie has also grown smaller over that same span. Far East firms in 1986 claimed 19.9 percent of the total truck market (all sizes) here in America. In 1997 that

The roots of the American minipickup can be traced back to the truly small American Bantam truck of the 1930s. Like the Crosley to follow, this minute machine was simply a car with a cargo box tacked on in back. *The National Automotive History Collection, Detroit Public Library*

In 1950, Crosley introduced its Farm-O-Road utility vehicle, a nice idea that never found a market.

Differentiating between import and domestic is no longer as cut-and-dried a proposition as it once was, what with so many "foreign" cars and trucks now being built right here in the good ol' U.S. of A. Nissan, the world's third leading automotive manufacturer, today operates one of this planet's largest auto plants not in Japan, but in America. Located just south of Nashville in Smyrna, the Nissan Motor Manufacturing Corporation facility takes up 5.2 million square feet of floor space and sits on 778 acres of fine Tennessee countryside. Inside are more than 620,000 men and women who annually bring home about $300 million in exchange for rolling out as many as 450,000 Nissan cars and trucks a year.

Pickup truck production was the Smyrna plant's initial priority, with the first American-built Nissan truck seeing the light of day on June 16, 1983. The Sentra car line was added in March 1995, Altima in June 1992, and 200SX in November 1994. Top production came in 1995, when 465,675 Nissan cars and trucks left Smyrna. 1997's total was 398,308. For four years running, 1994 to 1997, Nissan's Smyrna facility ranked as the most productive auto manufacturing plant in North America.

Company officials are understandably proud of this feat, as they also are of their American heritage. Stored within the Smyrna plant are various reminders of just how far Nissan's U.S. venture has come in only 40 years. The first Sentra is there, as is the very first truck built in 1983. But most notable is a small, pale-blue Datsun pickup that harkens back to the firm's humble Western market beginnings.

Restored by plant employees in the 1980s, this Datsun 1200 truck helps commemorate Japan's initial penetration into the American sales race, that coming in January 1958 at Los Angeles' Imported Car Show. While both Nissan and Toyota showed up that year with small cars, it was a Datsun 1000 pickup from Nissan that became the first imported compact truck in America—Toyota brought only its gremlin-ridden Toyopet sedan to the L.A. show.

Actual sales of Datsun trucks on the West Coast began early in 1959. Initial responses were slow, every bit as slow as the pickups themselves. Early tests showed that the Datsun 1000's 988-cc four-cylinder engine would never make the grade on those fast-paced SoCal freeways—37 horsepower wasn't nearly enough. Thus, after about 10 Datsun 1000 pickups were sold, Nissan upgraded its Austin-based power source late in 1959 to a stroked 1,189-cc four that put out 48 horses. Accordingly, this addition then changed the pickup's name to Datsun

Small and Spartan best describes the Datsun 1200 pickup interior. The optional radio, mounted below the dash, impinged greatly on driver legroom.

1200, of which approximately 45 were sold between 1959 and 1961. Smyrna plant people call their 1200 a 1958 model, which is probably correct, considering it was undoubtedly built that year in Yokohama. But from an American sales perspective, it is perhaps "more correct" to classify it as a 1959 model.

As for other numbers, the Datsun 1200, like its 1000 forerunner, was classed as a quarter-ton truck. It measured 61.4 inches high and 161.6 inches long, and rolled on a polite 99.2-inch wheelbase. Its bed was 53.9 inches wide and 66.9 inches long. An I-beam axle was suspended by leaf springs up front, the wheels were 15-inchers (wearing 5.60 tires), and the brakes were 10-inch drums. A column-shifted four-speed transmission with granny low sent 60.7 pounds-feet of torque to a stout 5.152:1 differential. Top speed was roughly 70 miles per hour.

These figures didn't exactly measure up by American standards, helping explain why Datsun's early little pickups were almost unknown anywhere outside of Southern California. But it wasn't long before Nissan began picking up the pace, especially so after Yutaka Katayama—the original "Mr. K" who inspired the caricature star of Nissan's recent "dogs love trucks" ad campaign—arrived in 1960 to promote Datsun sales. Mr. K rose to the president's chair at Nissan Motor Corporation U.S.A. in 1965.

Ray Lemke became the first Datsun dealer in America in October 1958. In the spring of 1959, Lemke's San Diego dealership sold the first imported Datsun pickup to retired Navy veteran Richard McCutcheon. In 1978, McCutcheon described his purchase to Nissan Motor Corporation U.S.A. officials:

"I had been driving a Crosley station wagon and was planning to sell it and get something else when I saw this truckload of Datsuns with a pickup truck. I followed the hauler to San Diego Datsun, determined to buy it. I had been over in Japan and I knew how rough their roads were and it figured that if the trucks could take that kind of a beating, they must be something. Well, Ray didn't want to sell it to me, 'cause he wanted to keep it for the showroom, but I talked him out of it. It ran great. I owned it for six or seven years and put 70,000 miles on it and the only things I had to replace were the radiator hoses and heater hoses. It still had the original battery and tires. I got $600 for it and traded it in on another Datsun pickup and I put another 68,000 miles on that."

McCutcheon paid $1,647 for his Datsun pickup. It was three months before Lemke received another from Nissan in Japan. Once in San Diego, it was

What a difference 40 years makes. Nissan's 1998 Frontier pickup stands as a far cry from the mundane Datsun truck that first landed in California in 1958. The Datsun 1200 truck shown here was sold in America in 1959.

proudly displayed on the showroom's roof. In 1965 Lemke's dealership became the first to sell 100 Datsuns a month in America. When he finally stepped down in 1984, he was selling 2,000 Datsuns a month.

The key to Lemke's success was a newfound need in this country for affordable, efficient, easy-to-handle practical transportation, a trend that at first grew slowly in the 1960s. By 1964, Datsun import truck sales had reached 3,524, then soared to 50,954 in 1970. The six-digit barrier was broken in 1979. Smyrna's best effort so far, 136,162 trucks, came in 1996.

Nissan sold its one millionth Datsun (cars and trucks) in America in 1973. Two years later it finally overtook longtime leader Volkswagen as this country's best-selling import, barely beating out rapidly rising Toyota, 335,425 vehicles to 328,918.

Today, Nissan offers its classy, comfortable Frontier pickup, obviously representing a far cry from its 40-year-old budget-conscious forerunner. But the bloodline had to begin somewhere, somehow. And starting small in this case proved to be just the ticket.

Willys helped popularize the forward-control light-duty truck design in 1957. The short-wheelbase F-150 offered off-road ruggedness in a compact package able to go where other 4x4s couldn't.

Willys' FC-170, a typically sized stretched version of the compact FC-150, was also rolled out in 1957. *Chrysler Historical Collection*

FORWARD CONTROL Jeep FC-150 PICK-UP

almost no such thing as an "import pickup" anymore. Toyota builds its small trucks in California, Nissan in Tennessee. Ford manufactures Mazda's pickups in New Jersey and GM does the same for Isuzu in Louisiana. Talk about strange bedfellows.

Actually they're not all that strange. Initial penetration of the American market by Eastern imports a few decades back may have caused considerable irritation then, but much has long since been forgiven. And forgotten. Homogenization eventually took over, not through natural forces but by plan. East indeed met West—by choice on both sides. A contentious domestic-versus-import battleground faded away in favor of a more user-friendly world market, which, although it too typically remains in flux, still better benefits all involved.

Forgive for a moment the oversimplification here. Discussing such things in 25 words or less probably leads more to consternation than conclusion. Foreign trade battles do continue. But the field in general is far more "level" than it was a few decades ago.

Arrogant American automakers learned their lessons the hard way and are still busy rethinking their position even as you read this. While Japanese manufacturers were hard at work expanding their horizons in the 1960s and 1970s, their Yankee counterparts were wasting time patting their plump bellies, confident that no one, from Europe or Asia, could ever eat their lunch. America's industrial might would always make right, right? Yeah, right. Underestimating the product 40 years ago was one thing. Selling Japanese industry short as a whole (with racist blinders on, perhaps?) was a whole 'nother bowl of rice.

And to think some automakers here in America actually had the jump on the Japanese before they got the jump on Detroit. The blinders worn by the Big Three blocked out more than the view across the Pacific. Small trucks were nothing new on these shores when that first little Datsun landed in Los Angeles in December 1958. Detroit's major movers and shakers just chose to ignore this stray breed whenever it popped out from under the porch.

The first most notable occurrence also came with a little overseas assistance, this time from

figure dropped to 14.2 percent. Today it's Ford's Ranger, Chevrolet's S-10, and Dodge's Dakota leading the way in the "bigger small truck" field, with Japan now playing catch-up. In truth, the game is no longer so easy to follow, as the players today aren't positioned on opposite sides of the field as they were not all that long ago. There's

across the Atlantic. In January 1929, Sir Herbert Austin arrived in New York from England to pursue the possibility of building his minute Austin Seven automobiles in America. These small, incredibly efficient, affordable cars worked well in Great Britain, and who was to say the same couldn't happen in the United States? Even with the Great Depression looming ahead, the Austin American Car Company was open for business in Butler, Pennsylvania, by the spring of 1929. Among the company's compact products was a pickup truck, a pint-sized cargo carrier that rolled on a 75-inch wheelbase and weighed a tad more than half a ton. Its tipsy track, made even more precarious-looking by tall 15-inch wheels, measured only 40 inches wide. Power came from a 14-horse 45.6-cid L-head four-cylinder engine. Like Ford's Model T pickups, the toy-like American Austin truck shared front-end sheet metal with its equally small passenger-car counterparts.

Whether or not the time was right for a U.S.-built compact pickup became a moot issue after October 1929. Unlike Detroit's entrenched big boys, American Austin couldn't survive the Depression, although the company did manage to struggle on until June 1934 before bankruptcy finally came. This little tale, however, didn't end there.

Sales guru Roy Evans, who had first tried selling American Austins with reasonable success in 1932, picked up the pieces and reorganized the Butler firm in June 1936 under the American Bantam Car Company shingle. Among his earliest moves as company president was to contract designer Alexis de Sakhnoffsky to restyle the American Austin into the American Bantam. This attractive compact arrived on the scene in January 1938, again in both car and truck forms.

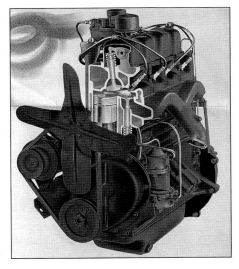

Along with its truly stylish facade, intended to complement "truly smart shops" according to factory brochures, the American Bantam pickup also incorporated various improvements over its Austin forerunner. Included was a beefier frame and a more powerful 20-horsepower L-head four. The price was $493. The same package rolled on almost unchanged (most notable was an increase to 22 horsepower in 1940) up through American Bantam's last production run early in 1941—reportedly as many as 138 left-over 1940 Bantams were marketed as those last 1941 models. Insufficient cash flow caught up to the company again, yet it was once more temporarily saved from certain death, this time by the coming of war.

Like various other doomed companies of the day, American Bantam received a reprieve, albeit brief, from Washington in the form of defense contracts. Bantam's main claim to fame was the military Jeep, which it developed in short order in the summer of 1940. Initial Jeep production put some life back into the firm, but it quickly faded again after the federal government turned to Willys-Overland and Ford to pick up the pace to meet sky-high delivery quotas, something little American Bantam couldn't manage. After building a few thousand Jeeps in 1941, Bantam lost the contract to its better-equipped, higher-production-rate rivals in Toledo and Dearborn.

Although another contract, this one involving lightweight Jeep trailers, did keep American Bantam busy during World War II, it was weak consolation. Car and truck production never resumed after the war, and the company was finally bought up by the ARMCO steel firm in 1956.

American Austin/Bantam's ill-fated struggle to survive should've represented enough fair warning to anyone interested in trying a similar

Willys trucks used the durable "F-head" engine, named because the intake valve was located overhead, while the exhaust valve was in the block. Squint your eyes a bit and this configuration supposedly appears in the shape of the letter F.

$20 during the 1920s when competitors' units cost more than $100. One of the many patents he bought from a small-time inventor resulted in the popular Crosley "Shelvadoor," the first refrigerator with shelves in the door. Meanwhile, down at Crosley Field, Powel's beloved "Redlegs" went from last place in 1937 to consecutive National League pennants in 1939 and 1940. His Reds won the World Series that second year.

"Almost" everything Crosley touched turned to gold. The only business venture Powel didn't master was building cars, although he gave it one helluva try for almost 15 years—after dreaming of doing it for more than 30. What tripped Crosley up was his decision to build small cars, really small cars. He didn't necessarily believe Americans needed cheap, easy transportation then. His premise involved the plain and simple fact that car buyers should be able to choose to be ultrapractical if they saw fit. "Have you ever stopped to think how ridiculous it is that one to four people require a ton-and-a-half motor car to carry them a mile or so to a picture show?," he once quipped. "It's like taking a battleship across the Hudson when a motorboat would be far easier." But as much as Crosley worked overtime trying to sell the American public on the concept of ultrapractical transportation, John Q. still wasn't buying. Not in the 1930s. Nor the 1940s. Nor the 1950s.

Full production of Crosley's first bug-eyed babies began in June 1939, to the proclamation of the coming of "the car for the forgotten man." The first Crosley cars were convertibles with 80-inch wheelbases and a price tag of about $325, considerably less than their only rival, Bantam. Crosleys weighed about 900 pounds, were only 120 inches long, and carried less than five gallons of gas. That meager fuel load, however, could keep things rolling for as many as 200 miles, thanks to the stingy nature of the 38-cid Waukesha two-cylinder engine. Output was equally stingy—13.5 horsepower.

A commercial-minded application of Crosley's small idea came midyear in 1939, identified as a 1940 model. Looking like a scaled-down panel van on the outside, the Parkway Delivery was pure Crosley automobile beneath the skin. The amount

The Corvair 95 Rampside pickup featured a clever loading gate in the passenger-side bed wall. With the engine in the rear, there was no drive shaft in the way, allowing a low bed floor that helped make loading even easier. The black container in the bed is an owner-added convenience.

International's little Scout, introduced in 1961, helped usher in two new eras for the American market: the age of the compact pickup and the early beginnings of the sport-utility craze.

tack in the 1930s. But not Powel Crosley, Jr. Radio mogul, refrigerator magnate, owner of the National League's Cincinnati Reds baseball team since 1934—almost everything Crosley touched turned to gold. Much of his fortune was made in the radio business, both as owner of "The Nation's Station," WLW in Cincinnati, and as the producer of the first low-priced radio sets in America. Crosley radios were selling for

Ford copied International's idea in 1966, introducing the Bronco. Broncos were offered in various forms, with or without doors and a top. A specific pickup model was also included.

of goods this commercial van could deliver was clearly limited, but big-time trucking wasn't the goal here. Powel Crosley saw these vehicles as ben-efiting inner-city shop owners who needed to get in and out fast on short-haul jobs. A Parkway Delivery would demonstrate its merits wherever parking was a problem, traffic was heavy, and the goods to be carried were light.

The same could be said for the Crosley pickup, which debuted midyear in 1940 as a 1941 model. "Here's the truck that makes sense and makes money on service and deliveries," bragged company brochures. Attractions included its "low operating cost," the fact that it "parks where no other truck can park," and

its ability to "give you 35 to 50 miles on a gal-lon of gasoline."

This roller skate of a quarter-ton truck was created by stripping off the Parkway Delivery's roof and side panels. The resulting cargo box measured only about 3.5 feet wide and almost 4 feet long.

All Crosleys were "assembled vehicles," that is, they were the sum of parts purchased from other manufacturers. As mentioned, the two-cylinder engine—which in 1940 was reduced to 35 cubic inches and 12 horsepower to help increase durability—came from the Waukesha Motor Company in Waukesha, Wisconsin. Waukesha powerplants were primarily produced

It was called the "People's Car," but Ferdinand Porsche's creation was much more than that. Designed in the mid-1930s at the request of Adolf Hitler, the Volkswagen was supposed to put an expanding Third Reich on wheels. Instead, after World War II, the VW eventually put the whole world on wheels in ways even Doktor Porsche never would have imagined.

After the war, the Volkswagen Werke began building the automobile that less than 150 Germans were able to purchase under Hitler's regime. Its popularity was immediate—by October 5, 1950, the 100,000th Beetle was built, a postwar miracle.

Another Volkswagen was introduced six months before. VW director Heinz Nordhoff had previously begun looking for other ways to expand the concept. In the late 1940s, Ben Pon, the Dutch importer who brought the first Beetles to the United States, sketched his idea of a second type of Volkswagen and presented it to Nordhoff. In March 1950 that idea became reality: the Volkswagen Type 2.

Based on the mechanical platform of the Beetle, the Type 2 "Transporter" was an all-new idea in automotive design. It rode on the same 94.5-inch wheelbase of the Type 1 Beetle, though the track was wider and ground clearance was raised to 9.5 inches. It also used the same engine as the Type 1, which produced 25 horsepower in 1950. But with the driver in front of the steering wheel and the engine hung out back, the Type 2 had a remarkable amount of room for its size. Available in a variety of configurations—including nine-passenger van, cargo panel van, and pickup truck—the Type 2 was unique at the time. Even more amazing, the Volkswagen staff created and executed this future classic design without the assistance of the famed Porsche Bureau.

The first Type 2 models began officially arriving in the United States in 1954, although a few were brought in earlier. Most were the popular nine-passenger window vans, which in the 1960s became an icon of the "flower power" generation and our highly mobile society. A few pickup variants were also imported, but with a much less enthusiastic reception. Compact, thrifty, and tough as nails, the Type 2 pickup just didn't find a niche in America.

Those first trucks were powered by the same 36-horsepower air-cooled flat-four that the Beetle received in 1954, and horsepower increases came slowly in small increments. In 1956, *Road & Track* tested a Type 2 nine-passenger van and found reaching 60 miles per hour from rest required a snail-like 75 seconds. Seventy-five miles per hour was also the vehicle's top speed.

While there was no mistaking the VW pickup's lack of power, there existed a not-so-true perception that these compact trucks could not handle a workload. In fact, they were rated at three-quarter ton and could actually haul a 4x8 sheet of plywood with 6 inches to spare on each side. The bed was shallow, but the drop-down sides made loading quite easy. Below the bed was a unique large, lockable storage area that appealed to city-dwellers. All this added up to a practical package that often found favor with city-based businesses like florists and delivery companies. Some VW pickups also found their way onto farms and ranches, where they were worked without mercy.

Although painfully slow, the VW pickup *was* reasonably rugged. A weak-kneed perception still persisted, however, and these trucks never became as popular as their Beetle brothers. Few buyers here found a use for this light-duty vehicle. In Europe, where roads are narrower, towns more confined and congested, and fuel more expensive, the unique Type 2 pickup was and still is very popular. In the Third World, too, the Type 2 found a home, where durability, low cost, high ground clearance, and mechanical simplicity are all highly valued. In America, however, the Type 2 pickup was just too slow and too limited in most minds to gain similar popularity.

But if imitation is the greatest form of flattery, then the Big Three paid Heinz Nordhoff and VW the highest compliment. When American manufacturers rushed into the compact car and truck market, they looked to the VW Type 2 as a source of inspiration for their small truck and van offerings. Ford's Econoline, Chevrolet's Corvair 95, and Dodge's A100 copied the Type 2 concept of "forward control." While the Ford and Dodge had conventional front-mounted engines and ladder-type frames, the Corvair went one step further, copying VW's rear air-cooled engine and four-wheel independent suspension. Again, the passenger vans found reasonable acceptance in the marketplace. But despite their more acceptable American-style features, the Big Three's compact pickups met with much the same indifference as the Type 2. By 1965 the Corvair 95 was gone, then the Econoline in 1968, and finally the A100 after 1970. Volkswagen, too, concentrated on marketing the popular Microbus passenger vans only, letting sales of the pickup basically die by the time a second-generation Type 2 was introduced in 1967.

Ironically, the pioneer of the compact truck market, the Volkswagen Type 2, was nowhere to be seen when the Arab oil embargo arrived in the fall of 1973. With gas prices soaring and gasoline rationing a common occurrence in many cities, truck buyers began to look at compact, more economical alternatives to the traditional American pickup. But it was Datsun and Toyota, not Volkswagen, that were ready with a product American buyers were willing to accept.

—Tom Glatch

Although few Americans noticed, it was Volkswagen that actually originated the forward-control pickup ideal in America. This 1960 VW model 261 truck is powered by a 40-horsepower four-cylinder engine located, of course, below the bed in back. *Tom Glatch*

Volkswagen pickups were rarely seen in America. Customers who did notice might've been attracted by the clever bedwall design. *Tom Glatch*

Ford's forward-control minitruck, the Econoline, debuted in 1961. This 1961 Econoline features the five-window Custom Cab option. *Tom Glatch*

for farm machinery. Also familiar to farmers was the Ross cam-and-lever steering mechanism. Other contributors included Spicer (rear axle), Timken (bearings), Warner (three-speed nonsynchronized gearbox), Rockford (clutch), and Murray (body and frame).

Hawley supplied the aircraft-style brakes, which were of the antiquated cable-operated mechanical variety. Unlike the equally obsolete nonsynchro "crashbox" transmission, which was retained right up to the end of the road for Crosley in 1952, the mechanical stoppers were superseded in 1949 by the industry's

first disc brakes. Crosley's innovative four-wheel Goodyear-Hawley hydraulic system looked good on paper, but failed miserably in real-world operation as it proved highly susceptible to infiltrating dirt. In 1950 the discs were replaced by 9-inch hydraulic drum brakes from Bendix.

Total Crosley prewar production, trucks and cars, from 1939 to 1942 was 5,757. Demand picked up considerably after the war, thanks to the company's "Roundside" restyle and the introduction of a water-cooled four-cylinder engine. Yet another off-the-beaten-path Crosley innovation, this little four was developed during World War II by Taylor Engines in San Francisco as a lightweight power source for portable generators. Its extremely low weight was achieved by manufacturing the block out of stamped steel sheets held together by oven-baked copper brazing. The resulting "Cobra" (for COpper-BRAzed) four-cylinder used an overhead cam and displaced 44 cubic inches. Its industry-leading 7.5:1 compression helped the Cobra four produce 26.5 warmly welcomed horses.

More power, coupled with modern styling, made the postwar Crosley pickup an attractive buy. Introduced in January 1947, this good-looking little truck found 3,182 buyers by the end of the year. Total production for all Crosleys hit 22,526 for 1947, inspiring Powel himself to predict the company would soon be building 80,000 cars and trucks a year. But it was not to be, thanks in part to one particular engineering snafu.

Like the disc brakes later in 1949, the Cobra engine quickly fell victim to gremlins in 1947. Extended use proved that the copper-brazed sheet-steel block and its liquid coolant didn't mix. Electrolysis soon took over, resulting in tiny rust holes that couldn't be patched. Uncontrollable coolant leaks led to the Cobra's downfall. In 1949 it was replaced by the more conventional "CIBA" ("cast-iron block assembly") four-cylinder. Displacement and advertised output carried over.

Commercial vehicle production (pickups and deliveries) remained strong in 1948 at 2,836 units. Another design change that year did away with those rounded rear fenders, replacing them with fully flush cargo box exterior panels, a style Chevrolet's classy Cameo Carrier would popularize seven years later.

A front-end restyle updated exterior impressions even more in 1949. But apparently looking good then wasn't better than running good. The Cobra engine fiasco, followed by the disc brake lash-up, left buyers leery of Crosley's small cars and trucks. Pickup production in 1949 nose-dived to only 287. And additional facade freshening did little to reverse this downward spiral

Powel nonetheless refused to give up. If the forgotten man couldn't remember to buy his cars, what about the forgotten farmer? Introduced in August 1950, the odd-looking Crosley Farm-O-Road was created for rural customers who just may have been looking for a cheap, easy way to both get around and do the chores. According to its creator, the Farm-O-Road was "designed to do big jobs on small farms—and smaller jobs on big farms." And when it was through doing that it could carry Ma and Pa Kettle to town as surely and quickly as any car at a mere fraction of the cost.

A Farm-O-Road cost only $795 and could motor nearly 40 miles on a gallon of gas. Highway speeds with both Kettles aboard could reportedly go as high as 60 miles per hour. At the same time, reasonably hard work off the highway was no problem, thanks to an auxiliary gearbox that funneled those 26.5 horses through a 4:1 torque multiplication. In the fields the dual rear tires, combined with the ability to lock either rear wheel, allowed the Farm-O-Road to go where almost no man had gone before—at least no man driving a standard full-grown pickup.

Optional hard-working equipment included a pickup bed with or without a hydraulic dump mechanism. For $150, a buyer could also add front and rear power take-offs, driven by a shaft in the auxiliary gearbox, and a hydraulic drawbar in back for mounting various farm implements. Available were a plow, disc harrow, planter, seeder, cultivator, and two mowers, one standard unit and one large commercial-type three-gang setup suitable for golf course duty. A top and side curtains could also be added at extra cost, as could a back seat.

Though obviously a wee bit small, Crosley's versatile Farm-O-Road did represent a viable choice for rural customers looking for a lot of utility for a little money. Sales, however, couldn't even match tooling costs. Like the rest of

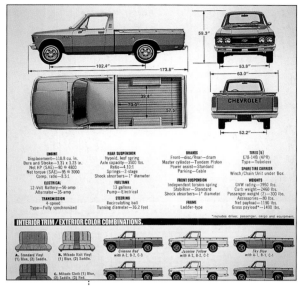

Ford and Chevrolet officials in 1972 apparently decided that if you can't beat 'em, join 'em. Both companies introduced compact pickups that year. And both models were created with Japanese assistance. Chevy's little truck was named "LUV," for light utility vehicle.

Dodge joined Chevrolet and Ford in the forward-control field in 1964. And like its Big Three rivals, Dodge also offered its A-100 pickup platform in van form. The A-100 later was fitted with an optional V-8. *Chrysler Historical Collection*

Crosley's four-wheeled creations, the Farm-O-Road quickly faded from memory even before it had a fair chance to make an impression.

A brief revival in 1959 fared no better. San Diego's Crofton Marine Engine Company that year repackaged the Farm-O-Road as the Crofton Bug. Only about 250 Crofton Bugs were sold—at a price about twice that of its Crosley forerunner—before the mini-off-roader was finally discontinued in 1962.

The Crosley Motor Company itself was discontinued in July 1952, its entire assets and properties going to the General Tire and Rubber Company for a reported $2 million. Luckily Powel Crosley knew how to sell radios and refrigerators.

Henry J. Kaiser was another big man who dabbled in small trucks. Henry J. knew how to sell ships, or at least he knew how to build them. During World War II, his shipyards launched 1,490 vessels destined for wartime service. Like Crosley, Kaiser could do anything he put his mind to—but on a much grander scale. Before the war, his construction company had played major roles in such monumental projects as the Hoover Dam and the Oakland Bay Bridge. Tunnels, canals, highways—

Henry Kaiser did it all. Then he met his stiffest challenge.

After the war, Kaiser teamed up with former Graham-Paige and Willys-Overland executive Joe Frazer to try his hand at automaking. The Kaiser-Frazer group got off to a glorious start, stunning Detroit's entrenched Big Three in 1946 with a line-up of cars that featured fresh, trendy "slabside" styling. Sales in 1947 and 1948 soared to 144,507 and 181,316, respectively. Then the money got tight. And the novelty wore off. The Frazer half of the team gave up in 1951. Kaiser continued building cars after that but at a dwindling rate until production shut down for good in 1955—in this country. Kaiser's automobile manufacturing venture then moved to Argentina.

Henry J.'s presence in America didn't exactly end there. While his cars were gone, his trucks remained. In 1953 the Kaiser company bought out Willys-Overland, known best in the postwar years for its various Jeep renditions (including a pickup version) and the creative Jeepster runabout. Jeep production continued under the Willys-Kaiser banner, although the various models were still labeled Willys Jeep, or later just Jeep. In 1963 the corporate name was changed to

Kaiser-Jeep, but the parent company for Jeep models and the new Wagoneer was still commonly identified as Willys. Then in 1970, Kaiser-Jeep merged with American Motors. Today's Jeeps, of course, are built by Chrysler Corporation, which bought struggling AMC in 1987.

Thirty years before Chrysler took over Jeep production, Willys was claiming the title of the "world's largest manufacturer of four-wheel drive vehicles." The ever-popular Jeep had been the company's bread and butter since the war. Then in 1957, Willys introduced yet another off-the-wall four-wheel-drive utility vehicle, a machine that may well have represented this country's first true compact pickup.

Unlike the Bantams and Crosleys before it, Willys' FC-150 was a truck through and through, not a car with a tiny cargo box bolted on back. Underneath was a rugged 4x4 chassis. Although its overall dimensions were certainly compact—wheelbase was a tidy 81 inches—its bed was six feet plus two inches long. Maximum gross vehicle weight was 5,000 pounds.

Willys designers managed to incorporate a full-sized bed in a compact pickup layout by utilizing a "cab-over" design similar to the style used by big-rig builders for years. With the 1957 FC-150 driver seated farther forward above both the front wheels and the 75-horsepower four-cylinder, a much shorter cab could be used. You do the math. A shorter cab meant more room on the frame for a longer bed.

Moving the driver atop the wheels also defined this new breed. The "FC" stood for "forward control," meaning the steering wheel was ahead of the wheels. The idea behind the forward-control design was to combine the agility of the compact Jeep with the broad-shouldered cargo capacity of a full-sized pickup. Throwing in Willys' proven 4x4 engineering was just icing on the cake.

The compact FC-150 pickup was also joined in 1957 by the larger FC-170, with its six-cylinder engine and 103-inch wheelbase. Crew cabs, dual rear wheels, and even a tractor-trailer rig using an FC-150 cab-chassis were offered. The last FC-150 pickup was built in 1965 by Kaiser-Jeep.

By then Detroit's prime movers had already done what they've always done best—copy someone else's idea and claim it for their very own. In 1961 both Ford and Chevrolet introduced compact forward-control pickups, although the two traveled in slightly different circles. While Ford's Econoline followed closer in the FC-150's tire treads, Chevy's forward-control pickup was more of a Volkswagen knock-off than a Willys redo.

Like the VW, Chevy's forward-control pickup kept its engine in the rear, a concession to its Corvair lineage. It was named Corvair 95 even though it actually shared few parts (primarily the engine) with Chevrolet's equally new compact car. The number referred to this unibody utility vehicle's relatively compact 95-inch wheelbase.

Thanks to its aft engine location, Corvair 95 cab comfort and seating capacity were superior to Ford's forward-control counterpart, since an Econoline driver and passenger had to share precious space up front with an inline six-cylinder powerplant perched between the seats. Four-wheel independent Corvair suspension was also used, although more suitable 14-inch wheels replaced the car line's minuscule 13-inch rims. Power came from the same air-cooled 145-cid "Turbo-Air" pancake six found behind the back seats of 1961 Monzas. Output was 80 horsepower.

Four Corvair 95 models were introduced in 1961. At the top was a six-passenger window van known as the Greenbriar Sport Wagon. Carrying Greenbriar script instead of Corvair 95, the upscale passenger van was actually marketed as a station wagon instead of a truck. Take away the windows and frills and you had the Corvan, which was marketed as a truck. Take away the roof and sides of the rear cargo area and add a back wall for the cab and you had a true Corvair 95 pickup. Two varieties were available, the Loadside and the Rampside.

The Corvair 95 Rampside pickup featured a unique loading ramp located behind the cab on the passenger side, a practical idea made even more practical by the Rampside's low main bed floor—remember, there was no drive

Chrysler's response to Japan's minitruck invasion arrived in 1980. Dodge's D-50 compact pickup was built with more than a little help from Mitsubishi. *Chrysler Historical Collection*

that probably helped limit its appeal. Whatever convenience the ramp gate provided was almost offset by the inconvenience of that multilevel cargo floor. Housing the air-cooled six in the rear created a raised ledge halfway back on the bed floor. Sure, you could roll your beer kegs up into the bed with relative ease, but driving away with a weekend's supply still required some dreaded lifting. Perhaps the back of the bed would've been a better place for lighter cargo. Like anvils.

A plywood "Level Floor Option" was offered, but it not only was a pain to place and remove, it of course also effectively negated the whole Rampside idea. In the end, a typical plank down the tailgate of a typical half-ton pickup with more cargo space and load capacity still proved effective, just as it had before the Rampside came along. Perhaps Chevrolet's unique side-loading pickup represented a solution to a problem that really didn't need solving.

The more conventional front-engined Econoline proved much more popular. Like the Corvair 95, it too was a unibody vehicle offered in both pickup and van forms. And it was powered by a comparable 85-horsepower 144-cid six-cylinder engine, this one of the typical water-cooled inline variety. Its cargo box was 85.9 inches long and 63 inches wide. The box sidewalls were 22.4 inches high. Unlike the Chevy, the Econoline used an age-old I-beam axle suspended by leaf springs up front. The curb weight was 2,555 pounds. The base price was $1,880.

First-year production was a healthy 14,893 units. Another 8,140 rolled out for 1962, when an optional 170-cid six-cylinder was added. A heavy-duty fully synchronized three-speed manual transmission appeared in 1963, as did an optional four-speed transmission and a heavy-duty package consisting of the 170-cid six, a beefier rear axle, stiffer springs, 14-inch wheels, and a reinforced frame. Econoline pickup sales hit their high this year at 11,394. From there, 5,184 followed in 1964, 7,405 in 1965, 3,090 in 1966, and 2,105 in 1967—a decent run for a decent little pickup.

Chrysler Corporation's forward-control response to Ford's Econoline and Chevy's Corvair 95 was slow in coming. Although design work

shaft running beneath. Loading beer kegs into a Rampside was as easy as dropping the side gate down and rolling the brew up the slight incline into the bed. Designers wrapped a ribbed rubber mat over the gate's upper edge to prevent paint damage to the area that made contact with the ground.

At a glance the Rampside pickup looked like a great idea, even more so considering the Corvair 95 truck topped Ford's forward-control rival where it counted. At 105 inches, a Rampside's cargo box was nearly two feet longer than an Econoline's. And the Corvair 95's 1,900-pound payload rating ranked at 250 pounds more than the snub-nosed Ford. The Rampside was lightweight (2,730 pounds) and relatively low-priced ($2,080), and some even felt it was better looking than the gangly Econoline, due to the Corvair 95's lower overall height; 68.5 inches, compared to 78.5.

The Rampside nonetheless never really caught on. After a good year in 1961 (10,787 sold), production dropped to 4,102 in 1962, 2,046 in 1963, and a mere 851 in 1964 before the Corvair 95 pickup line was canceled. Loadside models were only built for 1961 and 1962; production totals were 2,475 and 369, respectively. Why such a short run?

A full-sized half-ton truck was still a real man's machine in the early 1960s—the compact pickup's time had yet to come. But more specifically, it was the Corvair 95's rear-engined design

dated back as far as 1959, Dodge's final product didn't appear until 1964. Designers, however, put that lag time to good use by watching how Ford fared in the compact pickup race. They even went so far as to cut an Econoline van in half in 1962 to examine its structure. Lessons learned led to a stronger, more rigid unibody platform for Dodge's A-100 compact line-up, made up of vans and trucks. Gussets were heavier and welds, metal bends, and supports were more plentiful, all this done in the best tradition of Dodge toughness and durability.

In a side-by-side comparison the A-100 pickup outdid the Econoline in many areas. Although the A-100 was shorter than its rivals, it was wider, heavier, and taller. The added cab height combined with optional cab glass at the rear corners afforded excellent driver visibility in all directions. The cargo box measured almost 7 feet long and was 5.5 feet wide. The wheelbase was 90 inches. The base price was $1,752.

In standard form the A-100 half-ton's GVW was 3,800 pounds; the maximum payload was 900 pounds. Two optional GVW packages were also offered, one at 4,600 pounds, the other at 5,200. Bigger brakes, stiffer springs, a heavier clutch, and shorter 3.91:1 rear gears were included in these deals. With the right equipment, the A-100 easily represented the hardest-working forward-control compact.

The 1964 A-100 also featured the most standard power of the three competing compacts. Beneath that heavily insulated engine cover between the seats was Dodge's 101-horsepower 170-cid slant-six. Even more power was available in the form of an optional 225-cid slant six rated at 140 horses. At the time this was the largest engine available in the compact pickup field.

That changed in 1965, when Dodge introduced an optional V-8 for the A-100. Joining the two slant-sixes was the 273-cid small-block, rated at 174 horsepower. Dodge was the only player in the forward-control game to dare drop a V-8 into a compact pickup. A larger small-block, the 318 V-8, replaced the 273 in 1967.

Despite all its superior aspects, the A-100 pickup rolled on modestly in the shadow of its Ford counterpart. A-100 vans outsold their truck brothers by a wide margin, and not even a captive market seemed to help. Dodge was alone in the compact pickup field after 1967, probably for good reason. Extended demand for smaller light-duty trucks had still yet to materialize. Dodge finally retired its forward-control A-100 early in 1970.

By then attentions had turned to a new breed of compact utility vehicle, a less practical, more fun mode of getting off the beaten path. International had introduced this breed in 1961, and its four-wheel drive Scout soon inspired yet another round of Big Three copies. Ford's Bronco debuted in 1966, Chevrolet's Blazer in 1969, and GMC's Jimmy in 1970.

And with the 1970s came Detroit's modern compact pickups, the counterparts to all those Datsuns and Toyotas then crossing the Pacific. There were no rear engines, no forward controls, no new ideas here. These were just scaled-down renditions of typical trucks. They were also finally the right pickup for the right time.

Dodge introduced a new breed of minitruck in 1982. The Rampage was America's first front-wheel drive pickup. This 1984 model represented the end of the line. *Chrysler Historical Collection*

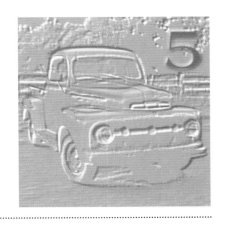

THEY CAME IN PEACE

PRODUCTION PICKS UP ON THE HOME FRONT

While World War II was an unspeakable tragedy for many parts of the globe, it was a major shot in the arm for this country's automaking industry. Still sluggish following the Great Depression, Detroit's various manufacturing firms suddenly found themselves lousy with work once America was pulled into the fray in December 1941. Bust quickly turned into boom as defense contracts abounded and the wealth was spread around for all to rake in. Ships, guns, and planes were soon being built in record numbers, with Detroit making a major contribution to the greatest industrial growth explosion of all time. Ford built B-24 bombers at a dizzying pace, Packard helped produce fighter plane engines, Willys rolled out Jeeps.

Detroit (and the independents) also kept building trucks, mostly big, brawny ones for the war effort. While automobile assembly lines were closed down tight early in 1942, truck production plants were kept open in order to supply the military with heavy-duty utility vehicles. Chevrolet, GMC, Ford, Dodge, Willys-Overland, Studebaker, International—all the big names took part in the fight, building everything from tanks to armored half-tracks, 10-ton troop transports, tandem-axle weapon carriers, ambulances, and scout cars. Even some pickups were found filtering into the flow of materiel heading overseas to Europe and the Pacific or to training bases spread from coast to coast here at home.

Boosting business alone wasn't the only benefit Detroit gained from its wartime service. Lessons learned and investments made, both in speeding up production and improving the utility breed, paid off in spades after peace returned in 1945. Manufacturing's prime movers and shakers weren't blind. They recognized long before the last shot was fired that Americans would be hankering for new vehicles, cars and trucks, like never before once the private sector was allowed to regain its privacy. Not only would all the boys come marching home after Berlin and Tokyo capitulated, but Washington would also surrender its grip on the American marketplace. Restrictions and rationing all would be quickly forgotten. Sure, a "shoot-fish-in-a-barrel" sellers' market was a strong possibility. But it would still be a race to see which company could be first out of the blocks with truly new postwar products.

Earth-shaking automotive developments were at first slow in coming following Hitler and Hirohito's final defeats in the late summer of 1945. A sellers' market did indeed dominate in 1946 and 1947, making it all too easy for American automakers to reap great rewards by simply repackaging existing prewar products. Save for the bold new Kaiser-Frazer, America's first postwar cars were clearly carry-overs from 1941 and 1942. It was left to Studebaker, the venerable independent from South Bend, Indiana, to shock Detroit's Big Three and become "the first by far with a postwar car" in 1947. Two other veteran independents, Hudson and Packard, followed with fresh faces of their own in 1948. General Motors finally got into the act that year with its all-new Cadillac. Chrysler, Lincoln,

Like those of all its rivals, Chevrolet's first postwar pickups for 1946 were simply carryovers from before World War II.

Ford, and Nash joined the modern postwar market in 1949.

The Big Three may have lost out in the race to roll out a totally new postwar car. But they curiously managed to get the jump on the competition with new postwar pickups. Chevrolet's highly touted "Advance Design" trucks debuted in the summer of 1947, joined a month or so later by their GMC counterparts. Ford's first F-series trucks appeared in 1948, as did Dodge's restyled "Pilot House" models. New trucks before new cars, what was up with that?

That fresh, modernized pickups from GMC, Chevy, Ford, and Dodge beat their car-line cousins out of the blocks in the reforming postwar market is not all that difficult to understand. According to most sources, the answer to the above question involved the fact that automobile production required additional start-up time following its wartime shutdown, while the truck manufacturing side remained well greased as it continued rolling through the war years to serve the military. Some pickups were already rolling off lines in 1945, about a year before automotive assembly began again in full force.

"Long before the war ended, the government permitted Chevrolet to begin production of trucks for civilians on the same lines on which military vehicles were being built," wrote Chevy Chief Engineer John Woods in 1947. "Hence, when the war was won, it was not necessary to reconvert lines, and continued production averted an acute truck shortage." Ford too was allowed an early start on postwar pickup production.

Dodge, perhaps the leader of the defense contract crowd during World War II, was also quick to trade its swords for plowshares. Almost a half-million Dodge military vehicles were built for American and Allied forces in the 1940s. And these weren't just trucks, they were hard-as-Sergeant-Rock beasts that were battle-tested tough like the soldiers they transported through war zones around the world. These heavy-duty all-wheel-drive (both 4x4 and 6x6) machines pulled, rescued, and fought. And they gained the

Here the all-new R-series Studebaker pickup for 1949 is shown mocked up in a design studio. Had this been a Ford or Chevy design, we'd probably all still be honoring it today. *Richard Quinn*

Studebaker's M-series pickup, introduced for 1941, reappeared for the postwar market. This 1947 M-5 Studebaker is powered by a 170-cid six-cylinder engine. *Tom Glatch*

trust of entire armies, from this country and in Europe and Asia.

So versatile, durable, and trustworthy were these workhorses that Dodge opted to continue production of the one-ton 4x4 version for civilian use. Reportedly the Dodge plant was converted over to peacetime production of its legendary Power Wagon within only a few hours after the last military 4x4 was completed.

Officially announced in the March 1946 issue of Power Wagon magazine, Dodge's big peacetime pickup was, according to factory

OPPOSITE: Financial limitations forced Studebaker to build the 2R-series in essentially identical fashion well into the 1950s. This 1953 Studebaker closed the book on Robert Bourke's original look. A new grille represented the only major change for 1954—sheet metal remained unchanged up until 1960.

promotional material, "the truck the boys wrote home about . . . now in civvies." Featuring a typical cab first used by both Dodge and Plymouth in 1939 for each company's light-duty trucks, the Power Wagon was, beneath the skin, everything an American fighting man remembered it as being.

The frame was battleship-like, with seven cross-members and reinforced side-rail channels. The wheelbase was a whopping 126 inches. In back, the hefty cargo box measuring 4.5x8 feet could hold 58 cubic feet of whatever you wanted to throw in it. An early Power Wagon's gross vehicle weight ratings were 7,600 pounds with the 7.50x16 eight-ply tires, and 8,700 pounds with the much taller 9.00x16 knobbies.

Power came from a 230-cid L-head six that produced 94 horsepower at 3,200 rpm and 185 pounds-feet of torque at a low, low 1,200 revs. Look up stump-puller in the dictionary and you'll see a picture of a Power Wagon. Transferring that torque to all four wheels was a four-speed transmission backed by a two-speed transfer case. Eight forward speeds and two in reverse were available. Adding to the Power Wagon's hard-working nature was an optional 7,500-pound-capacity winch up front and a tail-shaft drive feature for power take-off equipment.

Dodge marketed its original "army truck" Power Wagons in essentially identical fashion in the United States from 1946 to 1968—they were exported through 1978. In 1957 the big, brawny 4x4 was joined by more-civilized off-road versions of Dodge's standard pickup line, all wearing the Power Wagon nameplate. New model designations assigned that year were W100 for the half-ton Power Wagon, W200 for the three-quarter-ton, and W300 for the tried-and-true one-ton. W100 and W200 Power Wagons from then on used civilian pickup sheet metal, while the W300 motored on up through its demise in 1968 still wearing its military uniform. Style-conscious 4x4 Power Wagon pickups then carried on from there into 1980.

The civilian four-wheel-drive market was an unknown quantity when Dodge decided to dive right in in 1946, helping explain why it was 10 years before the company first tried marketing a 4x4 model more suited for the mainstream. Before those attractive W100 and W200 Power Wagons appeared in 1957, the Dodge boys were more than happy each year to roll out a limited number of its same old, same old monster trucks for customers who didn't give a spit about how fashionable they looked while rolling axle deep in the mud.

The two pickup leaders, Ford and Chevrolet/GMC, never even gave off-road possibilities a sideways glance during the 1940s and much of the 1950s. But that didn't mean 4x4 Ford and GM trucks weren't available in those years. Beginning in 1936, a Ford half-ton pickup buyer could have his machine converted into a tall, brutish four-wheel-drive vehicle by the Marmon-Herrington company in Indianapolis, Indiana. About a couple hundred Marmon-Herrington Fords were sold each year during the 1950s. And Marmon-Herrington conversions continued on even after Ford finally began offering its own factory-built 4x4 pickups in 1959.

Chevrolet went the same route in the 1950s, in this case through Napco in Minneapolis, Minnesota. Napco-converted Chevy 4x4 pickups were known as Mountain Goats and were very rare. GM began building its own light-duty four-wheel-drive trucks in 1957.

Dodge's only real off-road rival in the years immediately following World War II was Willys-Overland, somewhat of an ironic situation consider-ing the two company's hard-working products eventually ended up being stablemates within the Chrysler Corporation empire. The two initially were not direct competitors, however, as their approaches to four-wheel-drive utility differed like night and day. While Dodge opted for the big, powerful route, Willys chose a more humble angle.

Like Dodge, Willys simply kept on doing in peacetime what it had done best during the war—in this case, building Jeeps. After sharing military production with Ford, Willys kicked off its first run of civilian Jeeps—appropriately known as "CJ" models—in July 1945. CJ-2A production that first year was 1,823. It jumped to 71,554 in 1946. It wasn't long before Willys was the self-proclaimed world leader in four-wheel-drive vehicle production.

Willys was also among the first manufacturers to offer America a new postwar truck, as the

Ford restyled its half-ton pickup in 1942, just in time to allow it to be overshadowed by World War II's arrival. That same "waterfall" facade rolled on into the postwar market. *Ford Motor Company*

Ford dedicated its first new postwar assembly plant in Hapeville, Georgia, outside Atlanta in December 1947. It opened just in time to roll the new F-series pickups off the line. The Atlanta Assembly Plant ceased truck production in 1960. *Ford Regional Public Affairs Office, Atlanta*

THE NEW
DODGE
4-WHEEL-DRIVE
POWER-WAGON
The truck that needs no roads!

Only DODGE builds
Job Rated TRUCKS

W-O line-up was expanded in the summer of 1947 to include a pickup. Rudimentary and rock-solid like their quarter-ton CJ cousins, Willys' Jeep pickups were initially offered in two-wheel-drive form. A 4x4 pickup joined the fleet soon afterward, as did a similarly styled 4x4 wagon in 1949—all-steel 4x2 Jeep station wagons had been on the scene since July 1946.

Like the original Power Wagon, the Jeep 4x4 had a one-ton cargo capacity. But unlike the slow, hulking Mopar, a Jeep pick-up was far more maneuverable and much more suited to on-road use, thus their popularity easily overshadowed that of the less-friendly Dodge. Nearly 50,000 Jeep trucks had hit the road (or run off it) by 1949. Production of these familiar pickups with their squared-off fenders and CJ-like facade continued up through 1965.

On the downside, the Jeep pickup's bed measured only 6.5 feet long by 48.5 inches wide, considerably less cubic area than the Power Wagon's cavernous box held within. The reason here was obvious. At 118 inches, the Willys truck's wheelbase was 8 inches shorter than the Dodge's. But remember, these weren't toe-to-toe rivals; each had their own different niche to fill.

Like Willys with its Jeep CJ, Dodge simply took its military 4x4 truck and reissued it in civilian garb as the legendary Power Wagon, beginning in 1946. Military-style Power Wagons were built up through 1968. These were joined in 1957 by Power Wagon models using typical Dodge sheet metal.

Chevrolet's all-new Advance Design trucks appeared in 1947. GMC versions of the same pickups were of course also built. This 1950 GMC is a three-quarter-ton model wearing an owner-added 1948 grille.

The 4x4 Jeep's GVW was 5,300 pounds, compared to 4,700 for its 4x2 forerunner in 1947. An L-head four-cylinder, displacing 134 cubic inches and rated initially at 60 horsepower, was the first choice under the hood. In 1950 the unique "Hurricane" F-head four was introduced. Inside the F-head each cylinder featured one valve (exhaust) located in the block, the other (intake) suspended overhead. Displacement re-mained the same for the F-head four, but compression went from 6.4:1 to 6.9:1. An optional "high-altitude" head boosted the ratio even higher to 7.4:1. Willys brochures and ads were more than willing to brag of the "highest-compression engine in any farm truck." Output for the Hurricane four was 72 horses.

As powerful and durable as Jeep pickups were in the late 1940s, they were still rather mundane vehicles with relatively limited appeal. In many minds they had a face only a mother could love. But for the truly devoted Willys following, these purposeful pickups were friends for life.

Among the more widely recognized, highly publicized, two-wheel-drive world of the Big Three, it was General Motors that became the first firm to roll out a truly new postwar pickup. Some casual observers might have considered Ford a possible candidate for that honor—Dearborn does deserve some credit as the first to build postwar pickups, period. A small number were manufactured in May 1944 for a few civilian customers with high-priority needs. On May 3, 1945, common Ford customers were allowed to buy the first new trucks offered by any company after February 1942. With its attractive "waterfall" grille and beefier frame, this pickup looked and rode like an all-new truck from many perspectives. The design, however, actually dated back to the abbreviated production run of 1942.

Had the war not interrupted production, Ford would have indeed had something to crow about. As it was, the big news of 1942 was old news by the time anyone really got the chance to notice in 1945 and 1946.

Chevrolet civilian truck production fired back up again on August 20, 1945, with the same pickup that had debuted for 1941 wearing antiquated pod headlights. Like the carryover Ford, this truck too featured a waterfall-style grille. In Chevy's case, that latter item caught the eye with a wide, brighter "grin." It was a look truck buyers glimpsed only into the early months of 1947.

Production of Chevrolet's Advance Design trucks began in May that year. Identified as 3100-series models (three-quarter-tonners wore 3600 labels), these all-new half-tons were winners on looks alone. Overall lines were more pleasing, more modern, thanks in part to the deletion of those prewar relics perched atop each front fender in 1946. Advance Design headlights were now fitted nicely within those fenders. Proportions were also improved. Fender tops, hoodline, and cab roof seemed to work together aesthetically better than before. And door hinges were concealed within the sheet metal to help enhance the cleaned-up exterior.

Beneath the skin, the Advance Design pickup's main attraction came inside its strengthened, more durable cab, which welcomed drivers and passengers with real roominess and newfound outward visibility. Brochures claimed the cab used "Unisteel Battleship" construction. Increased glass area all around gave drivers "Observation Car Vision."

Increased comfort was the result of enlarged interior dimensions. Widening the cab translated into 8 more inches of hip room, 3.5 inches of extra shoulder space, and an additional foot for the feet. More springs in the new

BUILT-IN *power*

CHEVROLET'S FAMOUS VALVE-IN-HEAD TRUCK ENGINES

can do more work on a gallon of gasoline than any other type of engine of the same displacement in general use.

LOAD-MASTER engine, 235.5 cubic inches piston displacement, develops 192 foot-pounds of torque (pulling power) over a wide range of engine speeds from 1000 to 1900 r.p.m.

THRIFT-MASTER engine, 216.5 cubic inches displacement, develops 174 foot-pounds of torque at 1200 to 2000 r.p.m.

1—Valves in head provide faster intake of fuel mixture.
2—"Blue-flame" combustion—compact chamber design assures maximum economy.
3—Cast-alloy-iron pistons—close fit is assured.
4—Specialized four-way lubrication—prolongs engine life.
5—Individual cooling of cylinders—prevents waste of power.
6—Crankcase ventilator—removes harmful gases.

Chevy's Advance Design pickups continued using the old, venerable "Stovebolt" six-cylinder engine. Its merits continued to keep Chevrolet trucks out in front, even though Ford had been offering a V-8 since 1932.

Advance Design models continued on in similar fashion from 1947 to early in 1955. This is a 1954 model.

three-passenger seat meant less fatigue in your seat. And larger doors made it easier to move your seat, whatever size, in and out.

Modern styling and the bigger, better cab represented the Advance Design's main claims to fame. And those cab advances helped establish a new industry trend, as all manufacturers rushed back to the drawing board to create their own widened passenger compartments able to seat three humans in newfound relative comfort. Chevy's first new postwar pickup, considered really big news in 1947, was quickly lost in a crowd of competitive responses. Basically the same Advance Design trucks, wearing both Chevrolet and GMC badges, rolled on, year in and year out, into the 1950s. Another new Chevy/GMC pickup wouldn't arrive until 1955, again at midyear.

Ford's answer to Chevrolet's postwar challenge was the "Bonus Built" F-1, introduced in 1948. Few changes had been made by the time this 1950 F-1 came along.

Ford's response came in 1948 and typically mimicked many of the Advance Design selling points. Freshened styling, not nearly as far removed from the look it replaced as Chevy's 1947 update appeared, was of course a part of the plan, as was Ford's own restructured line-up labels. Dearborn's new "F-series" truck line started off with the F-1 half-ton. Three-quarter-ton models wore F-2 badges; F-3 for one-ton trucks. The series ran all the way up to F-8 in the three-ton range.

Ford's first F-series pickups were known as "Bonus Built" trucks—more for your money, get it? The company reportedly spent $1 million of its own cash to improve ergonomics, a term not yet invented then but clearly applicable from a modern perspective. The appropriately named "Million Dollar Cab" featured what promotional people called "Living-Room" comfort. This cab was not only taller (for hat-wearing drivers), it was also widened by seven inches to make room for a third rider, with or without a hat. All three could enter and exit with little worry of knocking knees on the door hinges thanks to doors relocated three inches farther forward.

A taller, one-piece flat windshield and enlarged rear glass aided visibility. And new seats with better springing and improved adjustment ranges enticed potential customers inside the F-1's cab with what Ford admen liked to call "Easy Chair Comfort." Just throw in a footstool, add a "See Rock City" ashtray, and the living room analogy would've been complete. Also enhancing comfort inside was the new Level Action Cab suspension system, which used rubber cab mounts to help insulate passengers from shocks sent through the frame. All told, the F-1 was definitely a better-riding, easier-to-drive truck.

Like Chevrolet, Ford was left to ride its kinder, gentler F-series pickup into the 1950s, although a new grille in 1951 did freshen up the F-1's face considerably. Chevy's Advance Design pickups meanwhile still looked very much the same each year until a radically new grille was finally added in late 1954. By then, Ford had already one-upped its GM rival with a truly new, totally restyled, redesigned truck.

In 1953, Ford's first F-100 stunned everyone, including Chevrolet, which needed two years to respond accordingly with a milestone of its own. But in 1948, Ford was not only not the first member of Detroit's truck triumvirate to bring out a new postwar pickup; it wasn't even the second. Bonus Built F-series trucks were introduced in January 1948. Dodge's first postwar update, in the two-wheel-drive mode, had appeared a few weeks before.

Heavily entrenched in big-truck production during the war, Dodge was allowed to resume building civilian versions of some of these beasts as early as May 1944. Peacetime production of half-ton pickups began in April 1945. These were of course prewar rehashes, in this case dating back to 1939. W-series Dodge pickups carried on almost unchanged up through 1947.

Dodge's new B-series trucks, the "Pilot House" models, appeared right about the turn of the year. The Pilot House name referred to—who would've guessed it?—an all-new roomier, more comfortable cab with extra glass area that afforded "360-degree vision," according to the promo crowd. The split front glass was four inches wider and three inches taller. Side windows were also enlarged, and rearward visibility could've been enhanced as well by optional cab corner windows similar to the Nu-Vue option Chevrolet offered for its Advance Design models.

Some felt Dodge's updated styling for 1948 outdid Chevy's for 1947. The look without a doubt represented a marked improvement over the company's own aging W-series appearances. Beauty beneath that fresh facade included a beefier frame with a shortened wheelbase (108 inches, compared to the W's 116) that helped better balance the load. That shortened stretch, working in concert with a widened front track and a new cross-steering design, also improved ride and handling and made the 1948 Dodge pickup's turning radius probably the smallest in its field.

on hills or with heavy loads. It wasn't an automatic transmission, but it was a start.

Freshened front-end styling featuring the first use of Dodge's long-established "Job-Rated" label (in the grille) came along in 1951. Two years later Dodge introduced the "Truck-O-Matic" option, an intriguing package that did the Fluid Drive equipment one better.

Truck-O-Matic used that same fluid coupling, a standard clutch, and Chrysler's M6 semi-automatic transmission. The clutch was only required for initial launching. From there, the M6 shifted on its own in various ways, depending on the driver's choice of either Power Range or Driving Range. Both ranges had two speeds, as did reverse. Shifts would come automatically at about 11 miles per hour. Putting a Truck-O-Matic Dodge in the Power Range meant the driver could hold her pickup in low gear until she let off the accelerator—at any speed greater than 5 miles per hour, the transmission would then shift up. Truck-O-Matic worked fine in everyday operation, but its hefty $110 asking price inhibited its popularity. Truck-O-Matic Dodge pickups are rare, to say the least.

Dodge also updated its pickup styling once more in 1953, just in time to wave good-bye to the B-series models. Another new model came in 1954, one year after Ford's second try and one year before Chevrolet's earth-shaking introductions.

But long before Chevy shook things up in 1955, before Ford was drawing raves for its F-100 in 1953, Studebaker was again amazing witnesses with another startling, new peacetime product. The same independent automaker that had beaten everyone to the punch in 1947 with a totally restyled postwar car pulled off a similar coup for its light-duty truck line midway in 1948. Studebaker in this case may not have been first—hell, it wasn't even third—but a case can be made that this was probably the best of the early postwar pickup restyling efforts.

"Studebaker sets a new truck style trend," claimed ads for the company's new-for-1949 2R-series pickups. "There is an unmistakable

F-series pickups were fitted with a new grille in 1951. This 1951 F-1 is powered by Ford's aging flathead V-8.

Like Ford, Dodge mounted its Pilot House cab on rubber mounts to improve driver/passenger attitudes. Inside, a new "Air-O-Ride" seat supported as many as three full-sized men quite comfortably on a cushion of air assisted by coil springs. Of course, those three men could fit in the cab (provided they got along) due to its typically enlarged size. It was 2.5 inches taller, 3 inches longer, and 6.375 inches wider.

Mechanical innovations included the introduction of Chrysler's Fluid Drive as a pickup option in April 1950. This unit used a fluid coupling, along with a clutch, to allow "semi-automatic" driving. While the transmission was still a manual shift, constant clutching wasn't required. A Fluid Drive Dodge pickup could be braked to a full stop without using the left pedal. It could idle at rest with the clutch engaged, as the coupling would allow a certain amount of slippage at lower rpm. Ads claimed Fluid Drive made for smoother operation and easier handling

distinction about these new Studebaker '49ers which establishes new style standards for the entire truck industry. Look at them from any angle. Stand back for an all over view of their balanced proportions. Come close-up and study the strong but graceful forms, the superior metal work. The unity of design in these new Studebaker trucks is as smart and as practical as that which distinguishes Studebaker passenger cars."

Brilliant designer Bob Bourke, of Raymond Loewy's avant-garde styling studio, was the main man behind the 1949 Studebaker 2R pickup. Just as his touch would later help create a modern classic in the form of Studebaker's Starliner coupe of 1953, Bourke's work in 1949 resulted in a true masterpiece—from a truck- or car-line perspective. This wasn't just a great-looking machine "for a truck." It was a great-looking machine, period.

Studebaker's expectations for its first new postwar truck involved an ability to bridge the gap between pickup purposefulness and car-like class. South Bend officials wanted a utility vehicle that could sweat like a dog on the job and still manage not to offend any sensibilities in polite society. Planners not only desired a pretty pickup, they wanted the prettiest pickup rolling—and this at a time when few customers recognized that they might want a truly attractive work vehicle, a truck that looked just as much at home in front of the church on Sunday morning as it did on the jobsite the following Monday.

Bourke didn't disappoint. The seductively rounded, superclean lines up front alone would've been enough to impress had he simply followed existing trends and only worked on the cab. Chevy, Ford, and Dodge's new postwar pickups at the time all had one thing in

Dodge introduced its "Pilot House" B-series pickups in 1948. This line-up continued with a few minor updates here and there up through 1953. Shown here is a 1952 B-3-B Dodge.

common: up front they were nicely restyled, but in back they were all function and next to no form. An age-old squared-off cargo box was, in all three cases, simply adorned with purposeful pontoon fenders to keep the mud down.

Bourke's '49er, on the other hand, was handsomely styled from nose to tail. It certainly ranks as this country's first "fully styled" pickup. The box in back was not just an afterthought. Its rakish rear fenders followed right along in integrated fashion behind all that smooth sheet metal up front. Overall impressions were low and sleek, thanks once more to a widened, airy cab, but accentuated even more by the fact that

Dodge's intriguing Truck-O-Matic option was introduced in 1953. Pickups equipped with this option still used a clutch for takeoffs, but most other operating situations were automatic.

Willys dominated the burgeoning 4x4 field in the 1940s and 1950s, thanks primarily to its popular CJ Jeeps. The veteran independent automaker also built heavy-duty four-wheel-drive pickups. This is a 1950 one-ton Willys. *Jeep/Eagle Division, Chrysler Corporation*

the flowing lines didn't just end at the back of the cab. Bourke even went one more step further, deleting the running boards normally found below all those other three-man-wide cabs running around in 1949. Truck buyers had never seen anything like it before. And it would be a while before they saw anything to top it. If there has ever been such a thing as a timeless pickup design, Bourke's 2R Studebaker may well have been it.

But its timeless nature also worked against it. Like the other downsliding independents in the postwar market, Studebaker simply couldn't afford to keep up with the Joneses in the 1950s. The company never had the extra cash to spend on retooling every other year or so like the Big Three boys could. As much as the 2R pickup looked like a classic in 1949, it could only impress customers for so long with the competition busy in the 1950s stealing more and more thunder at seemingly every turn.

While restyled trucks from Ford, Chevy, and Dodge were appearing almost every year as the decade progressed, Studebaker was faced with little choice but to build the exact same model up through 1953. Then it was only revised grilles and optional two-tone paint schemes that were added after that up through 1959. Was it any wonder Studebaker pickups survived in America only until 1963?

The other great independent truck-builder of the postwar era, International Harvester, fared much better, thanks undoubtedly to its great success in the big-rig market. International didn't give up on light-duty pickup production until 1980. As for the first new postwar model from I-H, that came in 1950, and it also turned a head or two in its day.

Introduced in October 1949, International's modern L-series pickups replaced the old K/KB models that had been on the road

since 1940. Though not as dramatic-looking as the 1949 Studebaker, the 1950 I-H light-duty truck still represented a major step forward from the past. Like the 2R Stude, its lines were long, low, and wide. And its enlarged cab—"the roomiest on the road," according to ads—featured a one-piece curved windshield, a first for the industry. Ford became the first of the Big Three players to add curved front glass in 1953. Equally notable was International's L-series rear glass, which was divided into two panes by a post down the middle.

The 1950 International's large, wide hood featured special latches that allowed it to open from either side—or lift off completely. Beneath that hood was a new overhead-valve six-cylinder, the Silver Diamond. Compared to its 214-cid Green Diamond L-head six predecessor, the 220-cid Silver Diamond was a real screamer at 100 horsepower. Green Diamond output had been 82 horses.

International lightly updated its L-model pickups in 1953, resulting in the R-series, considered a transitional step between the company's first new postwar design and its next major restyle waiting ahead in 1957. Interestingly, another transitional phase in 1956 brought along the S-series, a name that reminded many of International's popular "speed trucks" of 1921, the company's first S-series models. Those second S-series pickups were still very much L-models hidden underneath various updated tweaks. The S-series continued into early 1957, when it was replaced by a truly new International pickup to help mark I-H's 50th anniversary.

From high-wheelers to curved windshields—a lot sure can happen in 50 years. Or, in the case of the American pickup truck, a lot can happen in a decade, especially so if the decade was the 1950s. And the 1950s were only half over.

NEW AND IMPROVED

ENTER THE THOROUGHLY MODERN PICKUP

International Harvester began its 50th year in the business of building commercial vehicles not with a bang nor a whimper, just a steady hum. I-H's 1957 model year started with the same S-series pickups introduced for 1956, though that wasn't entirely a bad thing. S-series models had helped boost total sales by 5.7 percent that year, which ended with International thoroughly entrenched in the truck industry's No. 3 position behind Chevrolet and Ford. By 1957 the company had built more than 2.6 million trucks and officials in Chicago were claiming as many as 1.1 million of those were still hard at work. Too bad they chose to mark this achievement in their golden anniversary year with nothing new. Or nothing improved—at first.

In March 1957, International introduced its all-new, modernized A-series pickups. Fifty bucks to the first reader able to guess why the series designation that year went from S back to A. Sure, a natural alphabetical progression to T would have looked like a classic Ford knock-off. And, yes, the company had also gone back to the start of the alphabet in 1930 after its original S-series had run its course the first time. But a President Grant went to the first person out there (trust me, it's in the mail) who correctly answered the simple question, "What's the first letter in anniversary?"

The A-100 truck, which spanned the remaining half of 1957 into 1958, was the first totally restyled International pickup to hit the road since I-H Styling Chief Ted Ornas had set up shop at the company's design center in Fort Wayne, Indiana, in 1953. Trendy touches to Ornas' all-new look included an expansive wraparound windshield and front-end sheet metal that all but did away with the pontoon-style front fenders prominent in nearly all previous pickup designs. Fender tops rose up close to the hoodline and cabsides were cleaner and uncluttered, thanks to those smoothed-in fenderlines and the deletion of running boards. Ornas' team was the last of the major pickup players to drop their running boards, although Ford and Dodge stylists had only beaten them to this particular punch by roughly six months.

Antiquated pontoon fenders did remain astride the cargo box in back, but a stylish smooth-sided "Bonus Load" box was made available as part of the Golden Jubilee Custom Pickup package. Two-tone gold-and-white metallic paint and special trim were also included in this package, which made up for its late arrival for International's 50th birthday party with its smashing good looks. It took a few months but finally the candles were blown out.

Things weren't so happy to the west of Fort Wayne, over in South Bend, Indiana. Studebaker's birthday in 1957 was its 105th but no one was singing or wearing funny hats. Everyone essentially was busy mopping up red ink. Both car and truck sales declined considerably during the 1950s, creating a self-feeding situation (typical of the independent ilk) that only contributed to a continuing downward spiral. Ever-weakening cash flow meant Studebaker

Two years after Ford wowed the truck crowd with its first F-100, Chevrolet replaced its earlier ground-breaking Advance Design pickups with a sensational new package in 1955. "First-series" Chevy trucks (black at right) began the 1955 model year, then were superseded by the new "second-series" models (left) in March.

International Harvester celebrated its golden anniversary by unveiling its all-new A-100 pickup in March 1957. I-H trucks commonly ranked third—albeit a distant third—behind Chevrolet and Ford in the 1950s sales race.

Chevrolet's Task Force trucks were offered from 1955 to 1959. As was the case with the previously built Advance Design pickups, the base Task Force half-ton was the 3100-series model. New for 1955 was a 3200 series with its longer cargo box. This 3200 Chevrolet is a 1957 model. Also notice the optional wraparound rear window.

couldn't come up with the funds to tool up for critical redesigns. Buyers then grew weary of essentially the same models showing up year after year. No new models meant less money coming in. Less money meant no new models. Et cetera, et cetera.

As attractive as Bob Bourke's 2R trucks were, they simply couldn't keep up in a rapidly reforming modern marketplace that waited for no one. Sales of Studebaker's last 2R models in 1953 reached only 32,112, down from 58,873 the previous year. Updates such as a curved one-piece windshield and a big, new grille couldn't quite hide the fact that the 3R-series pickup in 1954 was still a masked 2R. Total truck production that year tumbled again to 15,608.

Studebaker and Packard joined forces in October 1954 in an effort to save these two once-proud independents, but the move only served to allow one ailing firm to drag down

The last of Ford's first-generation F-100s, built in 1956, featured a trendy wraparound windshield. This 1956 F-100 is also equipped with the rare automatic transmission option.

another. The handwriting was by then clearly on the wall. No one, however, wanted to read it. A new V-8 probably helped things in 1955, when truck sales temporarily steadied. Trendy two-tone paint schemes, on the other hand, did little to slow another slide. Nor did a large, toothy fiberglass grille added in 1957. The Studebaker-Packard Corporation as late as 1959 was still marketing the same pickup body introduced in 1949. That point was essentially rendered moot, though, as the 1950s came to a

close, because so few potential customers were even around then to notice.

What happened to South Bend's century-old-plus wagonmaker in the 1950s was the result of a fast-paced market leaving a handicapped runner behind. The Big Three's meteoric post-war rise to power didn't help matters, either. But which came first, the chicken or the egg? Did Detroit's ever-growing bullies push their weaker rivals away from the table? Or did the cash-strapped independents' weakening positions

Ford's second-generation F-100 Styleside pickup carried on in similar fashion up through 1960. A 292-cid V-8 powers this two-tone 1960 Ford.

Chevrolet in 1958 introduced two new image updates for its light-duty pickups. The Fleetside model, with its flush cargo box walls, followed in the tire treads of Ford's Styleside pickup, introduced the year before. This 1958 Fleetside is also equipped with the Apache deluxe trim package.

simply allow the Big Three to continually eat up more of the pie? Yes. To both.

Competitive pressures, the likes of which this country's demanders and suppliers had never seen before, came into play during the 1950s. What began as a pronounced sellers' market in the peaceful years immediately following World War II eventually reverted into the opposite once the automotive firms again found themselves fighting each other for customers, who seemed to be growing more plentiful by the day. More and more consumer cash was indeed out there, ripe for the taking in the early 1950s. But taking it proved to be a tougher and tougher task, as the consumer behind that cash began to grow more accustomed to seeing more and more choices. Car and truck buyers of the 1950s then became more discriminating, more wanting, more demanding. "What have you done for me lately?" became the prevailing attitude. "New" wasn't good enough in the postwar market; it had to be new *and* improved.

Keeping up in this atmosphere required deep pockets, more than ever before, because what was big news today quickly turned into old news tomorrow. Spending became the key to survival in the upward-spiraling postwar market. Those companies that had the green to invest in future advancements in the 1950s had a future. Those that didn't, did not. Independents that couldn't afford to run with the big dogs were not only left on the porch, but were earmarked for extinction.

Independent truck builders found the going easier than their counterparts on the car side of the fence for various reasons. Companies primarily (or totally) involved in automaking foundered first. Nash and Hudson prevented two untimely deaths by merging into American Motors in 1954. Continued survival for AMC then hinged on a quick jump into the burgeoning compact field in the 1960s. Kaiser's long-suffering automotive line-up finally retired from the American market in 1955. You know what happened to Packard.

In the truck world, it was International Harvester's wide diversity that kept it going strong in the face of Detroit's onslaught. The highly successful production of heavy trucks, heavier equipment, and farm machinery allowed International to stick with its pickup line-up through the 1970s.

On the flip side of the coin, Willys stayed healthy because it did one thing and did that one thing really well. The 40-year-old firm from Toledo, Ohio, owned the four-wheel-drive market in the 1950s, then remained a major player after Detroit jumped onto the off-road bandwagon big-time in the 1960s. Once freed of its four-doored deadweight, Henry Kaiser's automotive company managed to survive in this country after 1955 thanks to its 1953 purchase of Willys-Overland. Popular Jeep CJs and their pickup running mates later became the property of American Motors when Kaiser-Jeep merged with AMC in 1970.

Studebaker never found such a savior. George Mason had considered absorbing the company into his American Motors conglomerate once Studebaker and Packard were joined in 1954. But Mason died in October that year, and his replacement atop AMC, George Romney, wanted no part of the Studebaker-Packard mess. Cars or trucks, it didn't matter in South Bend. Neither line had a hope or prayer left after 1954.

Not even the impressive Lark in the 1960s could save the day.

While Studebaker was slowly falling victim to those ultracompetitive market pressures, its well-established rivals from Detroit were riding high above it all. Ford and Chevrolet took turns knocking truck buyers dead in the 1950s with seemingly one milestone advancement after another. Dodge also raised an eyebrow or two, although resulting sales for Chrysler's truck division never did come close to those of this country's two long-leading pickup builders. If Americans had thought those first new postwar models of the late 1940s were something, they had several surprises waiting for them in the 1950s. The first came from Ford in 1953.

When David E. Davis, Jr., announced "The 24 Most Important Automobiles of the Century" in Automobile magazine's September 1996 issue, one of his more intriguing choices was a pickup. This ground-breaking light-duty truck first appeared to wow the working crowd as Ford Motor Company was also celebrating its 50th anniversary. It debuted March 13, 1953.

"Every comfortable, driver-friendly pickup on the road today owes its existence to the original Ford F-100," claimed Davis. "Until the appearance of the restyled Ford F-100 pickup in 1953, trucks were thought suitable only for commercial uses. But Ford's 1953 F-100 was the first truck planned, styled, and engineered by a corporate management team, and suddenly pickup trucks became an alternative for personal transportation."

Ford reportedly spent $30 million on what undoubtedly represented Detroit's earliest use of an ergonomic study in a pickup design project—if not the earliest, surely the most comprehensive. Human comfort was this project's top priority. And Ford's top designers were assigned the task of making the F-100 the most posterior-friendly pickup in history. Stylists got into the act, too, resulting in a final package that balanced form and function like no other pickup ever before. Although it was still very much a work truck, the 1953 F-100 was a very smart-looking, truly stylish, much easier-to-use work truck.

Dodge introduced an optional V-8 for its trucks late in 1954, and promotional men couldn't help but tout this 145-horsepower hauler as the "world's most powerful pickup."
Chrysler Historical Collection

A truly major restyle finally came along for Dodge pickups in 1957. This same basic bodyshell would carry on (with differing nose treatments) up through 1960.
Chrysler Historical Collection

were more stylish, and the steering wheel was placed at an angle better suited to reduce driver fatigue. According to Mechanix Illustrated's Tom McCahill, the spacious three-passenger seat was "as comfortable as the average sedan's."

Mechanical advancements included "The Greatest Transmission Choice in Truck History," according to Ford brochures. Available was a synchromesh three-speed, a three-speed with overdrive, a four-speed with granny low, and the truck line's first automatic transmission, the Ford-O-Matic. The latter was only offered for half-tons in 1953.

Like Dodge's new pickups in 1948, the 1953 Ford relied on a restructured chassis (the front axle was moved back slightly to put engine weight farther forward) to better balance the vehicle and reduce its turning radius by about 19 percent. International discovered this trick in 1957.

The first F-100 stuck with the same power sources offered for the last Bonus Built F-1 in 1952. Buyers in 1953 again could choose either a 101-horsepower, 215-cid overhead-valve six-cylinder, or Ford's venerable flathead V-8. "Flattie" displacement was 239 cubic inches; the output was 110 horsepower. The second-edition F-100 in 1954 was treated to two new engines. The first was a bored-out, higher-compression six that displaced 223 cubic inches and produced 115 horses. The second was Ford's first modern overhead-valve V-8. While the OHV V-8's displacement equaled the flathead it replaced, its output was a healthy 130 horsepower.

All this power and added comfort made the F-100 irresistible. Sales in 1955 surpassed Dearborn's best pickup effort, established in 1929, by almost 20,000 trucks. Ford still finished second again behind Chevrolet that year, but its market penetration topped 30 percent for the first time in the postwar era.

Additional upgrades included a switch from a 6-volt electrical system to a 12-volt setup in 1956. A minor restyle that year also added a more trendy wraparound windshield. If that wasn't enough glass for you, an equally trendy

Advertising ink claimed the F-100 offered "more power, more comfort, more economy," the middle feature resulting from the "driverized" cab that included sound deadener in the doors, an even wider seat with improved shock-absorbing capabilities, and a larger, one-piece curved windshield that both improved visibility and helped make exterior appearances more pleasant to the eye. A 4-foot-wide rear window also contributed to a 55 percent increase in total glass area.

Ford spent most of that $30 million on the new "Driver Engineered" cab. Instruments and control locations were improved, appointments

wraparound rear window was introduced as an option in 1956 as well.

All that new glass came as part of an effort, however humble, to keep pace with rival movements, those of Chevrolet to be exact. After making all the headlines in 1953, Ford officials found themselves on the back page by 1955 as the Bow-Tie boys rolled out a milestone pickup of their own. Chevy called its latest new line Task Force trucks. Critics called them sensational.

As the whole world knows, 1955 was *the* big year for Chevrolet. An incredibly exciting restyle on the car side, coupled with the introduction of the division's first modern V-8 with overhead valves, overnight transformed Chevy's Bel Air into the "Hot One." Triple-digit speeds had never come this cheap, nor had this much style and flair. Average Joe would've been happy enough with that big news. But GM's price leader didn't stop there.

Pickup production for 1955 began with a mildly updated version of the same Advance Design package introduced in 1947. Then on March 25, that first-series was replaced by Chevrolet's second-series 1955 models, the modernized Task Force trucks that did the F-100 more than one better. While Ford executives were bragging about breaking into the 30 percent market share club, Chevy beancounters were busy clicking off pickup after pickup, including the six millionth sold since the beginning of time. When the dust finally cleared, about one out of every three trucks sold in 1955 was a Chevrolet.

Who cared how comfortable the second-series Chevy pickup's spacious cab was in 1955? Stunning, even sexy, styling was the main selling point, although the beauty found beneath the skin was nothing to sneeze at. Mechanical firsts (for Chevrolet) included the same OHV power-plant that made the Hot One so hot. In pickup guise, Chevy's high-winding 265-cid small-block V-8 was known as the Trademaster 265, rated at 145 horsepower. Behind the Trademaster V-8 a customer could've also added a four-speed Hydra-Matic automatic transmission. Among additional

optional firsts introduced in 1955 were power steering and brakes, passenger car-style full wheel covers, a factory-installed radio, and an illuminated cigar lighter.

The standard "Panoramic" wraparound windshield was yet another first for Chevy trucks. Optional Panor-amic glass was available in back for those who preferred maximum visibility—and maximum style.

New as well were 13 different exterior paint choices and 12 two-tone combinations. The restyled sheet metal that that paint went on mimicked the 1955 Bel Air's, especially so with its egg-crate-style grille, a feature un-abashedly borrowed from Ferrari. Overall lines were seductively sculptured with softened, rounded corners. Up front were hooded headlights and "fadeaway" front fenders in place of the old, archaic pontoons. Chevrolet wasn't the first to trade in its pontoons—Dodge had been working on this transition since 1948—but an argument can be made that Chevy made its first jump from prewar trends to smoother modern lines better than any other manufacturer.

The division sold pickups better than any other company, too. Chevrolet's Task Force trucks continued to top the industry with more than 30 percent of the market for all five years they were around. Included for the first time in this mix in 1957 was a factory-built four-wheel-drive model. In 1958 quad headlights were added to the Task Force design and exterior model designations dropped the two zeroes—a typical half-ton was now simply a "31." An upscale trim package called Apache was also introduced that year.

Dodge never did sell trucks well in the 1950s, though not for a lack of trying. Chrysler Corporation's truck division surely could've been credited with being on the cutting edge, at least from a style perspective, with its new post-war pickups in 1948. Studebaker in 1947 had been the first to integrate pickup styling into one meaningful package from nose to tail.

THAT RED HOT SWEPTLINE...

TODAY IT'S REAL SMART TO CHOOSE
DODGE TRUCKS

Dodge typically finished third in the race to introduce a modern-looking, stylized pickup with a flush-walled cargo box. The attractive Sweptline debuted in 1959, one year after Chevy's Fleetside and two years after Ford's Styleside.

Dodge closed out the 1950s with a few minor facelifts of the same shell introduced in 1958. This body also carried over into 1960, to finally be replaced by a truly new Dodge pickup the following year. After the trendy Sweptline's appearance in 1959, Dodge trucks with the old-style pontoon fenders, like this 1960, became known as Utiline models.

Dodge's B-series trucks weren't all that far behind the following year. Okay, they were no great shakes as far as their typically crude cargo box was concerned—nobody even came close to Studebaker in this department until 1955. But, despite their smooth, flowing lines, Studebaker's 2R pickups still stuck to the old prewar "modular" plan up front. All trucks to that point were put together like building blocks: a separate cab and box with clearly defined functional fenders bolted on at all four corners. Studebaker's front fenders were still very much present and accounted for in the 1950s. Dodge's, on the other hand, lost nearly all vestiges of that prewar pontoon image, as their more subtle fender tops faded away straight back into the doors.

A polite restyle in 1954 cut even more ties from the past. A modern, mildly curved one-piece windshield replaced the old twin flat panes, and those fender tops moved up closer to the hoodline, making overall impressions up front appear even more integrated. Not only did this Dodge "fenderless" design beat Chevrolet by a year, it also in some minds represented a more modern departure from the old delineated cab/fender layouts. But such claims mattered little considering that Chevy pickups always sold like hotcakes while Dodge's simply sold.

Few probably noticed when Dodge added its own wraparound windshield in 1955 as part of yet another keep-up-with-the-Joneses ploy. Harder to miss was a truly serious attempt to follow in Ford and Chevrolet's history-making tire treads two years later.

Dodge's 1957 pickup restyle featured a bit of styling guru Virgil Exner's "Forward Look" influence. Modernized lines and a truly dramatic nose characterized the new D-100 design, which still portrayed much of the previously seen Dodge pickup heritage. Totally new, however, were the hooded, "frenched" headlights. These sported a forward slant that supposedly gave the D-100 pickups that same distinctive look of motion-while-standing-still possessed by Chrysler's 1957 passenger cars. Standard wraparound glass (optional in back) and an updated grille typically found their way into the D-100 look.

That look remained nothing at all new in back, at least for standard Dodge pickups in 1957. The D-100 Sweptside (see Chapter 7) complemented its modern front end with an out-of-this-world cargo box sheathed in station wagon rear quarter panels complete with Dodge's trademark sky-high fins. This odd creation was born in response to Chevrolet's superclean Cameo Carrier, introduced in 1955 with the industry's first flush-sided cargo box. Actually Crosley was the first to completely delete pontoon fenders in back in 1948, followed by the Powell pickup in 1955. So why does history honor the Cameo in this respect? Simple. Chevy is GM and little Crosley and Powell aren't. Enough said.

As it was, the Cameo was a high-priced, limited-production model anyway, so its claim to that claim—like Roger Maris' 61st home run initially in 1961—was marked by an asterisk. But unlike Maris, the Cameo deserved its qualification. Chevy may have originally toyed with the idea. But the first truck builder to strip the pontoons off a mainstream, typically priced, mass-produced pickup was Ford in 1957.

While Dodge chose a quick-fix, low-production copycat response to the Cameo in 1957, Ford designers incorporated a smooth-sided cargo box into a complete redesign called Styleside, and then fitted all standard 1957 F-100s with this slick sheet metal. If you still wanted pontoons, you had to special-order what was now known as a Ford Flareside truck.

Dearborn designers additionally tied together its Styleside pickup in a fully integrated package that represented the first leap into yet another thoroughly modern market. The 1957 Styleside instantly left the 1950s behind in a flurry. Not only were the rear fenders deleted, so too were the fronts. Running boards were axed as well. Lower and wider than its forerunners, Ford's first Styleside pickup was clean and concise. The design elements worked together better, from all angles, than any truck's before it—and many to come. Though detractors liked to refer to it as a refrigerator on wheels, it was a damned fine-looking 'fridge.

The idea looked so good, Chevrolet copied it back in 1958, adding a stylish Fleetside bed (walled in steel, not fiberglass) to its Task Force truck cab. New front-end styling to match didn't come until 1960. As for Dodge, its decision-makers finally tired of the weak-selling Sweptside early in 1959 and replaced it with the up-to-date Sweptline, it too with smooth bodysides completely devoid of running boards or fenders.

So it was that the stage was again set for yet another new decade. High-stakes competition in the pickup field didn't end with the 1950s. On the contrary, the race had just begun. And no matter what the result, truck buyers were guaranteed to be the real winners.

Canadian-market Dodge trucks and vans were sold under the Fargo banner from the late 1930s through 1972. *Chrysler Historical Collection*

A TOUCH OF CLASS

GUSSIED-UP PICKUPS WERE BORN IN THE 1950s

We Yankees certainly are spoiled. Having our cake in both hand and mouth at the same time is the American way. Consider the vehicles we drive. A generation or so ago there were cars and there were trucks, with never the twain to meet. Cars were (and always will be) convenient, mostly comfortable, and sometimes classy. Trucks were just trucks, plain and simple. Haul this, carry that. The sky was almost the limit for a car buyer looking for a little (or a lot of) prestige and/or performance in his practical transportation. Spartan, yeoman-like utility represented a pickup's prime selling point. That, however, was then.

Today's light-duty pickups—hell, even many 4x4s—offer every bit as much class, comfort, pizzazz, and performance as their passenger-car counterparts. And they have for almost as long as anyone born after 1968 can remember—which is no more than five minutes ago, but you get the picture. Conceived in the 1950s, nurtured in the 1960s, well grown in the 1970s, and full blown in the 1980s, the concept of a truck working hard and looking as good as a car at the same time is simply taken for granted in the 1990s. At this point, we are already seeing more than one long-running automotive bloodline finding its way onto the endangered species list as pickups are rolling their way farther and farther into the daily transportation mainstream. Who needs a car when a truck offers much the same features and attractions and so much more?

Tracing the roots of this trend takes us back to the 1950s, the birthplace of so many popular movements, automotive and otherwise. Rock 'n roll, suburban sprawl, and upward mobility all got cooking during this fabled decade. So too did horsepower, as Chevrolet in 1955 introduced the "Hot One" with its low-priced, high-winding overhead-valve V-8. Detroit at the same time also began toying with the idea that pickup trucks could be practical and stylish.

That's not to say, however, that pickups built before the 1950s were completely devoid of style. Remember, in the beginning many light-duty trucks were more or less half car, half truck. Car-type styling in front was followed by a no-nonsense cargo box in back. Yet it was still plainly obvious that form fully followed function. This tradition dominated truck production through this century's first three decades because it represented a purely practical, relatively inexpensive way for pickup builders to offer purely practical, relatively inexpensive utility vehicles to buyers who probably couldn't have cared less about making fashion statements. Individual identities, new-model status—who cared? Hard work and no play was the plan. Nary an eyebrow was raised when reportedly new trucks debuted wearing old-news facades from previous model years.

Ford attempted a marked departure from the old plan in 1937. Dearborn-bred half-ton pickups then began featuring a look all their own, thanks to their large "barrel-nosed" grilles. Customers apparently didn't want to change the way they looked at their pickups though. In 1940 Ford went back to borrowing passenger-car looks. Barely anyone noticed when Ford tried

Dodge's Spring Special pickups were simply dressed up with two-tone paint as "gate attractions" for dealers desiring to leave the winter sales doldrums behind. This 1953 Spring Special, which is equipped with the Truck-O-Matic option, was painted in nonstock shades of blue.

another pickup restyle just before World War II shut things down in 1942.

A new movement began right after the war. In 1949 hardy independent Studebaker first demonstrated (with great flair) that trucks could turn heads on their own. While Ford did beat this Detroit outsider to the punch with an attractive new model of its own in 1948, the restyled F-series models still carried serious ties to the past in back. On the other hand, the totally new R-series Studebaker was truly fresh from head to tail. Critics loved the look. Too bad Studebaker was stuck with it for too long while its Big Three rivals were riding away on thoroughly modern restyled bandwagons of their own.

Form still followed function after 1949, but suddenly there was more form to admire than ever before. Truck builders almost overnight discovered that pickup buyers too could be influenced with a little prestige or pizzazz. Studeba-ker's R-series models proved that individualistic styling did have a place

International Harvester began offering trendy two-tone paint schemes for its new S-series pickups, introduced in 1955. *Navistar International*

International's Golden Jubilee anniversary A-100 model appeared in 1957 with special two-tone gold paint and a stylish cargo box reminiscent of Ford's new Styleside design. *Navistar International*

in the workaday world of the American pickup truck. From there, it was only a matter of time until competitive forces led the way toward other new and improved tactics to market pickups.

All pickup producers seemed to be bragging about the latest, largest, and most comfortable cab as the 1950s dawned. Once that particular claim lost weight, it was left to stylish exterior touches to do all the profiling.

Dodge was among the earliest to try the high-profile image game with the first of many "Spring Specials." The idea was to break out of the wintertime sales doldrums with an eye-catching promotional piece come each spring. Offered from 1948 to 1953, the rare Spring Special Dodge pickup brought customers in from the waning cold with its attractive two-tone paint treatment. Two-tone trucks were nothing new; mixing and matching bodies and fenders in contrasting colors had been common before the war. But this time the trick was truly artistic. A Spring Special pickup did not get lost in a crowd, which was the whole idea.

International began turning to brighter colors and stylish two-tone finishes in 1955, that latter touch serving the venerable company's top-line pickups in proud fashion into the 1970s. International Harvester's most noteworthy use of two-toning came in March 1957 to mark the 50th birthday for I-H utility vehicles. The "Golden Anniversary Special" A-100 model featured a trendy "slab-side" cargo box (mimicking Chevy's Fleetside and Ford's Styleside models) and a metallic gold-and-white finish set off with exclusive chrome trim.

Studebaker also began offering "purpose-built" two-tone trucks midyear in 1955. At first, these high-profile pickups used a demarcation line quite similar to International's. Then, in 1956, Studebaker's renamed Transtar trucks were treated to a much more trendy color split that separated the two tones vertically instead of horizontally. A two-tone Transtar in 1956 featured one color up front, another contrasting finish for the cargo box, with the two shades set apart by an inverted "L" delineation on the door's lower rear quarter. This practice may have gone one step beyond, for the South Bend firm

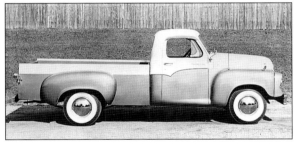

brought back a more conventional upper/lower horizontal split in 1957.

A third two-tone truck, this one from Chevrolet, also debuted in 1955. Only in this case, there was far more to the attraction than one color atop another. Painting on a stylish image was one thing. Creating a truly stylish pickup was another story entirely.

Chevy's Cameo Carrier easily represents the most significant step up into the world of pizzazz and prestige for the American pickup. It may well stand as the first truck able to play as hard as it worked, although true hard work was clearly never among the intentions for this high-class hauler.

Studebaker began using high-profile two-tone paint schemes to attract fashion-conscious buyers in 1955. Shown here is the 1956 style. *Richard Quinn*

Studebaker may have taken some flack for its 1956 two-tone layout, because its 1957 scheme emerged in far more restrained fashion. *Richard Quinn*

Chevrolet easily deserves credit for introducing this country's first truly classy pickup, the Cameo Carrier, early in 1955. Custom-built fiberglass exterior walls for the bed made all the difference. Full car-line wheel covers and exclusive two-tone paint represented icing on the cake.

The real goal was to make a big splash, something pickup drivers in 1955 weren't accustomed to. Nor had Detroit watchers ever seen anything like it. This pretty pickup looked like the perfect utility vehicle for the "suburbanization" movement then gathering steam in America. It could fit right in, whether down on the farm or up in front of the club. Suddenly city slickers didn't have to be afraid of being seen behind the wheel of—dare we say it?—a pickup truck. At the same time, country folk could feel right proud heading into town in their Sunday-go-to-meeting workhorse.

Honest-to-goodness high style was the key to the Cameo Carrier's appeal. In a reversal of pre-war plans, the Cameo was all pickup up front, partially car-like in back. Unlike previous pick-ups, which carried a typically crude, squared-off cargo box sandwiched between two bulbous "pontoon" fenders, the Cameo's exterior bed walls flowed uninterrupted from cab to bed. Gone, along with the pontoons, were the conventional "steps" behind the cab. In their place were clean, continuous bodysides that echoed the then-fresh "slabside" styling that was all the rage among car designs of the time.

Longtime General Motors Design Executive Charles M. Jordan was the genius behind the idea. Having first joined GM as a young apprentice in late 1949, Chuck Jordan had basically cut his teeth on light-duty truck design, working briefly under Chevrolet truck studio head Luther "Lu" Stier before being called to duty in 1952 as a second lieutenant in the Air Force. As Jordan later recalled, the federal government initially sponsored the Cameo pickup's creation. When not completing assignments in a military art studio at Cape Canaveral in Florida, he would doodle away, putting on paper his ideas for various exceptionally stylish pickup trucks. These were eye-catching, sleek stunners with one-piece cab/bed bodies that easily would be able to compete for a customer's attention right alongside most cars.

Once Jordan returned to Detroit in 1953 it didn't take much to put the wheels in motion. As luck would have it, Stier's crew was already hard at work on Chevrolet's completely modern facelift for the 1955 truck line. All-new ideas were more than welcomed. Stier showed Jordan's drawings to Chevrolet Chief Engineer Ed Cole, who was no stranger to promoting narrowly focused pet projects—he had just finished helping rush the Corvette to market. With Cole's weight behind Jordan's proposal, there was no stopping it.

The resulting design eventually evolved into what Chevrolet in 1958 would call its Fleetside style—"evolved" because things didn't go exactly as Jordan had hoped. Full-sized mockups of his drawings were certainly attractive. But Chevy engineer Jim Premo needed only one look to predict a major shortcoming. An integral cab/bed construction would never work in the real world—at least in Chevrolet's world—as torsional stress on the frame would surely warp that super-smooth sheet metal where the back of the cab and the front of the cargo box met. It was a problem that almost derailed the project right there.

As Lu Stier told *Special Interest Auto* editor Mike Lamm in 1978, "At that point, the division was practically ready to abandon the idea, but our studio insisted we could separate the cab and box without losing the desirable exterior appearance." It was also then that Chevrolet's ever-present beancounters determined the division couldn't afford to produce the smooth-sided cargo box out of steel. "The cost of new tools and dies [would have been] too much for the projected low production volume," Stier remembered. His solution?

"We were then able to convince the division that we could keep the existing stepside box and simply add fiberglass panels flush with the cab sides. We also added a fiberglass cover to the existing tailgate." Saving extra costs by using the existing box structure as a skeleton also helped save the project. As for those fiberglass panels, producing them was no problem, especially since Chevrolet already had a working relationship with the Moulded Fiberglass Company in Ashtabula, Ohio. Moulded Fiberglass' top priority? Corvette bodies, of course. As the joke goes, Chevrolet had a lot of extra fiberglass lying around anyway since Corvette buyers were then staying away in droves.

Once the bed was made, the rest was gravy. Chevrolet's 1955 pickup redesign already included an attractive front end reminiscent of the equally new car-line facade. Present were an egg-crate grille, hooded headlights, and GM's trendy Panoramic wraparound windshield. From there, only the best would do for the Cameo's first appearance, which came in March 1955. Custom Cab features—chrome grille and bumpers, an airy full-width rear window, and extrabright trim inside and out—were standard for the Cameo, as were full wheel covers that also made a connection between pickup and passenger car.

Rearward impressions were especially car-like. The graceful wheel openings in those crisp, clean fiberglass bedsides, that unique rear bumper, and those distinctive taillights all reminded most witnesses of automotive styling touches, as did the fiberglass-clad tailgate with its big red Bow-Tie emblem. The bumper below was as functional as it was stylish—the center section hinged downward to allow access to the Cameo's spare tire. At the other end of the cargo box, a piece of chrome trim was added to help hide the gap between bed and cab.

Completing the Cameo package was an exclusive two-tone paint scheme. Bombay Ivory was the only finish available in 1955; this bright white paint was accented by Cardinal Red touches around the cab's glass. Red paint also graced the wheels and the bed's interior walls. The red-and-white scheme carried over inside the cab, where special upholstery and chrome knobs added to the attraction.

Standard power for the 1955 Cameo Carrier was the proven 235-cid six-cylinder, advertised at

119 horsepower. Chevrolet's brand-new OHV V-8, displacing 265 cubic inches, was an option.

The price for the 1955 Cameo was about $1,900, compared to $1,500 for a standard 3100-series pickup. You might have thought a 30 percent premium would have inhibited the Cameo's appeal—its scope was already limited by the plain fact that probably no one would ever put this polite pickup to work down on the lower 40. Chevrolet nonetheless sold 5,220 Cameos in 1955, numbers that to no one would sneeze at. But popularity quickly waned from there. Seven optional paint schemes joined the traditional Bombay Ivory and Cardinal Red combination for a nearly identical Cameo encore in 1956, when only 1,452 were sold. Even more paint schemes were offered the following year as sales jumped to 2,244.

By then Ford had already begun cutting in on Chevrolet with its first slabside pickup, the 1957 Styleside, a truck that offered a bit of the Cameo's sleek flair at a much lower price and in a form better suited to what utility vehicles did best: utilize their cargo capacities. No one ever worried about banging a milk can over the steel bedsides of a Styleside pickup. Chevy then responded with its stylish steel-bodied Fleetside in 1958.

With the readily affordable, ready-to-work Fleetside on the scene, it became obvious Chevrolet would no longer have a place for its highly modified, high-priced, high-profile pickup. The Cameo Carrier's work was done. When the ax fell

Car-style taillights were a Cameo trademark. The contrasting two-tone trim was added to the bed in 1957.

Dodge copied Chevy's Cameo ideal in 1957, introducing the Sweptside. These "half-truck, half-cars" were built for three years and were powered by either an L-head six or a V-8. This 1957 Sweptside has the 314-cid V-8. Those are actually 1957 Dodge station wagon rear quarters, complete with high-flying fins and "signal-tower" taillights. Wedged between that stylish sheet metal is a typical Dodge pickup cargo box.

midyear in 1958, the final tally for the fourth-edition Cameo read 1,405.

Diminishing sales figures, however, didn't tell the true tale of the Cameo's success. Classifying the Cameo Carrier as a big hit involved not so much how it alone behaved in the marketplace, but more of how the market itself changed once this prestigious pickup had made its first impression. The Cameo not only inspired rival knockoffs, it also led to a rethinking of the basic pickup package. Although the addition of a smooth-sided cargo box may not look like much from a turn-of-the-millennium perspective, those simply stylized responses from Ford and International in 1957 represented the humble beginnings for the long-developing trend that has made the modern American pickup what it is today—a classy combination of pizzazz, performance, and practicality. Chevrolet's Cameo indeed helped usher in a new age.

Yet another competitive response to Chevy's car-styled truck came from Chrysler Corporation in 1957. Sagging sales had left the boys at Dodge watching on the sidelines as the pickup market pulled away from them in the 1950s. The division's restyle for 1957 was the first step toward catching back up. But something more, something truly special was needed to draw attention

the way the high-profile Cameo had. Dodge, however, didn't have the deep pockets of Chevy, nor did it have Chuck Jordan. What Dodge did have was the Special Equipment Group, managed by a clever idea guy named Joe Berr.

The SEG was where Dodge truck buyers could go for special treatment. Fleet sales represented the group's prime target market, but individuals could also have their needs met by the SEG. Beefed frames, heavy-duty wheels and tires, driveline modifications—whatever the request, if it helped make a sale, the men of the SEG were ready, willing, and able to make it happen.

As head of the SEG, Berr was clearly no stranger to custom-built special orders. He was also keenly aware of his company's dire need to keep up with the Joneses. Although a costly retool was out of the question, especially in light of the recent effort expended on the new 1957 front end, it was clear the old cargo box with its typical pontoon fenders wouldn't stand a chance running up against those attractive new Fords and Chevrolets.

Berr's solution to Dodge's dilemma was incredibly simple—and wonderfully inexpensive. The first step involved pulling the bulbous rear fenders off a standard 116-inch-wheelbase D100 pickup. Next, he paid a visit to Dodge's main assembly plant, where he copped a pair of 1957 Suburban station wagon rear quarter panels, along with the bumper. SEG employee Burt Nagos then welded the passenger car sheet metal to the truck bed, resulting in a custom pickup that might've made even George Barris proud. Dodge called it "Sweptside."

The Suburban wagon's bumper and rear quarters, complete with fins and "signal tower" taillights, amazingly fit as if they belonged. Doing away with the passenger car fuel filler door and adding trim to the cab to match the existing Suburban beltline brightwork was no sweat. The only hard work involved cutting down the D100's tailgate to fit between the station wagon fins. Though a little more imagination could've been used to help the Sweptside's patchwork tailgate match its snazzy surroundings, you can't blame Berr and crew, knowing the budget they were working with—next to nothing. "Afterthought" represents high praise for their closing efforts, a fact made painfully clear when looking from dead-on behind. But from a profile view, the Sweptside impressed many witnesses with its clever combination of high-flying automotive styling and Dodge truck toughness.

Introduced in May 1957, the Sweptside pickup was all D100 half-ton truck up front. Two-tone paint, full wheel covers, and a chrome-plated front bumper to match the rear completed the Sweptside package. "Straight out of tomorrow," bragged brochures, although beneath the skin, a 1957 Sweptside was still a basic 1957 Dodge pickup. Spartan cab appointments didn't exactly bring 'em running in from the fields. However, a small collection of comfort and convenience options did help spruce things up a bit for those willing to open their wallets a little wider.

A push-button Loadflite three-speed automatic transmission (a Torqueflite specially prepared for truck use), power steering and brakes, a Custom Cab, and wide whitewalls were prime promoters of the Sweptside image. Custom Cab equipment included dual armrests and sun visors (Standard cabs accounted for only the driver), a locking glovebox (Standard owners apparently kept their gloves on for safe-keeping), a rayon-covered foam rubber seat cushion (Standard drivers sat on cotton sisal), two-speed wipers, and trendy wraparound rear glass.

Standard Sweptsides were powered by the yeoman 230-cid L-head six. Optional power came from the healthy 204-horsepower 314-cid Power-Dome "polyhead" V-8, priced at $105. This engine inspired brochures to again brag, this time of "the most V-8 power of the low-priced three." "Polyhead" referred to the polyspherical combustion chambers, which fell somewhere between the standard wedge design and the famed "hemi-head" with its hemispherical chambers.

It could brag all it wanted, but promotional paperwork still couldn't convince Dodge customers to buy a truck disguised as a car. Unlike Chevy's Cameo, the Sweptside never did attract a following. Although high price and limited function did play a role (again, would you want to ding those fins?), so too did the plain fact that

not all that many buyers were flocking into Dodge truck dealerships to begin with in the late 1950s. Blaming the Sweptside alone for the weak response isn't entirely fair. Dodge officials apparently recognized this, as they came back with a second-edition Sweptside in 1958. Reality then took over and they quietly discontinued the intriguing design in January 1959.

As it was, Dodge by 1959 had its own standard-issue stylish pickup, the Sweptline, to compete with all those smooth-sided rivals then out strutting their stuff. Dodge's Sweptside, along with Chevrolet's Cameo, were soon forgotten as the 1960s marched on. But adding more and more class into the light-duty truck equation continued on. More comfort and more convenience also began entering the pickup picture, leading up to today's multipurpose vehicles, which are now able to work hard, play hard, and make the neighbors jealous with a vengeance.

Are we spoiled or what?

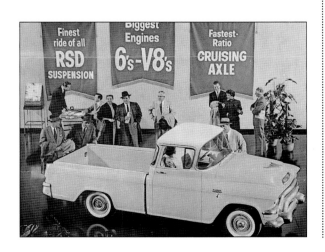

Dodge quietly discontinued its Sweptside pickup early in 1959. *Chrysler Historical Collection*

A GMC rendition of Chevrolet's classy Cameo, the Suburban, was offered with Pontiac powertrains.

Chevrolet proved in 1955 just how well a touch of car-line class could transform a workaholic pickup truck into an out-of-this-world dream machine. Dodge then demonstrated how easy it always has been in Detroit to snatch another's great idea and take it for a trip on the wild side. Dodge's Sweptside pickup of 1957 looked more like something out of a Buck Rogers sci-fi flick, less like a forward-thinking sign of things to come. Perhaps the lesson learned here was that a manufacturer should be more careful choosing candidates when trying to mate car with truck. Or was it that it just might have been wiser to mate truck with car?

Ford had stood curiously by when Chevrolet first tried mixing and matching pickup practicality and passenger-car prestige. In 1955 Dearborn officials were just two years into resting on their laurels, these delivered by their headline-making F-100. Why try to fix a milestone?

Actually Ford at the time was considering a response to the Cameo's appearance; it just wasn't a direct response. There would be no jumping on Chevrolet's glamorous bandwagon, no upscale copycat model like Dodge's Sweptside. Dearborn designers did take note of the Cameo's trend-setting flush-sided cargo box. Ford's Styleside, unveiled in 1957, did replicate that look and dared others to follow. But this restyled model was simply a typical F-100 with a modernized bed. Although the Styleside did one-up Chevy in the mainstream, it was left to an entirely different breed of utility vehicle to put Ford back on the front page.

This new breed also debuted in 1957. Ford called it "Ranchero." Average Joes on the street weren't quite sure how to describe it. Was it a truck that looked like a car? Or was it a car that worked like a truck? Was the intention to allow the working man a touch of class? Or was the goal to let higher-class buyers do their own personal hauling in place of the hired help?

Any way you looked at it, this better idea from Ford was a good one, if proven only by pure longevity. Rancheros appeared annually for 23 years. Along with that, this half-breed also inspired an almost immediate copycat response from Chevrolet, the El Camino. Debuting in 1959, Chevy's "car-truck" did even better, surviving through 27 model runs, although not consecutively—the El Camino went on vacation in 1961. Returning to the road in 1964, the second-generation El Camino rolled on with great success until shrinking sales finally convinced Chevrolet decision-makers in 1987 to close the tailgate. Official production actually ended during the 1988 model year, with only 420 El Caminos built in a brief run. This end came a decade after Ford had retired its Ranchero in 1979.

Transformations were common during both long careers. After three years as a full-sized model, the Ranchero was reborn in 1960 as a variation of Ford's all-new compact Falcon. In 1967 the Ranchero jumped up a notch into Dearborn's intermediate ranks, first as a Fairlane, then a Torino (until 1977), and finally an LTD II. Like its rival, Chevy's El Camino was also

WHEN CAR MET TRUCK

FORD'S RANCHERO AND CHEVROLET'S EL CAMINO

Ford designers simply sawed off the roof of a 1957 two-door station wagon to create the first Ranchero—it was almost that simple.

Many critics felt Chevrolet's copycat response to the Ranchero, the 1959 El Camino, came off a bit more stylish than its rival. It too was the product of "de-roofing" a two-door station wagon. *Robert Ackerson collection and Chevrolet Motor Division*

Chevrolet stuck with its full-sized El Camino into 1960, even as Ford was downsizing its Ranchero into a Falcon model. The El Camino was then retired temporarily while a new plan was put into action. *Robert Ackerson collection and Chevrolet Motor Division*

born a full-sized model, then was downsized upon its return in 1964 when GM's all-new A-body intermediate was introduced. The fresh, exciting midsized Chevelle was joined by a similarly adorned El Camino running mate, a sporty utility vehicle that quickly soared in popularity, outselling its Ford counterpart by at least a 2–1 margin almost every year.

GMC also offered an El Camino variant, first the Sprint, debuting in 1971, then the Caballero, introduced in 1978. GMC's Caballero carried on through 1988, too, with the final tally that year reading only 325.

From a numbers perspective, the copy easily stole the show from the original. Including 36,576 Sprints and 37,719 Caballeros from GMC, total El Camino production surpassed 1 million by 56,424 units. Ford's record showed "only" 508,355 Rancheros: 45,814 of the

1957–1959 models; 139,694 Falcons; and 322,847 for the rest. Both Ford and Chevrolet hit their peak in 1973, with 45,741 Rancheros and 64,987 El Caminos rolling off the line. Sprint production, at 6,766, also reached a high that year. GMC's actual zenith came in 1979 when 6,952 Caballeros were built.

Thirty years and 1.5 million vehicles, who would have thought it? Certainly not Ford officials in 1957. No one then could've predicted such a long, successful run for such an unproven entity. At the time, Dearborn executives had proven themselves more than willing to briefly dabble in specialty-car shenanigans, more or less on a whim, then move on. Consider the 'glass-top Mercurys and Fords of 1954–1956, those fabulous two-seat Thunderbirds, and the gizmo-crazy retractable-hardtop Skyliner of 1957–1959. Hit and run appeared to be the marketing tactic here.

Who was to say similar intentions didn't apply to the first Ranchero? Was there really a need for a car able to work like a truck? Did late-1950s buyers want to split the difference between automobile and pickup? Or were the original Rancheros and El Caminos simply the latest curiosities in a long line of 1950s fads and fantasies? Did they only survive initially because they inspired trend-conscious customers to be the first on their blocks to show off Detroit's newest, coolest creation?

Any worries about skeptics accepting this new breed were undoubtedly eased by the fact that this multipurpose machine would be so easy to build. Like Chevrolet's later response, the Ranchero was not much more than a two-door station wagon with its rear roof area chiseled away to reveal the pickup-style cargo bay always hidden within. Michelangelo couldn't have done it any better. A tailgate was already present. The job appeared so easy, why not just do it? Start-up costs were so low Ford simply couldn't lose, regardless of whether or not a solid market materialized.

But that market did show up, albeit not all that solidly, for both Ford and Chevrolet. As Chevy's Assistant General Sales Manager

Albert Olson, Jr., described it in 1959, the El Camino was a response to a need on the West Coast for a "comfortable pickup." Potential customers would include businesses serving higher-class clientele, those who recognized that image was everything. Wealthier, high-placed customers who might need a truck but demanded convenience, class, and style were also targeted. Of course even as Olson was making these claims, Ford had already tested the market and returned to the drawing board.

Dearborn's initial assumptions two years before had read much the same as Olson's. As Pickups and Vans' Spence Murray wrote in 1972 about the Ranchero's introduction, "A need had been instantly created for a utilitarian, around-town light-duty truck with a sporty automotive flair." Continued Murray, "establishments that delighted in putting up a strong front grabbed Rancheros for one-upping their commercial rivals. Service stations wanted a fleet, handsome errand-runner, and repair shops and other trades felt a yen for a practical

GMC rolled out its own El Camino, called the Sprint, in 1971. Shown here is a 1973 Sprint Sport (thus the "SS" grille badge) armed with a 454-cid big-block V-8.

A Royal Knight El Camino was a real head-turner, but the beauty of this bad, black 1981 model runs more than skin-deep. It is equipped with the rare V-8/four-speed combination.

Chevy's El Camino returned for 1964 based on the new A-body Chevelle platform. The midsized El Camino quickly soared in popularity.

This 1965 show vehicle represents the only El Camino that year to hit the streets with Chevy's new 396-cid Mark IV big-block V-8. Chevrolet did build 201 SS 396 Chevelles for 1965, but regular-production El Caminos didn't receive an optional big-block until 1966.

That crossed-flag fender emblem identifies this 1967 El Camino as a 396-equipped model. El Caminos in 1966 and 1967 could've been equipped with all the Chevelle SS 396's equipment except the exterior identification.

service vehicle that wouldn't be an eyesore among a background of high-priced passenger cars."

Indeed the need for such vehicles did exist, but filling it was a matter of determining just how much the market could stand. How much size, how much capacity, how much price. As both Ford and Chevrolet people discovered, bigger

wasn't necessarily better—perhaps in this case because carrying a really big load wasn't what potential customers had in mind. Nor was spending a lot of money on a vehicle that could straddle the fence between the car and truck worlds but couldn't really stand tall on its own solely on either side. Rancheros and El Caminos found true success once they settled into a comfortable niche, a place all their own where expectations weren't all that great, where the jobs weren't all that tough.

Once established, the Ranchero and El Camino represented more icing than cake. Throughout their long careers, they served their masters best in figurehead roles. Each looked nice showing off company logos on their doors while the boss toured jobsites hauling along nothing more than a clipboard. Neither really was ever capable of working all that hard. Even with optional heavy-duty suspensions, their passenger-car heritages still prevailed. Recreational usages and household chores basically represented the limit as far as earning their due was concerned.

Both were still cars, too. Many customers simply chose a Ranchero or El Camino as attractive everyday transportation with no intentions of ever putting them to work. And why not? This two-timing pair could always impress with their good looks as easily as their car-line counterparts, which were no help at all should a stray washer and dryer ever want for a new home.

They could also supply some certified status when fully loaded down with all the bells and whistles. Comfort and convenience options were plentiful, as was performance on occasion. It was possible in 1957 to fit Ford's first Ranchero with either of the Thunderbird's hottest 312 V-8s, one fed by twin four-barrel carburetors, the other topped by a supercharger. Available beneath an El Camino's hood in 1959 was an optional tri-carb 348 V-8, the formidable forerunner to Chevy's fabled 409. Later Ranchero variants included GT models armed with muscular Cobra Jet big-block V-8s or red-hot Cleveland small-blocks. Chevrolet also offered the El Camino in SS 396 or SS 454 in the 1960s and 1970s.

Both Chevy and Ford traded horsepower for imagery once high performance began fading away in the early 1970s. Two-tone paint, tape stripes, and simulated woodsides took over. Although not nearly as powerful as their original renditions, Ranchero GTs and El Camino Super Sports also hung around right up to the end. Less popular appearance packages included the El Camino's Conquista paint option, offered from 1974 to 1977. Chevy's Royal Knight and GMC's Diablo emerged in 1978, each featuring a large Trans Am-inspired hood decal. High-profile promotions from Ford included the White Sales Special in 1971 and Explorer in 1976. The end of the road for the Ranchero in 1979 was also commemorated with a Limited Production model, a dressed-up variant that acknowledged its owner with an exclusive exterior plate engraved with his or her initials.

By the 1970s, Ranchero and El Camino buyers were long past questioning how such frivolities as vinyl roofs, air conditioners, and eight-track players fit into the equation, a contrasting relationship that supposedly involved a working partner. These two vehicles, of course, were never meant to be all work and no play. On the contrary, it was their playfulness that helped make them so popular.

And to think buyers in 1957 didn't even know they would want the comfort of a car combined with the practicality of a pickup. It was left to the original Ranchero to convince them. Luckily Ford already had some experience mating trucks with cars.

Like various other early American light-duty pickups, Henry Ford's Model T and Model A trucks were nothing more than car-line noses trailing a cargo box in back. Ford in 1931 even created a stylish pickup with a one-piece cab/box body. Listed as type 66-A, this rare truck was built (with the aid of the Briggs Body Company) for General Electric as part of a new refrigerator promotion, explaining why all 293 examples sold were painted bright white.

Car-style noses were still found on Ford's half-ton trucks as late as 1941. And other similar combinations carried over after World War II. Light-duty pickups from Studebaker, Nash, Willys, and Hudson-Terraplane during the years 1936 to 1948 would all resemble their automotive counterparts from their cabs forward. Less memorable was the crop of business coupes carrying small cargo boxes in their

Few noticed when Ford created an integral cab/bed body for this 1931 pickup, built specifically as part of a General Electric refrigerator promotion. Less than 300 were produced. Its model code, 66-A, would later reappear as a Ranchero designation. *Ford Motor Company*

trunks. Plymouth and Chevrolet tried this combination in 1936. Ford's "Tailbox" business coupe conversion debuted in 1937, as did the Terraplane utility coupe.

More significant to the historical progression of the "comfortable pickup" was the "Ute," Ford of Australia's legendary half-breed introduced Down Under in the 1930s. The target market here consisted of Aussie ranchers and farmers, who soon shortened the vehicle's official "Utility" label into its more affectionate moniker.

Ford's passenger-car-line restyle for 1958 carried over to the Ranchero, but only in front. The 1957-style tail remained, as designers apparently didn't want to fret with splitting the new 1958 taillights for the Ranchero's tailgate. *Ford Motor Company*

Yet another restyle, this one for both ends, graced the 1959 Ranchero, the last of the full-sized breed. *Ford Motor Company*

Utes originally were Ford roadster car bodies joined to a flush-mounted cargo box, a combo reminiscent of the 1931 "General Electric" pickup. A Ute coupe appeared in 1933 and soldiered on up through 1958. The topless variety was dropped after 1938. Utes marketed in Australia after 1958 were based on the American-style Ranchero.

Unlike the Ranchero, the original Australian Ute was a no-nonsense workhorse. Yet in its lack of refinement, the Ute helped demonstrate that the whole car/truck thing was by no means rocket science. Accordingly, designing the original Ranchero was a piece of cake.

No, legendary Cord designer Gordon Buehrig did not do the honors. Buehrig was responsible for Ford's first modern steel-bodied station wagon, the 1952 Ranch Wagon, an accomplishment he was more than willing to take credit for. Commercial vehicles he left to his underlings, one of whom first sketched a car-truck proposal when Ford's new 1952 line-up was being drawn up. This concoction mimicked the Ute but had more style and flair. In Dearborn it was named the "Roo Chaser." Persistent rumors named Buehrig as the man behind the Roo Chaser. Not true. Buehrig himself denied any ties to the Ranchero.

It seemed Ford's brain trust was put off by the idea as much as Buehrig. At first. They shot the Roo Chaser down in its tracks. Then along came Robert McNamara, who was made Ford Division general manager in early 1955. Later considered too conservative, McNamara was willing early on to go where few automakers had gone before. The division's 1957 restyle was then under way when he took the general manager seat, a situation that opened the door for creative opportunities. The retractable-roof Skyliner was one result. The Ranchero was another.

Simply fashioned from Ford's 1957 two-door wagon, the first Ranchero shared the wagon's tailgate, rear compartment subfloor (hidden beneath the cargo box floor), and wheelbase. At 116 inches, the Ranchero's front-to-rear stride was 2 inches less than the 1957 Fairlane's.

Almost everything else was pure 1957 Ford, right down to those round taillights and short fins in back.

Major differences, of course, included the truncated roofline and the cargo bed found between the nicely sculptured rear quarter panels. Among sheet metal stampings unique to the Ranchero were the roof, upper cab panel (with its exclusive rear window), double-walled cargo box, bed floor, and tailgate inner panel.

The spare tire location was also unique. It was behind the seat on the passenger's side, where it displaced valuable, lockable interior storage space. Some clever Ranchero drivers had a better idea. Remember, the station wagon's rear substructure was still there beneath the Ranchero's bolted-down bed floor. Part of that structure contained the wagon's spare tire mounting area. By rigging up a hinge, or simply undoing all those bolts, a Ranchero owner could stow his spare where it belonged, freeing up precious in-cab storage area.

Stowing other cargo was made possible by 32.4 cubic feet of bed in back. Bed length measured 8 feet with the gate dropped, payload capacity was 1,190 pounds, and maximum gross vehicle weight was 4,600 pounds. Ford classed the 1957 Ranchero as a half-ton pickup.

Promotional people called it "America's first work or play truck." Public introduction came on November 12, 1956, in Quitman, a rural community just west of Valdosta in southern Georgia. There, Ford public relations people awarded a 1957 Ranchero to Wesley Patrick, a

Like its El Camino rival, the Ranchero took on some serious sporty appeal in the late 1960s. Real performance was also offered in the form of the optional Cobra Jet big-block V-8. A Ranchero GT also emerged to do battle with the Super Sport El Camino. Ford's 1971 utility line-up, showcased here, demonstrates the Ranchero GT's aggressive good looks. *Ford Motor Company*

"Star Farmer" then being honored by the Future Farmers of America. From Dearborn's perspective, a young farmer like Patrick was the perfect choice as the first Ranchero owner. Wesley, however, felt otherwise. He quickly traded his four-wheeled FFA award for a 1957 Ford passenger car.

Paying customers could chose from two different Rancheros in 1957, the yeoman standard model and upscale Custom. The base prices were $2,098 for the Ranchero and $2,149 for the Custom Ranchero. The Custom Ranchero, in typical fashion, was treated to extra interior appointment choices and a more distinctive exterior, thanks to the addition of the Custom 300's body-length trim spear. Along with the trim came the optional Style Tone paint scheme. Colonial White went on top of the spear; below was a choice of 11 different shades. Since standard Rancheros had no trim, they only came in solid colors. In 1957, Custom sales dominated, 15,277 to 6,418, demonstrating that the Ranchero's appeal probably involved more play than work.

Practically everything a Ford car buyer wanted in 1957 was available as a Ranchero option, including air conditioning, power steering and brakes, and electric seat and windows. The 144-horsepower 223-cid "Mileage Maker" six-cylinder backed by a three-speed manual transmission was standard. Overdrive or a Ford-O-Matic automatic were also available at extra cost, as were two V-8s, a 190-horsepower 272-cid powerplant or its stroked, 212-horsepower 292-cid running mate.

All these parts added up to a sum worthy of high marks in press critics' opinions. "For the person who has always wanted a pickup," opened Motor Life's July 1957 report, "but is balked by the looks or riding qualities inherent in normal trucks, Ford has come to the rescue." As Motor Trend's Walt Woron put it, "the Ranchero gives the room and 'personal' feel of a Thunderbird, the comfort of a sedan, and the load-carrying capacity of a small pickup." Woron also touted the Ranchero's ability to appease both the frugal (with its six-cylinder fuel economy) and the fast-thinking (with optional 292 V-8 power). A prestige factor was mentioned, too. "Any company that needs a pickup could do much worse than advertise its name on the side of a Ranchero," concluded Motor Life's review.

Compliments may have been plentiful, but customer responses weren't nearly so. After a great start, the Ranchero stalled in its second year. Sales for 1958 fell by 50 percent to 1,471 for Ranchero, 8,479 for Custom Ranchero. A national economic recession was mostly to blame. But marketing strategies probably didn't help matters. The Ranchero looked like a car and drove much like a car, yet it was sold through Ford's Truck Division and was promoted primarily in truck brochures. Perhaps Dearborn should not have tried to attract pickup buyers to a car that could work a little like a truck, but instead have turned its attentions to car customers looking for the best of both worlds.

Ford did try to turn customers' heads in 1958 with fresh, Thunderbird-inspired styling, although only up front. The 1957 tail carried over into 1958, just as it did for the sedan delivery line on which the Ranchero was based. Ford designers apparently didn't want to mess with running pesky weatherproof wiring into the tailgate for the inner halves of the new 1958 taillights. Fortunately engineers weren't so willing to sit on their hands. New drivetrain features for 1958 included an optional 352 V-8 and a Cruise-O-Matic three-speed automatic transmission.

Ford's original Ranchero ran one more year before the flag was transferred to the compact Falcon. Another restyle appeared in 1959 and the wheelbase went from 116 inches to 118. A 7-inch-longer cargo bed, a trendy compound-curve windshield, a new optional 332-cid V-8, and a "floating star" grille were the main attractions. A Custom Ranchero, priced at $2,312, was the only model offered in 1959.

Longer and leaner, the third-edition Ranchero did revive interest. Production for 1959 jumped to 14,169. The future, how-ever, was already predetermined. The all-new down-sized Ranchero was by then waiting in the wings. As it was, what appeared to be a positive sales gain for Ford's car-truck ended up becoming lost in the shadows cast by a competitive response from Chevrolet. Walt Woron had seen this coming in 1957. "I'll go on record with a proclamation that the Ranchero will be copied in principle by other manufacturers," he wrote. "It's too good to pass up."

Once Ford got the ball rolling, Chevrolet had no choice but to kick it back. In typical disregard for the facts, Chevy's promotional people called their 1959 response "the brightest new idea of the year." New idea, eh? Even its Spanish name—"El Camino," "the road" to you Yankees—was an unabashed knockoff of Ford's south-of-the-border-sounding name.

As much as the El Camino was an obvious copy, a lot could be said about Chevrolet doing Ford's idea one better. Introduced to the public on October 16, 1958, the 1959 El Camino was comparable to the 1959 Ranchero with an advertised maximum payload of 1,150 pounds. Although Ranchero's bed was longer, El Camino's was wider.

What gave the first El Camino an edge involved first impressions. Most critics picked the Chevy over the Ford in the image category. "Good looks never carried so much weight," claimed Chevy brochures. Forget for a moment what most innocent bystanders have long said about Chevy's 1959 styling effort, which even the late Claire MacKichan later apologized for, telling Automobile Quarterly in 1983 that "we just went farther than we should have." Many witnesses felt Chevrolet designers managed to combine car and truck features in a more pleasing fashion. According to a May 1959 Motor Life review, "while the El Camino resembles a passenger car in every way, except for the short cab and stylish pickup bed, even the cab has rakish lines—more so, one might say, than the Ranchero, inasmuch as the rear window is not squared off but has a graceful forward slope."

Indeed, the Ranchero's "squared off" cab appeared more like an afterthought than an integral styling element. El Caminos, on the other hand, were crowned by an attractive, airy "greenhouse," a cab featuring expansive glass area and minimal posts at the four corners. Mimicking the "flyaway" roofline of the four-door Impala Sport Sedan, the El Camino's cab also featured GM's distinctive rear roof overhang and sloping, wraparound rear glass.

From the cab down, the first El Camino was pure 1959 Chevrolet with the obvious exception of the bed in back. The rear quarter sheet metal and tailgate came from the two-door Brookwood wagon, the long sidespear was a Bel Air piece, and the high-flying fins were seemingly not from this world. Ford stylists called the redesigned 1959 Chevy a "Martian Ground Chariot," kicking off a long line of jokes and gags starring what was probably Chevrolet's wildest creation ever. But whether you hated the look or loved it, you had to admit 1959 Chevys did turn heads wherever they went—on this planet, or any other.

Critics might've also been forced to admit there was something different about how the controversial sheet metal fit the El Camino form. Maybe it was the abbreviated cab, an arrangement that allowed the sweeping horizontal fins more room to stretch back and less

The last Falcon-based Ranchero was built for 1966, by which time Ford officials no longer wanted to associate the breed with frugality. In 1967 the Ranchero moved on up to the midsized Fairlane line. *Ford Motor Company*

Dearborn closed out the Ranchero run with a special Limited Production model in 1979. About 1,000 of these were built with special color-keyed trim and leather interior appointments. Customers got a choice between wire wheel covers, Magnum 500 five-spokes, or these turbine wheels.

opportunity to stick out like sore thumbs. Maybe it was the truck-style bed, which also helped draw attention away from those "batwings." Whatever the case, many kibitzers liked the look. As Motor Life's judge and jury pointed out, the 1959 El Camino's "gull-wing fins blend in with the pickup bed better, perhaps, than they do with any other body style in the Chevy line."

Beneath that look was Chevrolet's rigid X-member chassis with coil springs at all four corners, a design introduced for 1958. El Camino updates included station wagon rear springs and shocks, while all 1959 Chevys got a revamped rear suspension featuring a new upper control arm layout, an additional frame cross-member, and a lateral anti-sway bar. Overall, the 1959 El Camino was still softly sprung, a concession to the passenger car side of its split personality. Body roll was considerable in the turns and load capacity wasn't all that great. Motor Life reported a noticeable squat with the bed full of 700 pounds, more than enough weight to induce bottoming out of the suspension over even the smallest bumps. Although heavier springs were available at extra cost, the trade-off was a distinctive forward rake, something long-time

pickup owners were well acquainted with, but a stance not all car buyers would've settled for.

Car buyers might've also been disappointed by the El Camino's standard interior, which carried on in the best Spartan truck-like tradition. The basic gray upholstery was blah at best, and typical car-like conveniences like armrests, padded dash, a right side sun visor, foam-filled seats, automatic interior light, and a cigarette lighter were not included unless the customer forked over a few extra bucks. These missing items would've been no big deal as far as a practical-minded owner interested in putting the El Camino's utility to good use was concerned. But many interested parties among the newly formed car-truck market didn't look at Chevrolet's contribution to the trend from that perspective. They considered it instead a vehicle along the lines of the Cameo Carrier, a classy pickup more at home carrying clubs to the front nine than spreading manure on the lower 40.

Not helping the situation at all was the 1959 El Camino's price tag, which started out at about $2,500—a definite jump up from your average pickup. Adding to that bottom line was a host of powertrain choices, including everything available to your average Impala buyer, from the basic 235-cid thrifty six, to the tried-and-true 283-cid small-block V-8, all the way up to the hot-blooded 348 "W-head" big-block. Transmission choices were equally wide, beginning with the standard three-speed manual. Overdrive, a four-speed with Chevrolet's first passenger-car floor shifter, and the two automatics, Powerglide and Turboglide, waited just one optional check-off away. Clearly, driving off the lot with a $3,000 El Camino in 1959 was a strong possibility if loading up was the buyer's intention.

Chevrolet's potent 348 could transform a 1959 El Camino from a polite pickup into a hell-for-leather hauler in a hurry. In basic form fed by a single four-barrel carburetor, the Turbo Thrust 348 V-8 injected 250 horses into the equation, while at the top of the pecking order was the tri-carb Super Turbo Thrust, a V-8 "almost too potent for normal driving," according to Motor

Life. Fed by three Rochester two-barrels, the muscle-bound Super Turbo Thrust 348 featured 11:1 compression, a solid-lifter "Duntov" cam and various beefed internals. Output was 315 horsepower at 5,600 rpm, more than enough muscle to make some serious hay.

Hot Rod's Ray Brock did just that, putting a 315-horsepower El Camino fitted with a floor-shifted four-speed and 3.36:1 gears through its paces. Limited severely by poor traction primarily due to the El Camino's nose-heavy 57/43 weight bias, Brock's test subject still dashed through the quarter mile in 16 seconds, topping out at about 90 miles per hour. Driving the same El Camino, *Motor Life* recorded a 0–60 clocking of 8 seconds, at the time outstanding performance in anyone's field. Potential promised even more. "With a gear ratio of about 4.55 to 1 and the optional positraction differential," wrote Brock, "this car would break 100 miles per hour in the quarter and come close to 14 seconds flat."

Performance, practicality, or pizzazz; it was your choice. As for Blue Oval or Bow-Tie, more than half as many more customers preferred the El Camino over the Ranchero in 1959. Chevrolet sales hit 22,246 that first year. But like Ford, Chevy also quickly encountered slow going. El Camino production for 1960 fell by 50 percent to 14,163. Chevrolet then copied Ford again, returning to its own drawing board after 1960.

That the first El Caminos and Rancheros rode down dead ends was by no means a matter of a risky proposition not finding a market. This was more a story of a good idea being released slightly ahead of its time in a form slightly off target. Customers probably first came running to see what all the fuss was about. Once they grew tired, once the novelty wore off, the attraction was over. Short attention spans prevailed.

Attitudes changed in the 1960s. Form had tended to dominate function in the 1950s. Bigger was apparently better. A new decade introduced a new trend bent more toward practical application and cost-consciousness. Less was now more. Compacts like Chevy's Corvair and Ford's Falcon were the new craze,

as were multiple model lines offering widely varied prices and appeals. Chevrolet by 1964 had five such stair-stepped lines.

This newfound market segmentation gave the car-truck breed a second life. Affordability became Ford's latest, greatest selling point. Using the same model designation (66A) as the 1931 "General Electric" pickup, the all-new Falcon Ranchero debuted for 1960 with a base price of less than $1,900. "New way to vacation . . . Great way to save!" was the advertising claim. So too was 30 miles per gallon from the Falcon Ranchero's only available power source, a 90-horsepower 144-cid six-cylinder.

The 1960 Ranchero was 19 inches shorter that its full-sized forerunner. Its wheelbase was 109.5 inches. Its cargo box was 6 feet long—8 feet with the gate down. Cargo volume was 31.6 cubic-feet, advertised payload was 800 pounds.

Creature comforts were also on the short side, just what you'd have expected from a compact budget buggy. But even though pizzazz and prestige were traded for pure practicality, reborn Ranchero popularity quickly blossomed. Falcon Rancheros sold like clockwork at about 20,000 a year. The best results came in 1966, when 21,760 hit the road.

Falcon Ranchero refinements came steadily as the 1960s progressed. An optional 101-horsepower 170-cid six-cylinder arrived in 1961. An optional V-8, the 164-horsepower 260-cid Windsor small-block, was added two years later, along with a fully synchronized four-speed transmission. Classier inside and out, a Deluxe Ranchero also debuted in 1963. Freshened styling and a third model—a Deluxe with the Ranchero's first bucket seats—appeared in 1964. Model choices expanded to four in 1965, as both standard and Deluxe versions came with or without buckets. A more powerful 225-horsepower 289 V-8 replaced its smaller Windsor brother that year, too.

The last Falcon Ranchero came in 1966, although many have commonly mistaken this one for Ford's first midsized car-truck. Nameplates didn't help. While all 1960–1965 models were officially tagged "Falcon Rancheros," the slightly larger and flashier 1966 version was simply labeled "Ranchero." Dearborn's image-makers by then wanted to cut all ties to the budget-conscious compact crowd.

By 1966 the Ranchero wasn't so compact anyway thanks to some chassis shuffling. The 1966 Falcon rolled on a 110.9-inch wheelbase; the midsized Fairlane's was 116. Meanwhile, both Falcon and Fairlane station wagons shared a 113-inch chassis. Since Rancheros had always been based on Ford station wagons, the longer 113-inch wheelbase became the platform of choice for 1966. Complicating matters were exterior styling touches that appeared more Fairlane than Falcon.

Ford's half-breed did become a full-fledged Fairlane in 1967, meaning Ranchero and El Camino were direct rivals once more, this time in the intermediate field. Chevrolet had reintroduced its El Camino as part of its midsized A-body line-up in 1964, a downsizing move nowhere near as radical as Ford's in 1960. The Chevelle-based El Camino technically was now a notch below Chevy's full-sized ranks. But the 1964 model still compared favorably with its 1959–1960 forefather. Although weight and wheelbase were down, the cargo box was actually larger both in length and height. The maximum payload was 1,200 pounds.

The 1964 El Camino's base price was $2,276 with a six, $100 more with the 283 V-8. Another $80 bought a classier Custom El Camino. Total production was 36,615 that first year, more than double the 1964 Ranchero's figure.

El Camino appeal continued growing, especially so once more and more performance began piling on. Almost everything muscle car buyers found in their SS Chevelles was available as an El Camino option by 1966. This included the hot 396-cid big-block V-8, which could supply 375 horses in top form. Exceptions included Super Sport nomenclature. Even though a 396 V-8 may have been beneath the hood, El Caminos didn't gain full "SS 396" status until 1968.

Sales of the 1968 SS 396 El Camino reached 5,190. Total production went up 20 percent from 1967's figure to 41,791, then an all-time high. By 1969, the high had reached 48,385. In 1970 the SS 454 joined the SS 396 El Camino, leading to a new high for performance. Most SS 454 El Caminos were equipped with the 360-horsepower LS-5 big-block. But a meager few featured the 450-horse LS-6 454, commonly considered the top dog among the performance powerplants of Detroit's muscle car era.

The El Camino's rise up the prestige and performance pecking order left Ford no choice but to follow. Newfound prestige for the Ranchero in 1967 came by way of the classy Fairlane Ranchero 500 with its extrabright trim outside. Another step up was the Fairlane Ranchero 500 XL, which featured sporty bucket seats and a console inside. Optional performance was supplied by a 390-cid big-block V-8.

The Fairlane reference was dropped in 1968 and the top-line XL was traded for the Ranchero GT, a sporty machine wearing high-profile badges, stripes, and styled-steel wheels. A 325-horsepower 390 was initially the top power source. Like the SS 396 El Camino, the 390 GT Ranchero was rolling proof that play had superseded work in the car-truck class.

"El Camino and Ranchero have established a new trend in the fun car market," wrote Motorcade's Lee Kelley in December 1967, "and people all over the country are getting on the bandwagon." Ford added even more fun early in 1968 in the form of the 335-horsepower 428 Cobra Jet V-8, an optional big-block more than capable of leaving an SS 396 El Camino driver eating dust.

The 428 CJ V-8 was replaced by the 370-horsepower 429 Cobra Jet in 1970. High-profile, highly reflective "laser stripes" also debuted that year for the Ranchero GT. Joining the GT that year was the Ranchero Squire, a "personal luxury" pickup dressed up in simulated woodside panels. Prestige temporarily overtook performance in 1970 as Squires outsold GTs, 3,943 to 3,905. Ranchero GTs took back the lead in 1971, the last year for a big-block Cobra Jet version.

In truth, performance-minded customers always were a minority among the El Camino and Ranchero crowd. They were warmly welcomed into the fraternity, but they represented more a sign of the times than a driving force behind the growing popularity of the two car-trucks. More important to the legacy's continuance were buyers looking for comfort, convenience, and class. It was these men and women who were the true impetus behind soaring sales.

Ranchero sales rose each year after 1968, reaching 24,946 in 1971. A restyle and a switch to a full-frame chassis (unibody construction had been used since 1960) in 1972 helped up the production ante dramatically to 40,334. The breed's peak performance of 45,741 units then came two years later.

A major makeover also contributed to the El Camino's zenith in 1973. By then the "midsized" classification no longer fit, as both rivals had grown every bit as big and heavy as the first El Caminos and Rancheros of 1957–1960. This wasn't a bad thing, though, it was just what the customer had ordered—more room, more comfort, more class.

More growth eventually contributed to the Ranchero's demise. Even with the gentlemanly wood-sided Squire and sporty GT still leading the way through the 1970s, the end of the line was clearly in sight. The Ranchero's crowning success just happened to come in the same year as the Arab oil embargo. Changing attitudes fueled by the ensuing gas crunch helped deflate Ranchero demand almost overnight. Sales in 1974 dove 28 percent to 32,925. Another 50 percent drop came the following year. A facelift in 1977 briefly revived the legacy, as sales rose back above 20,000 and then actually increased each year for the last three Ranchero runs. But such success still couldn't offset the fact that the Ranchero's low-volume, specialty-vehicle nature would never conform with Ford's plans for automated production lines. Detroit's first car-truck wouldn't see another decade.

The Ranchero's higher-volume competitor did, although it remained in steady decline through the 1980s. Like Elvis, Chevy's El Camino and GMC's Caballero just wouldn't die.

As late as 1986, El Camino sales were still topping 20,000. But GM planners knew too that they finally had run out the string. Their reasoning differed from Ford's. Two new 1980s trends had begun drawing customers away from their car-truck. One involved the growing popularity of the minivan, and the other encompassed an emerging breed known as the sport utility vehicle. So it was that the El Camino trail reached its end in early 1988.

Many El Caminos and Rancheros still can be seen on the road today. And they continue to work and play as hard as ever.

GMC replaced its Sprint in 1978 with the Caballero, which then continued, like its El Camino cousin, into early 1988 before the ax finally fell. The Caballero appearing here is a 1985 model.

PICKING UP THE PACE

KINDER, GENTLER TRUCKS EMERGE

The proverbial handwriting was clearly visible on the walls of the tired, old Studebaker works as the 1950s wound down. By 1958, sales had fallen off to their lowest levels since the war. Both product lines were still using the same bodies introduced too many years before; trucks in 1949, cars in 1953. Bob Bourke's lovingly sculpted sheet metal was lauded then as classic, perhaps even timeless. Time, however, demonstrated that no mere mortal can capture it in a bottle. Though they remained quite attractive, Studebaker products in 1958 still represented old news in a marketplace that seemingly grew more competitive by the day.

Being the "first by far with a postwar car" in 1947 mattered little once all the other new postwar models were up and running by 1950. Seniority also counted for nothing. Buyers in the late 1950s couldn't care less that Studebaker was the oldest manufacturer of wheeled transportation in America. What they wanted was new—all-new—and the aged, cash-strapped independent couldn't afford to give that to them. Officials marking the company's 106th birthday in 1958 undoubtedly couldn't help but long for the good old days.

Those days began in the 1850s when John C. and Rebecca Studebaker moved their family from Ohio to a village on the St. Joseph River in northern Indiana. Once known as Southold, it was now called South Bend. There, sons Henry and Clement bought a blacksmith shop in February 1852. They built their first wagons that year and soon found business booming as all those fabled Forty-niners soon supplied a demand for the means to haul their shovels and picks westward to the California gold fields.

California's calling also claimed one of Henry and Clem's brothers, John Mohler. John M. Studebaker, however, didn't have to dig for his fortune. After arriving in California in August 1953 he went to work for a local wagonmaker building wheelbarrows, which the gold-crazed miners bought up just as fast as they were pieced together. Within five years, "Wheelbarrow Johnny" had amazingly saved up $8,000. He then took his windfall home to South Bend.

Once back east, John M. bought out brother Henry and invested his cash in the family company, which also eventually signed on siblings Jacob and Peter as secretary and sales manager, respectively. All that extra cash, combined with John's experience, immediately led to incredible growth. Covered wagons were rolling out of the South Bend works by the thousands in 1860. Civil War demands led to even greater production, although "at prices which almost eliminated profit," according to an 1870 U.S. Bureau of Census report.

Peace brought more prosperity for this patriotic outfit. By 1868 the Studebaker Brothers Manufacturing Company was grossing about $350,000 a year. Sturdy, trustworthy farm wagons and fashionable, classy carriages also joined the product line as the demand for cross-country "Conestogas" waned. When John C. Studebaker died in 1877, he left this world satisfied in the knowledge that his sons were the finest craftsmen in their trade in America. Studebaker Brothers

Studebaker dusted off an old tradition in 1960, using the new Lark automobile body as a base for its equally new Champ pickup. The Champ finally ended the tenure of the same Studebaker truck body introduced in 1949.

Ford pickups rolled out with a new body in 1964, then were fitted with the company's famed Twin I-Beam front suspension in 1965. The short cargo box and two-tone paint help make this 1966 F-100 a real looker.

Ford in 1961 introduced a new pickup body that integrated cab and bed, a trick Dearborn had previously tried in 1931. The look was certainly clean, but a conventional separate cab-body layout returned two years later. *Ford Motor Company*

Wagon Manufacturing Company in Louisville. Kentucky Wagon then continued its powerless production into the early 1940s.

The growing presence of the horseless carriage around the turn of the century made it obvious to the Studebaker brothers that continued survival in the 1900s would require jumping onto this new bandwagon. But John M. had no use for internal-combustion machines, claiming they were "clumsy, dangerous, noisy brutes [that] stink to high heaven, break down at the worst possible moment, and are a public nuisance." Thus, the company's first horseless venture involved electric cars. Studebaker began building electric autos in 1902 and continued doing so up through 1912.

Electrics were joined by the gas-powered Studebaker-Garford automobiles in 1904. Four years later, Studebaker hooked up with another automaker, the Everitt-Metzger-Flanders company, to market E-M-F automobiles. The two merged to form the Studebaker Corporation in 1911.

Studebaker trucks were rarely seen early on. A three-ton electric hauler was built as early as 1906. Light-duty, car-based delivery vans began appearing on the gas-powered side soon afterward. In 1913 Studebaker became perhaps the first company to use the term "pickup" in its factory literature when it advertised a half-ton express truck. One-ton trucks followed in 1916.

The company temporarily suspended utility vehicle production in 1918. Studebaker reentered the truck field in June 1927 with the introduction of a new three-quarter-ton chassis. Attempts to produce trucks through deals with Pierce-Arrow in the late 1920s and then with White in 1932 failed in short order, although Studebaker did manage to build medium- and heavy-duty trucks on its own in the 1930s. By 1936 the South Bend firm stood as the country's 10th-leading truck builder in a field of about 20 established competitors leading a handful of minor fly-by-nights. Sales in 1937 surpassed 5,000.

Studebaker's first modern, light-duty pickup debuted that year. This Coupe Express was more car than truck, but it was a start—or a stopgap measure until the company could get its M-series

by then was the world's largest manufacturer of horse-drawn vehicles.

Ads in 1896 proclaimed the Studebaker wagon was "first in war, first in peace, first in the hearts of farmers, freighters and teamsters." Reportedly Studebaker built its last wagon in 1920, after which time the horse-drawn-vehicle end of the business was sold to the Kentucky

pickup in production for 1941. More than 50,000 M5 Studebaker trucks were built before Bourke's stunning 2R restyle superseded them in 1949. Total Studebaker truck registrations for that year alone reached the 50,000 neighborhood. But the yearly population fell off rapidly after that. By 1959, 4E-series (half- to two-ton) production was down to 7,737. Studebaker's market penetration went from a high of 5.7 percent in 1949 to 0.96 in 1959.

Studebaker-Packard's last gasp came in the fall of 1958. An all-new automobile, the compact Lark, debuted then to hopefully turn the company around. New hope for the truck line appeared in 1960 in the form of the Champ pickups. These were half- and three-quarter-ton trucks that recycled Studebaker's quick-change trick of 1937–1939. In back, the Champ used the same bed Bourke had originally styled in 1949. But up front, it was almost all Lark automobile. Except for its grille and bumper and the fact that it was chopped off behind the doors, the Champ's "T" cab was identical to the Lark sedan's leading half. Comparisons disappeared from there. Unlike those Coupe Express models of the 1930s, which rolled on car-line frames, a Champ pickup used an honest-to-goodness pickup chassis.

The Champ may have looked like a car, but it was all Studebaker truck where it counted. But whether or not it could've changed the course of Studebaker truck history was rendered a moot point when a steel strike and other production delays pushed the Champ's debut back into the spring of 1960. The ensuing short model-year run produced no sales improvement. A new bed didn't help matters, either. The cab-wide Spaceside cargo box, created by using Sweptline tooling purchased from Dodge, was introduced in January 1961 to finally update rear-half appearances. Studebaker's old pontoon-fendered box remained for those who just couldn't leave the past behind.

Sales did increase slightly for 1962. At $1,870, the third-edition Champ was the lowest-priced light truck (5,000-pound GVW) built in America that year. Who knows what might have happened had more Studebaker dealers made an effort to at least let Americans hear about that fact. Most

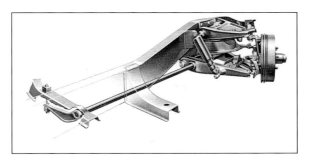

The New Passenger Pleasing Light-Load Carriers of Generous Capacity

INTERNATIONAL C-100 SERIES

Vehicles that serve partly as passenger carriers and partly as light load carriers have proved immensely popular. Station wagons, including the INTERNATIONAL TRAVELALL®, are seen everywhere. Pickup trucks are used more and more for family driving as well as load-hauling.

In designing the new light-duty C-100 Series, International engineers have made this dual use their guide. They have avoided the purely passenger car approach which sacrifices capacity and road clearance for an exaggeratedly low silhouette. They have avoided the purely truck approach which can make riding comfort subordinate to load-hauling strength. They thus have achieved a happy medium—two models in the 4,200 to 5,000-pound gross vehicle weight range that are ideal dual-purpose vehicles.

The overall height of C-100 Series models is lower by five inches than any previous full-size INTERNATIONAL model. This conforms with styling trends while leaving the same generous interior height. Yet, chassis units remain high enough to prevent scraping bottom when one or more wheels must drop several inches below road level or straddle obstructions.

A new, contoured grille and horizontally-mounted dual headlights give the C-100 Series models fresh, sparkling appearance. The low, gracefully-sloping hood increases the visible area seen through the large Sweep-Around windshield. Upon opening either door, one easy step takes you directly into the seat area, without any interference from windshield or fender projections.

Independent Front Wheel Suspension

Most significant mechanical feature of these new models is their new front wheel suspension that assures a softer, smoother ride than ever before offered. Each front wheel is mounted on a torque arm, not on the end of the front axle. Thus it is able to rise and fall on uneven roads without pulling or pushing other chassis, cab and body units along with it. The wheels, torque arms and stabilizing torsion bars, supplemented by shock absorbers, cushion out road-induced jolts and bounces, minimizing their effect on riders above. The torsion bars supply needed spring action without the tendency of coil springs to recoil excessively. This suspension system is the most effective of its kind on any vehicle.

Other mechanical components—notably the INTERNATIONAL V-266 standard engine which supplies smooth, quiet, fast-accelerating and economical power for the C-100 Series models—are described on following pages.

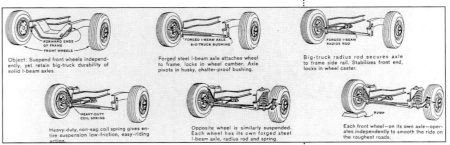

Object: Suspend front wheels independently, yet retain big-truck durability of solid I-beam axles.	Forged steel I-beam axle attaches wheel to frame, locks in wheel camber. Axle pivots in husky, chatter-proof bushing.	Big-truck radius rod secures axle to frame side rail. Stabilizes front end, locks in wheel caster.
HEAVY-DUTY COIL SPRING — Heavy-duty, non-sag coil spring gives entire suspension low-friction, easy-riding action.	Opposite wheel is similarly suspended. Each wheel has its own forged steel I-beam axle, radius rod and spring.	**BUMP** — Each front wheel—on its own axle—operates independently to smooth the ride on the roughest roads.

Chevrolet and GMC pickups in 1960 became the first American trucks to use independent front suspension, in an attempt to marry a relatively nice ride with workaday toughness. GM chose torsion bars instead of coil springs for its initial design, then later switched over to the more conventional coils.

International Harvester's advances into the 1960s not only involved fresh styling, but a new front suspension, too. Like their Chevrolet counterparts, I-H engineers in 1961 opted for an independent torsion bar design. Suddenly soft rides had become important in the light-duty truck field.

Ford tried to sell us all on the idea that its Twin I-Beam front suspension, introduced in 1965, offered a superior truck ride. Although this arrangement was a step up from the old solid axle, it still fell short of a true independent layout. Even so, its durability and ruggedness convinced Ford to stick with Twin I-Beams up until 1997.

dealers barely lifted a finger to sell trucks in the 1960s. Of course we all know that had these guys not ignored the truck market, South Bend still would've only delivered a few more additional trucks before the inevitable arrived. Studebaker's 1962 market share might've hit something like 1.2

The many rugged merits of the new D-100 pickup, introduced by Dodge in 1961, were demonstrated by this show vehicle. Overall solidness had become a major pickup selling point by the 1960s. The engine shown is a 200-horsepower 318-cid V-8. *Chrysler Historical Collection*

One of this country's first sporty half-ton pickups came from Dodge in 1964. The Custom Sports Special featured twin racing stripes and a bucket seat interior. The hot 426-cid wedge-head V-8 was also an early option. *Chrysler Historical Collection*

percent instead of the actual 1.14. The ink on those walls had longsince dried before the Lark and its cargo-carrying alter ego arrived.

While the Lark would carry on briefly north of the border, the Champ threw in the towel in 1963. Studebaker's last pickup rolled off the South Bend line on December 27 that year. Trucks were left behind when the company then moved to Canada, where Lark production continued in Hamilton, Ontario, until 1966. Three years before that last hurrah, a proud, century-old heritage of hard work and stylish innovation had ended with less than a whimper.

Meanwhile, Detroit's Big Three truck-builders were growing ever stronger. Chevrolet, Ford, and Dodge's products rolled out of the fad-conscious 1950s and braced themselves in preparation of being loaded down with even more convenience, comfort, and class in the progressive

1960s. In truth, the correct reference should've been the "Big Two and Dodge." As they did before and have since, Chevy and Ford dominated truck production in the 1950s, together annually holding anywhere between 53 and 68 percent of the market. This left Dodge, GMC, and International Harvester to grapple for the bulk of the rest. International had a heavy-duty niche all its own; it didn't need to put up the monster numbers like the Big Two. I-H's best effort, 12.8 percent, came in 1959. GMC of course also had its own role to play as part of General Motors' truck tag-team. It managed a market-share high of 10 percent in 1951.

Dodge trucks, on the other hand, were alone in their work. There were no corporate coat-tails to ride. Nor were there big-time heavy truck sales to fall back on. Chrysler's truck division, like Chevrolet and Ford, primarily built pickups. But it built them in much smaller numbers than its Big Two rivals, which commonly rolled out three or four or even five times more trucks in a given year. Dodge's market share went from 8.7 percent in 1950, up to 12.6 in 1952, then back down to 6 in 1957. By 1961, the company's piece of the pie had been whittled down to 5.7 percent.

As feeble as these numbers appeared, they denoted what has long been Dodge's accepted lot in life: to play a distant third fiddle to Ford and Chevy. While the Dodge boys back then would've certainly preferred a heftier hunk of that pie, none of them had a gun to their head or stood perched at the open window on the 29th floor. This wasn't Studebaker, this was Chrysler Corporation. Its truck division wasn't going anywhere—it certainly wasn't going up, nor was it heading to Canada any year soon. Dodge truck men simply took what they got and learned to like it. As Chrysler Chief Bob Lutz later said in 1993 after introducing the alarming, all-new, balls-out Ram pickup, "we don't care if half the buyers hate it; if 15 percent of them can't live without it, we've tripled our market share."

Back in the 1960s, Dodge waited a year then kicked off the new decade with a superclean restyle in 1961. The company then stuck with this boxy body up through 1971. Chevrolet the year

Willys pickups, both Jeeps and forward-control FC models, continued to soldier on into the 1960s looking very much like their 1950s forerunners. But along with the Kaiser/Willys arrangement's transformation into the Kaiser-Jeep Corporation in 1963 came a truly new breed. Two model lines were offered: the ground-breaking Wagoneer "station wagon" and its Gladiator pickup running mate. Discounting certain variations on Willys' FC platform, the Gladiator was the first Jeep truck to feature a stylish "fenderless" cargo box. Fashion-conscious buyers could have the Townside model with its cab-wide box, while purists could buy the Thriftside Gladiator with its flareside fenders in back. Even with obvious family ties to the original Jeep pickup image unveiled in 1947, the Gladiator ranked right up with the nicest-looking light-duty utility vehicles of its day.

New looks and new models weren't the only big news-makers in the 1960s truck market. Modern, mainstream compact pickups also debuted. First came Chevy's Corvair 95 and Ford's Econoline in 1961, followed by Dodge's A-100 in 1964. Like Willys' FC-150, these three extralight trucks were of the forward-control genre. And, in the best tradition of Powel Crosley's truly tiny trucks of the 1940s, Detroit's forward-control trio failed to make any real lasting impact on the market, despite decent early sales. The compact pickup idea didn't officially begin to stick in Americans' minds until 1972, when Chevrolet and Ford each introduced a minitruck manufactured with Japanese assistance.

Another almost unprecedented new breed (although Brooks Stevens' Willys Jeepster from the 1940s probably qualifies as a forerunner) first made the scene too in 1961. International's little Scout that year helped kick off two different hardworking legacies that later rose to prominence in the 1980s truck market. The Scout line-up included both a compact pickup and a pioneering 4x4 sport utility model. Helping to shape the progression toward today's modern SUV were Scout responses from Ford and Chevrolet—Bronco and Blazer. The Bronco debuted in 1966, the Blazer three years later. A fourth contender, Kaiser-Jeep's modern reincarnation of the classic

By the 1970s, Ford was offering various dress-up packages for its F-100 pickup, including the Explorer variety shown here. Bed rails, special trim, side mirrors, and exclusive paint—the Boss 302 Mustang's Grabber Blue on this 1973 model—were just some of the Explorer's attractions.

Chevrolet restyled its pickups in 1960 and changed the half-ton designation to C-10. The 4x4 versions of the same trucks began using a "K" code. This is the system Chevy still relies on today. Shown here is a 1963 C-10 Stepside.

before was the first to offer a fresh face for the 1960s, with an aircraft-inspired look that remained in a holding pattern until 1967. Ford joined Dodge in 1961 with new Styleside sheet metal featuring one-piece cab/bed construction that harkened back to Dearborn's "General Electric" pickup of 1931. International pickups in 1961 also received a major makeover, although these lower, wider models still echoed many similar impressions made by their predecessors. A truly modern I-H restyle followed eight years later.

Chevrolet introduced a new optional 327-cid V-8 for truck buyers in 1965. This 1965 C-10 Fleetside has the smaller 283-cid "High Torque" V-8.

Yet another new body appeared for Chevy's light truck line in 1967. Even more pizzazz was available in the form of the Custom Sport Truck option, which added various special trim features. The CST Chevy pickup was later upstaged in 1971 by the truly flashy Cheyenne.

FLEETSIDE CUSTOM SPORT TRUCK CST

A new concept in personalized pickups.

Here's Chevrolet's new 1967 Fleetside Custom Sport Truck. Available for all Fleetside and Stepside pickups and Chassis Cabs, Custom Sport Truck equipment literally transforms the truck's appearance and comfort to something more akin to that of a passenger car. On the cab exterior, extensive use of bright metal around grille openings, headlights and windshield add a flair to conventional truck appearance. Also, a tastefully designed emblem with CST designation is mounted on both doors just below the window sill. Inside, the transformation is more dramatic. Bucket seats are provided for both driver and right-hand passenger with a center console-type seat for the third passenger. Padded backrest may be folded down when not in use to provide an armrest. Additional Custom Sport Truck (CST) equipment includes floor and fuel tank carpeting, chrome front bumper, bright metal frames for clutch, brake and accelerator pedals, chrome trimmed instrument knobs and horn button, right-hand padded sunshade, underbody coating and more.

Willys Jeepster, appeared in 1967 in Jeep Commando guise. A pickup model was included in the Jeep Commando 4x4 line-up.

For the bulk of the pickup market, that is, those offered by Chevrolet, Ford, and Dodge, the 1960s and 1970s represented a time for refined refinement. Some of the work needed to put the American pickup more in line with its car-line cousins in its ability to serve as everyday transportation was done in the 1950s. Uncharted areas explored by truck builders then didn't end with those various all-new styling adventures. Mechanical advancements included modern V-8 power and the convenience of automatic shifting. Chevrolet's all-new

Task Force pickups in 1955 became even more attractive when fitted with the division's first V-8.

Ford's V-8 pickups dated back to 1932, but they relied on the venerable flathead for more than 20 years. A modern overhead-valve V-8 finally appeared as an F-100 option in 1954. Ford-O-Matic automatic transmission trucks debuted in 1953. Dodge pickups began receiving V-8s in 1954, and the Fluid-Drive Truck-O-Matic equipment was also joined by a true automatic transmission the next year. Studebaker's first V-8 pickup came in 1955; International's in 1959. Kaiser-Jeep offered an automatic transmission for its 4x4 pickups for the first time in 1963.

Eight-cylinder pickups began to gain ground on their six-hole brothers in the 1960s. More than 86 percent of Chevrolet's trucks in 1960 were sold with six cylinders. Roughly 50,000 V-8 Chevy trucks were built that year. That figure jumped to nearly 250,000 in 1966 when the breakdown shifted to 60/40 for sixes versus V-8s. Chevy V-8 trucks outsold their six-cylinder counterparts for the first time in 1968. By 1971 Dodge was installing V-8s in 70 percent of its trucks.

Other signs that Americans were changing the way they looked at their pickups included the emergence of more car-like convenience options. By 1971 Chevrolet was installing automatic transmissions in trucks 50 percent of the time. Air conditioning and power steering and brakes also became more common in the 1960s. Chevrolet's first factory-installed air conditioning option appeared in 1965. Ford's first in-dash cold air option came two years later. Ford also made note of the light truck's "fun factor." By the 1960s, reportedly two out of three pickups were doing double duty as a work truck and a recreational vehicle. Dearborn responded with the industry's first Camper Special package in 1965.

Improved standard ride and handling became major selling points, too. Although some 1950s pickups had started appearing at least partially as stylish as cars, they were still very much

A lot can happen over three decades. The 1954 Chevrolet 3100 pickup at left was cutting edge for its day. By 1970 Chevy trucks were sporting damn near as much style as many of their car-line counterparts.

trucks beneath the skin, especially up front. The straight axles found there were essentially identical in concept to the wooden beams used by the Studebaker brothers' wagons a century before.

Chevrolet in 1960 became the first to offer independent front suspension beneath its trucks. Light-duty Chevy pickups that year used coil springs in the rear, torsion bars up front. Packard had pioneered torsion-bar suspension in the postwar era in 1955—for both ends. Front torsion bars became a Chrysler chassis feature in 1957. According to brochures, Chevrolet's front torsion bars gave its trucks car-like ride qualities. Steering effort was also lowered by exchanging king pins for ball joints.

It took Dearborn five years to respond. Ford's highly publicized Twin I-Beam front suspension debuted in 1965 to reportedly help a Blue Oval pickup roll over bumps and jolts like no truck before it. Although this double swing-

Dodge's flagship pickup in the 1960s and 1970s was the Adventurer, shown here in 1973 form. Three trim levels were offered that year, the base Adventurer, Adventurer Sport, and Adventurer SE.

axle arrangement was by no means cutting-edge technology, Ford hypemasters still touted it as the next great thing in pickup design. And they carried on a running battle with their Chevrolet counterparts as to which design

139

International's smooth-sided cargo box option was called Bonus Load. The basic body introduced in 1961 was used for the last time in 1968.

International stopped making conventional light-duty pickups in 1975, choosing instead to run with its playful Scout on its own. In 1976 the Scout Terra was introduced on a lengthened 118-inch wheelbase. Scout Terra production itself ended in 1980, and I-H was finally completely out of the light truck field.

made for a better ride while still retaining typical truck ruggedness. "Drive like a car—work like a truck," read Ford ads for its Twin I-Beam pickups. Arguments wouldn't cease until all pickup competitors finally began featuring the typical coil-sprung short-arm/long-arm (SLA) design long used by cars. Chevrolet traded its torsion bars for coils in 1963. Ford finally gave up on those twin I-beams when the new 1997 F150 model was introduced with an SLA setup.

On the shinier side, pickups began to grow more and more image-conscious in the 1960s. Truck builders in the 1950s had proven that their products didn't have to look bad to be good. But paying more attention to standard styling treatments was just a start. A decade later designers expanded further on those basic good looks with optional enhancements that added even more prestige into the equation.

Dress-up touches weren't unknown before —and we're not talking about Chevy's Cameo or Dodge's Sweptside. Optional "big windows" in back, two-tone paint, Custom cabs, more colorful upholstery, bright knobs on the dash—such humble offerings did a nice job of freshening things up for everyday, mainstream pickups in the 1950s. At least at first. Adding a little chrome around the windows only could've been counted on to turn heads for so long before the "what-have-you-done-for-me-lately?" attitude kicked in.

Chevrolet in 1958 became the latest truck maker to again pick up the pace in the image department. Along with the new Fleetside cargo box, Chevy that year also created a new name for its top-line, trimmed-out trucks— Apache. Various other fancy pickups were offered through the 1960s, including the Custom Sport Truck, introduced in 1967 with bucket seats and center console. Then Chevrolet's classy Cheyenne option debuted in 1971. A fully loaded Cheyenne pickup in the 1970s was every bit as sporty as most Camaros.

Ford's first image package, Ranger, debuted along with a new F-100 body in 1967. Even flashier Ranger XLT and Explorer upgrades soon followed. Dearborn's basic truck line-up was also expanded in 1978 with the introduction of the F-150 "heavy-duty half-ton." In 1984 the F-150 supplanted the F-100 as Ford's base half-ton.

Chevrolet's designation system was restructured in 1960, resulting in the "C/K" labels still used today. "C" represents two-wheel-drivers, "K" is for 4x4s. Numbers were also assigned to denote load capacity. Typical half-tons were C-10 models, while the C-30 was a one-ton. Those number codes now are four digits long.

Dodge in the 1960s tried a different approach to turning customers' attention toward its front-running pickups. Chrysler's truck division in 1964 introduced its Custom Sports Special, a half-ton hot rod featuring racing stripes and bucket seats. While the yeoman 225-cid slant-six engine was standard, optional power even included Dodge's muscular 426-cid wedge-head V-8. The rare Custom Sports Special was offered up through 1967. Though all but forgotten, this hot-to-trot

In 1977 Dodge picked up where the Custom Sports Special left off in the 1960s, introducing the D-100 Warlock. Gold spoke wheels, accent pinstriping, and wooden bed rails were included in this rare package. *Chrysler Historical Collection*

Setting the stage for later performance trucks like GMC's sizzling Syclone and Ford's SVT Lightning was Dodge's Li'l Red Truck, or Li'l Red Express, as some call it. These wood-trimmed, exhaust-stacked pickups were as hot as any car in their day. Rectangular headlights identify this Li'l Red Truck as a 1979 model—1978 versions had round headlights.

hauler represented Detroit's first performance pickup.

The second major muscle truck to come along was also a Dodge—a much more memorable Dodge. You had to be blind to miss the Li'l Red Truck, or Li'l Red Express as it was commonly called. Offered in 1978 and 1979, these red-hot half-tons announced their presence in no uncertain terms with chrome wheels and twin big-rig-style exhaust stacks behind the cab. These trucks also backed up their bark with some serious bite. A high-performance 360-cid four-barrel V-8 helped make the Li'l Red Truck one of the fastest factory machines, car or truck, of the late 1970s.

In between the Custom Sports Special and the Li'l Red Truck, Dodge also applied a softer touch to its top-line truck image. The Adventurer options package debuted for 1968 with var-

ious exterior dress-ups and interior upgrades. Dodge only offered the Adventurer option on its Sweptline pickups. This was done for two reasons, the most obvious being that the more stylish smooth-sided cargo box represented the logical choice from an aesthetic perspective. But company officials also were eager to see more buyers pick that easy-to-build all-steel box over its more narrow, labor-intensive Utiline counterpart with its pontoon fenders.

International Harvester really never did go in for the high-profile pretty pickup approach in the 1960s and 1970s like its Big Three counterparts, although its top-line half-ton trucks were no strangers to extra trim and optional baubles. Such shenanigans essentially didn't appear until after the company discontinued its standard light-duty line in April 1975. This move then left the big heavies and

Kaiser-Jeep's first Gladiator pickup debuted in 1963. It carried on into the 1970s as an American Motors product after AMC acquired the former Willys product line in 1970. Shown here is a 1970 Gladiator. *Chrysler Historical Collection*

the little Scout to carry on the International truck tradition.

A new Scout II pickup was introduced in 1976. Named "Terra," this light truck rolled on a lengthened 118-inch wheelbase. The standard Scout II stretch was 100 inches. Those extra 8 inches translated into 11 cubic feet of storage space behind a Terra's seat. A 6-foot-long cargo box followed in back. International continued offering the Scout II Terra pickup, with various appearance packages, up into 1980, before closing the book for good on its light truck legacy.

International's withdrawal from the light-duty market in 1980 meant the Big Three were by then the only three. Jeep pickups from AMC were still around but rarely seen, primarily off on their own well out of the mainstream. Few truck buyers noticed them,

except perhaps for the four-wheeler crowd. Dearborn grabbed the truck market lead in the late 1970s and hasn't let go since, with Chevrolet/GMC right in Ford's tire tracks every year. Then there's Dodge cruising along—with no complaints, nor excuses—as the perennial third-place finisher in a three-truck race. At least the Ram is still running.

Studebaker, Willys, Hudson, Plymouth, Crosley, Mack Jr, Reo—these and other pickup players weren't so fortunate. In their places in recent decades have come names like Nissan, Toyota, Mazda, and Isuzu. Many of today's beloved pickups are no longer as American as apple pie and baseball. And they're also now overshadowed in the light truck realm by the family-friendly sport utility vehicle. Where will history take us from here?

That's all up to truck buyers like you.

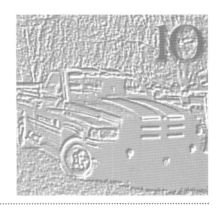

Today's light-duty trucks certainly don't look all that bad for their age, whatever that may be. As was the case with Hall of Fame baseball pitcher Satchel Paige, there's no telling exactly how old the great American pickup really is. The truck breed itself celebrated at least its 100th birthday in 1998—that is, if you agree that Winton's first gas-powered utility vehicle of 1898 qualifies as the forefather. As for the birth of the pickup we know today? Let's just say it has been around the block a few times.

The same can be said about America's top pickup maker. Along with being the long-time sales leader, Ford also claims the senior position in Detroit's truck triumvirate, by one year over Chevrolet and about a half a year over Dodge. Dearborn officials in July 1997 marked the 80th anniversary of "Ford's permanent entry into truck manufacturing." That legacy began with the one-ton Model TT chassis in 1917, which was joined by America's first factory-built half-ton pickup eight years later. By 1930, both Dodge and Chevrolet were offering their own complete-from-the-factory half-tons. And the race was on.

The Blue Oval brain trust celebrated a golden trucking anniversary in 1998. Ford's wildly popular F-series pickup turned 50 on January 16, to the sounds of birthday praises being sung at assembly plants in Norfolk, Virginia; Louisville, Kentucky; Kansas City, Missouri; Oakville, Ontario; Cuautitlan, Mexico; and Valencia, Venezuela. The company's official fandango actually began well in advance in October 1997 at the State Fair of Texas in Dallas.

"The State Fair of Texas is the biggest fair in the world and F-series is the No. 1 selling truck in the world," explained Ross Roberts, then Ford Division general manager. "I can think of no better place to celebrate the 50th birthday of America's favorite truck than right here in Texas, the heart of truck country." Indeed the Lone Star state represents the world's largest light truck market—more than 10 percent of all full-sized pickups sold annually hit the road in Texas. That's not to say, however, that the other 49 states haven't done their fair share helping promote the F-series' popularity and longevity over the years. "We have millions of customers to thank for this milestone," said Roberts. "Last year alone, more than 780,000 customers drove home an F-series truck, the most since 1978."

But Texans seemingly always do things in a big way, as did Ford on October 1, 1997. A huge 50-foot-tall, three-layer mock birthday cake was served up that day to mark the occasion. Concealed in its second layer was the new 1998 F-150, still this country's best-selling vehicle, car or truck. Ford's F-series truck also now stands as the best-selling nameplate of all time after having surpassed the Volkswagen Beetle in 1995. More than 26 million F-series trucks were sold by 1997, and more than 8 million of those were still on the road that year.

"Without a doubt, the explosive growth of the truck market over the past few years has been one of the biggest stories in business," continued Roberts. "Even with the popularity of minivans and SUVs with consumers, full-size pickups are

TRUCK TRENDS TODAY

WHERE HAVE WE GONE FROM THERE?

What a difference 50 years make. Even today's monstrous Super Duty 4x4s from Ford offer more comfort, convenience, and class than the company's light-duty half-ton F-series trucks did when first introduced. And when the 1951 F-1 shown here was built, the biggest engine available was a little flathead V-8. That 1999 F250 Super Duty is powered by a V-10.

Flash and flair have especially become prime selling points in the smaller truck field, as demonstrated by this 1995 Ranger Splash from Ford. Roomier cabs are also of greater importance today, whether the truck is a compact or full sized.

purchased by more customers than any other kind of truck."

In 1996, for the first time in history, three of the top five best-selling vehicles in America were full-sized pickups. Ford also has led the way in the compact pickup class, with the Ranger having topped its rivals for a dozen years now. The truck market as a whole established yet another calendar-year sales record in 1997, the fifth straight year it has done so, and the ninth time in the last 13. Trucks early in 1998 were leading cars in the sales race by a 60/40 ratio. If that trend continues, it will result in the first-ever truck-dominated marketplace. What a difference 50 years makes.

"Today's F-series competes in a marketplace that has changed considerably since the name-plate's introduction in 1948," added Joel Pitcoff, Ford strategic market analysis manager. "No longer strictly a workhorse, the present F-series has taken its place as a family member and a pleasure companion. The new F-series has the potential to make lifelong friends through the years as entire families grow up with it."

Did Studebaker admen right after World War II really know what lay ahead when they first began showing off artwork that depicted their pickups in everyday driving situations? Okay, 1949 might have been a bit too soon for a continued on page 152

Dodge in 1994 was especially proud of the way its all-new Ram pickup impressed like a big-rig. The feel behind the wheel was also "semi-like." *Dodge Division, Chrysler Corporation*

In 1991 and 1992 it was GMC's V-6 Syclone pickup that had truck buyers swooning with its all-wheel-drive performance. Then, in 1993, Ford's Special Vehicle Team demonstrated what a V-8 could do. Nearly 12,000 of these 351-powered SVT Lightning pickups were built during a three-year run. Shown here is a 1995 model. *Ford Special Vehicle Team*

Truck popularity today is a product of one simple addition equation. So many utility vehicles now are able to offer buyers all the comfort and convenience of a car, coupled with the ability to work and play like a pickup. Trucks can haul, they can tow, they can go off-road. They can also carry the kids quite safely, they can do the town with flair, they can go to the office everyday. And they can put you head and shoulders above the rest, in more ways than one. Just as the modern truck's tall, confident presence on the road is a major selling point, so too is its status appeal. Pickup prestige? You betcha. It all adds up: Why buy a car and be stuck on the path well traveled when you can have a truck and go anywhere and do anything you want with just as much style?

Actually, the truck market's rise in the 1990s is a result of more than just growing pickup popularity alone. Much more. Included in the mix are two other types of utility vehicles, both of which have played major roles in that rise. The first, the minivan, exploded on the scene in the 1980s, then peaked in the early 1990s. The other variety, the wildly popular sport utility vehicle, is still rolling stronger every day, thanks to its ability to combine car and truck qualities better than anything else on four wheels. SUVs represent the main reason trucks have all but matched cars one-to-one in today's market. And their ever-growing presence will soon tip that ratio in favor of trucks. How far is anyone's guess.

Industry experts claim we'll never see a 100 percent truck market no matter how strongly trends seem to be pointing in that direction. But we're already witnessing some automotive segments falling by the wayside as SUVs steal more and more attention from car buyers. GM's once-beloved F-body platform, home to Chevrolet's Camaro and Pontiac's Firebird since 1967, is only one-call-from-the-governor away from extinction. Sales simply no longer support the two-door "pony car" sport coupe, although Ford's long-running Mustang remains in no present danger. Ford's Thunderbird, on the other hand, has already retired, with Dearborn's last upscale two-door sport coupe rolling off the Lorain, Ohio, line in September 1997.

Ford officials closed the door on 43 years of high-flying success without so much as a bye-bye birdie. It was nothing personal; on the contrary, it was all business. Market trends overshadowed nostalgic allegiances. "Two-door coupes used to be familiar to family types in the market for utility and versatility," explained Ford Public Affairs man Jim Bright in 1997. "But a greater number of customers are now turning to light trucks instead of cars."

Those light trucks include Ford's own Explorer, Detroit's best-selling SUV dating almost back to its debut in 1990. More than 400,000 Explorers a year are now hitting the streets. Yet even though Ford has the top-seller, it was GM that led the way through the 1990s atop the SUV field—"was," as in past tense. Thanks to all-new, more upscale models from Mercury and Lincoln, Ford Motor Company finally grabbed the sport-ute total calendar-year sales lead in 1997 with 670,570 units, compared to GM's 666,454. Chrysler's piece of the pie,

now stuffed with new Durangos from Dodge, amounted to 493,135 sporty utilities for calendar year 1997.

Such lofty numbers would've never come about if not for the diversity that rapidly developed in the SUV field in the 1990s. Four-door sport-utes, appearing first among the imports, initially helped widen the breed's appeal among the family set. The scope was broadened even further once competitive pressures inspired a pricing pecking order. Today's SUV market breaks down into four categories; subcompact, compact, full-sized, and heavy-duty wagons. While imports are present, they are scattered over a wide range. European models do top the high-end segment, at least as far as the bottom line is concerned. But Detroit's luxury sport-utility line-up is presently emerging, led by Lincoln's lavish Navigator, introduced in 1997. A Cadillac counterpart is in the works as we speak.

Also spied behind proving ground fences in 1998 was a brutish Ford counterpart to the Chevrolet/GMC Suburban, long entrenched as the largest SUV on the road. The Suburban is also the oldest, although claiming that title represents somewhat of a stretch, as the sport-ute breed didn't really come into its own until the 1980s.

The essence of the concept, however, was first concocted in 1935, when Chevrolet introduced what also could be considered Detroit's first all-steel "station wagon." According to Chevy brochures, the all-new Carryall Suburban combined the advantages of a passenger car and a light delivery unit. "As you desire it," added advertising copy, "this all-purpose vehicle serves you in business or in pleasure."

Unlike the mundane sedan delivery it was based on, the Suburban featured side glass, added so the eight adults seated inside could have a view with their room. Practical transportation (for a baseball team minus the pitcher perhaps?) was the goal here, although the rear seats could be removed if hauling cargo was preferred. This was no station wagon. Underneath was an able light truck chassis. And the dual-purpose Suburban was marketed under Chevy's upscale Master Truck banner. Upscale was a relative term, as the Suburban's only deviation from its sedan delivery lineage for years remained that extra glass and the slightly-better-than-bleachers seating. It was left to competing firms to refine the concept.

Additional ground-breaking SUV forerunners included Willys-Overland's Jeepster, introduced in 1948. This nicely stylish, wonderfully rugged roadster was created by noted designer Brooks Stevens. Much more crude, yet plainly practical was the station wagon version of the Jeep that Willys rolled out in 1946. Jeep wagon production would continue in reasonably popular fashion long after Henry Kaiser bought out Willys-Overland in 1953. The last Willys Jeepster was built in 1951.

In 1956 International Harvester introduced its Travelall, a Suburban knock-off. Again, loads of glass and added seating represented the main attractions

Chevrolet built its first Suburban in 1935. But calling this innovative vehicle America's first SUV doesn't exactly add up. For one thing, the sporty utility concept itself didn't begin evolving until the 1960s.

Ford Motor Company was first to offer an American-built luxury SUV, originally in the form of Mercury's Mountaineer (back) and then in full force by way of Lincoln's Navigator.

Chevy's family-sized Suburban legacy continues on today. It presently stands all but unchallenged as rivals have yet to dare to build a bigger SUV—for now.

for this utility vehicle, which also was meant more for people than products. Travelalls became more comfortable and stylish through the 1960s.

Kaiser-Jeep (Willys) was responsible for taking this concept to all-new levels in 1963 when it rolled out its first Wagoneer, truly a candidate for the honor of "father of the modern SUV." This off-road wagon looked like no other off-roader ever seen before; it was stylish, sporty, classy, and tough. "Long a builder of strictly, almost starkly functional, utility-type vehicles, Willys adds a whole new dimension to the line with the Wagoneer," claimed *Motor Trend*'s Jim Wright. "Up to this time, almost all of the four-wheel-drive enthusiasts have been faced with the problem of two cars in the garage. With the new Willys station wagon in the garage, the other car is no longer a necessity." Such is the case today with the latest sport-utes.

Yet another notable moment in SUV prehistory came from International Harvester in 1961. That year I-H introduced its Scout, Detroit's first off-road, multirole sport pickup. Available in either 4x4 or 4x2 form, this quarter-ton utility vehicle could be fitted with various tops or could be stripped down with no doors or roof. Its windshield also folded flat across the hood, Jeep-style.

Ford copied International's formula in 1966 with its little Bronco, the so-called "stablemate of Mustang." Three versions of this fun four-wheeler were offered: a full-roofed wagon; a roadster pickup with a full soft top (and no doors); and another open-air pickup, this one with a removable hardtop for the front seating compartment only. Dearborn officials apparently wanted to set their mini-4x4 apart from (and above) the rough-and-ready Jeep set, thus the steel top and real doors with roll-up windows added to the last of the those three models. This more-civilized, split-personality pickup also was given its own unique name—"Sports Utility."

Chevrolet's response, the Blazer, came in 1969. Chevy labelmakers three years later then contributed another piece, however obtuse, to the SUV puzzle when they reached into the acronym pile for an appropriate name for their next new minipickup. In 1972, LUV wasn't just a cute moniker, it was short for "light utility vehicle." From there, similar connections were made to help bring the "sport utility vehicle" badge into vogue about a decade later. Only this time, transforming this particular acronym into a three-letter word all its own was thankfully skipped. That's "ess-you-vee" to you.

Or, in Detroit terms, it's "ess-you-em"—show us the money.

One thing is for certain: Ford does deserve credit for at least partially originating the SUV moniker. One of its Bronco models introduced in 1966 was called "Sports Utility." *Ford Motor Company*

Introduced in 1963, the Jeep Wagoneer probably best exemplifies the modern SUV spirit in pioneer form. *Chrysler Historical Collection*

Ford jumped on the aero bandwagon in 1997 with this redesigned F-150. Is everything old new again? Pontoon fenders still survive, however meekly, after all these years.

Detroit's Big Three truck makers seem to be falling all over themselves these days trying to be the first with this or that. More seats and more doors were prime targets in this race to one-up the competition. Shown here is Ford's convenient third door for its 1997 F-150 Supercab. Four doors are now all the rage.

continued from page 146
Sunday-go-to-meetin' truck. But a half century later most customers take for granted the multi-role aspects of today's kinder, gentler, yet still-tough trucks.

"Traditional assumptions about pickups and pickup buyers don't apply any more," continued Pitcoff. "In days gone by, pickups were primarily work trucks, used in farming, construction and building trades or as delivery vehicles, rather than for personal use. In recent years, however, about 90 percent of all the new full-size pickups have been sold to individuals. Certainly, some of these people may be carpenters, electricians, plumbers or contractors. Yet less than one-third of the individual full-size pickup customers surveyed during the 1996 model year reported ever using their trucks in their 'line of business'—with merely 13 percent identifying that as their primary use."

Pitcoff also pointed out the obvious fact that many old, familiar demographic stereotypes are also obsolete. "No longer are full-size pickup customers predominantly rural residents," he said. "Today, pickup trucks are commonplace in the driveways of suburban subdivisions." Median income is essentially equal between car and truck buyers now, too.

Another new trend involves the way the market's pie has been sliced up in recent decades. Customers in the 1990s appeared more willing to consider all truck companies, not just the Big

Two. Chrysler is no longer such a distant trailer as it was in the 1950s, 1960s, and 1970s, although much of the gains made in recent years can be credited to the 1987 purchase of American Motors, a move that added the desirable Jeep line into the Mopar mix.

As late as 1982, the Chevrolet/GMC tandem was wolfing down 40.2 percent of the truck pie, with Dodge managing only 12 percent. While Ford kept a steady pace at about 30 percent, plus or minus, over the following 15 years, GM's truck sales carried on in a slow decline. The Chevy/

A popular trend today involves putting pickups in the limelight at racing's top venues. Dodge offered this official Indy 500 truck in 1996 with its Viper-like paint scheme.

Big, brawny 17-inch wheels and tires and a 250-horsepower engine were just a few of the Dakota R/T's attractions in 1998. Dodge engineers typically fitted their latest R/T rendition with a playful, purposeful chassis. *Dodge Division, Chrysler Corporation*

GMC share in 1997 was 28.8 percent. On its own, Dodge began to surge in the 1980s, going from 11.3 percent in 1983 to 16.3 the following year. The slice grew to 18.4 percent in 1987, then peaked at 23.4 in 1996. The Dodge/Jeep percentage was 21.7 percent in 1997, compared to Ford's leading figure of 31.1.

The bulk of the remaining slice went to the various Far East companies. It's interesting to note that while Japanese cars claimed 30.9 percent of

the pie in 1997, their pickup counterparts only scored a 14.2 share. The recent decline of the compact truck market partially helps explain this differential.

In the full-size pickup world, yet another ever-growing trend has developed over the last 10 years or so. With competition running as tight as it ever has between the Big Three domestic truck manufacturers, it was discovered in the 1990s that a company didn't have to be first to be

first. Most witnesses for years now have automatically conceded the top spot in the annual sales race to Ford anyway. So what has been left for the competition to brag about? Plenty. Just ask the Dodge boys.

Hands down, Dodge's promotional people are the busiest today, proclaiming all the "firsts" their trucks have registered on the pages of pickup truck history. The first available V-10 pickup engine. The first full-sized pickup to offer optional four-wheel antilock brakes for all models. The first full-sized 4x4 with a coil-spring/link front suspension design. These are just a few, and they all came in 1994, when an alarming, totally redesigned Dodge Ram pickup debuted to help "change all the rules."

Chrysler officials had initially hoped to rewrite the pickup rule book in 1992, but a change of heart delayed the plan by two years.

Other vehicle development programs took a higher priority. Lengthening the design schedule, however, turned out to be a blessing. "In my view, it was one of the most valuable things the corporation did," said Bernard Robertson, general manager of the Jeep/Truck Platform Team. "That allowed us to go back and revisit all the earlier assumptions of what we wanted this truck to be."

What everyone from Chrysler Chief Robert Lutz on down wanted was not any old new truck. This would be a machine the likes of which pickup buyers had never seen—yet they would recognize as a Ram-tough truck.

"We felt we needed to leapfrog the competition, not play catch-up," said Jeep/Truck Design Office Director Trevor Creed in 1994. "The target for us was not where Ford and Chevrolet are now, but where they would like to be in the future."

While Ford explores alternative alcohol fuels, GM continues to investigate electric power as a way to save our environment. In 1997 a specially prepared Chevy S-10 electric pickup was sent to Colorado to tackle the famous Pikes Peak Hill Climb.

The National Hot Rod Association debuted its new Pro Stock Truck pickup drag racing class at the Southwest Nationals in Houston in March 1998. *Steve Statham*

A second sanctioning body, the High Desert Racing Association (HDRA), followed. Over the next few years desert racing established itself as a viable entity in the racing world, offering a variety of classes for truck competition. There were classes for two- and four-wheel drive, stock and modified, and everything in between—not to mention varying degrees of factory participation. The sport's heroes have included such racing giants as Parnelli Jones, Rod Hall, Walker Evans, and Ivan Stewart, and such memorable vehicles as Bill Stroppe's "Big Oly" Broncos.

In the 1990s though, where every sport seeks the all-important television package, desert racing has struggled. It is, after all, difficult to televise a 1,000-mile endurance race across the desert. Other truck racing series have found ways around that problem, though, through stadium and short-course racing. One such series was the Mickey Thompson Off-Road Stadium Series. Another is the SODA off-road series, based in the Midwest.

With pickup trucks put to just about every stressful duty under the sun, it was only inevitable that someone, somewhere, would hit upon the idea of racing them. While trucks have traditionally lacked the sophisticated powertrains, aerodynamics, and braking systems found on cars, little things like that have never stopped Americans from engaging in speed contests. Witness the unique spectacle of diesel-powered semi rigs racing on stock car ovals.

The genesis of modern truck racing was, appropriately enough, in the desert. In the minds of the founding fathers of the sport, running flat out across the dunes was a lot of fun, and the desert seemed the ideal venue for truck, bike, and dune buggy competition. The 1965 Riverside Grand Prix in California, one of the first organized off-road races, staked its claim to fame by featuring side-by-side racing over a variety of types of terrain.

But the grandfather of all off-road racing is the Baja 1000, run the length of Baja, California, from Tijuana to La Paz. First named the Mexican 1000, it was sanctioned and run by the newly formed National Off-Road Racing Association (NORRA) on October 31 and November 1, 1967. The first event was won by Vic Wilson and Ted Mangels in a Myers Manx dune buggy. Two years later, the shorter Baja 500 joined the schedule, as did the Mint 400 in Nevada.

In 1973 Mickey Thompson's Short Course Off-Road Events (SCORE) organization assumed control of Baja and most other desert racing events.

Ford truck successes in the grueling Baja races date back some 30 years now. Here, Dave Ashley and Dan Smith kick up a little sand on the way to a SCORE Pro Series overall title.

Chevrolet's NASCAR stock car success carried right over into the truck racing division. Chevy pickups won 50 of the first 70 races during the Craftsman Truck Series' first three years.

Away from the dirt and on a more local level are assorted mud drags, in which two trucks, rocker-panel-deep in muck, race down the swampy trenches, tires spinning, mud flying. While mud drags represent grass-roots truck racing at its grassiest, these trucks make big money for the automakers and attract considerable corporate attention. Proving that trucks clean up real well, too, is the NASCAR Craftsman Truck Series. NASCAR's truck series showcases full-sized pickups from Ford, Chevy, and Dodge running truck sheet metal over what are basically Winston Cup car chassis. The trucks run 5.9-liter V-8s with a lower compression ratio (9.5:1) than Winston Cup cars run. Horsepower factors out to between 650 and 700.

After running an exhibition schedule in 1994 as the Super Truck series, the inaugural 1995 season championship was captured by Mike Skinner, who won 8 of the 20 races in his Chevy C1500. The series is contested over a variety of ovals and road courses, sometimes in conjunction with Winston Cup events, but usually not. Although no threat to dethrone the Cup cars in popularity, the Craftsman Truck series has seen steady growth in its short life, and has moved to the front of the line as the most popular truck racing series in the United States. By 1997, the NASCAR Craftsman Trucks attracted more than 920,000 fans through the course of its 26-race schedule, up 13.5 percent from the year before.

Taking a cue from NASCAR, the National Hot Rod Association (NHRA) instituted a new pro drag racing class, Pro Stock Truck, in 1998. After a year of exhibition runs, the class debuted March 20–21, 1998, at the NHRA Southwest Nationals in Houston. Making the history books as the first winner was David Nickens in a 1998 Dodge Dakota. In Pro Stock Truck, the vehicles of choice are compact pickups, powered by 358-cid small-block V-8s. Elapsed times for the new Pro Stockers flash by in the mid-to-high seven-second range at 170 miles per hour. The NHRA is counting on brand-versus-brand competition to excite the fans, as truck owners are known for their loyalty to their favorite nameplates. It all makes perfect sense—"My truck is faster than yours" is the battle cry that started this whole mad dash to race pickup trucks in the first place.

—Steve Statham

While the American pickup truck may now be on the upswing as far as big-time professional racing is concerned, there's still room for old-style dirty fun, such as the mud-bogging event shown here. *Steve Statham*

Everything about the all-new 1999
Silverado, according to Chevrolet
promotional paperwork, is "bigger,
faster, stronger and smarter." More is the
only fair description here—a more
rugged frame, more power from three
new Vortec V-8s, more performance in
the braking department, and more
comfort by way of improved ride
characteristics. *Chevrolet Motor Division,*
General Motors

Power, comfort, and convenience were main priorities, but so too was a new image that would
leave Ford and Chevy people wondering what
had hit them. That image borrowed both classic
lines and big-rig impressions to turn heads as
few other trucks have ever done.

"All of us were pleasantly stunned when we
saw the full-size clay for the first time,"
recalled Bob Lutz. "We knew we were on to
something. We knew we had something very
new and very exciting, something that was
potentially controversial. Something that not
everybody would like.

"When we sent the fiberglass model out to
research, we got much more polarized results
than before," added Creed. "It was a real love or

hate thing with no middle ground." Fortunately
the final product inspired more love than hate.
Dodge truck calendar sales in 1994 soared
upward by 140 percent compared to 1993's total.
Plant managers quickly found they couldn't build
the all-new Rams fast enough. The newly introduced Club Cab version sold out completely midway through the 1995 run, convincing Chrysler
officials to add a fourth plant to the three over-
worked Dodge truck facilities. The new St. Louis
assembly line helped boost production to more
than 450,000 trucks a year, with as much as 60
percent of that run expected to be Club Cabs.

Comfortable cabs as big as living rooms have
become all the rage among truck builders in the
1990s. Ford's F-series SuperCab dates back to 1974,

a time when such things as added room and comfort were just beginning to be valued. Today they're a priority, as is a need to get passengers and cargo easily in and out in sedan-like fashion. Chevrolet in 1996 became the first to offer a passenger-friendly third-door option for its family-friendly big-cab trucks. Ford's SuperCab in 1997 then became the first to offer a third door as standard equipment. A four-door cab sits atop the bandwagon all truck builders are presently jumping on.

Earth-shaking styling has also become the order of the day in Detroit since Dodge threw down the gauntlet in 1994. Ford's aerodynamic F-150 restyle of 1997 earned it "Truck of the Year" honors from Motor Trend. And Dearborn's new-for-1999 Super Duty trucks—offered with four doors, incidentally—are even more dramatic. They also can be fitted with an optional V-10 engine.

Chevrolet's all-new Silverado also debuted with stunning good looks for 1999, just in time to itself haul home a "Truck of the Year" trophy from Motor Trend, making Chevy the first company to cop five straight MT awards.

"Motor Trend has written that 'Chevrolet completely reinvented its pickup' and that Chevrolet 'clearly raises the pickup standard,' and that's pretty high praise from one of the most prestigious publications in the auto industry," said Chevrolet General Manager John Middlebrook. Chevy's compact SUV, Blazer, won "Truck of the Year" in 1995, as did its full-sized SUV running mate, Tahoe, the following year. Malibu and Corvette scored "Car of the Year" honors in 1997 and 1998, respectively.

Chevrolet officials had stuck with their previous C/K design since 1988, all the while laying claim to their own brand of industry-leading honors. "We already offer the trucks with the highest resale value, the best long-term quality and the most satisfied owners," said Middlebrook in August 1998. "The only way you follow up that kind of product is to make it bigger, faster, stronger and smarter." The latest C/K's list of upgrades, improvements, and other such firsts is far too long to even put a dent in here. As Middlebrook explained it, "Silverado is the epitome of the Chevy Truck brand image. It takes quality, dependability, performance and comfort to a whole new level."

It will also lead Chevrolet trucks into a new millennium. "We're looking forward to building our reputation for dependability for another 80 years in the truck business," he added. "Silverado gets us off to an excellent start."

What awaits pickup buyers in the next century? More trucks undoubtedly—more trucks with more of everything that customers long have taken for granted in their cars. We're probably already trained to expect such things from our trucks now. What more could we ask for? Cleaner-running trucks perhaps?

Just as carmakers are busy exploring low-emissions and alternative fuel possibilities on that side of the fence, so too are their truck-line counterparts, even though utility vehicles at this point remain exempt from the low-emission vehicle (LEV) requirements presently awaiting automobile designers. Ford designers are already ahead of the field seeking out yet another first.

"Next on the list is to give U.S. customers the 'greenest' sport utility vehicles and minivans in the industry," said Ford Division General Manager Jim O'Connor in June 1998. This means the 1999 Ford Explorer, Expedition, and Windstar will meet LEV requirements ahead of schedule, a move intended to draw the attention of the ever-growing environmental-conscious consumer segment. "Our customers drive Ford's product innovation," continued O'Connor, "so we're looking for opportunities to improve and expand our industry-leading truck line-up."

Meanwhile Chevrolet engineers continue toying with GM's pet concept—electric vehicles. Chevy built 250 battery-powered S-10 pickups during a brief 1997 production run, and plans call for a significantly larger number to appear in 1998.

"We're excited to be on the leading edge of providing an alternative to gasoline-powered vehicles for commercial use," explained Chevy's Commercial Specialty Vehicles Director David Spence in 1997. "The S-10 Electric was engineered to be a real-world, hard-working commercial vehicle that will also enable fleet operators to demonstrate their concern for air quality."

First they became driver friendly, then family friendly, and now atmosphere friendly. How much more friendly can the American pickup truck get? Stick around for another 100 years and find out.

INDEX